The International Library of Sociology

ORGANIZATION AND BUREAUCRACY

Founded by KARL MANNHEIM

The International Library of Sociology

THE SOCIOLOGY OF
WORK AND ORGANIZATION
In 18 Volumes

ORGANIZATION AND BUREAUCRACY

An Analysis of Modern Theories

by

NICOS P. MOUZELIS

Routledge
Taylor & Francis Group

LONDON AND NEW YORK

First published in 1967 by
Routledge

Reprinted in 1998, 2000 by
Routledge
2 Park Square, Milton Park, Abingdon, Oxon, OX14 4RN
711 Third Avenue, New York, NY 10017

Transferred to Digital Printing 2007

Routledge is an imprint of the Taylor & Francis Group, an informa business

First issued in paperback 2013

© 1967 Nicos P. Mouzelis

The publishers have made every effort to contact authors/copyright holders
of the works reprinted in *The International Library of Sociology*.
This has not been possible in every case, however, and we would
welcome correspondence from those individuals/companies
we have been unable to trace.

British Library Cataloguing in Publication Data
A CIP catalogue record for this book
is available from the British Library

Organization and Bureaucracy
ISBN13: 978-0-415-17682-8 (hardback)
ISBN13: 978-0-415-86358-2 (paperback)
The Sociology of Work and Organization: 18 Volumes
ISBN 0-415-17829-0
The International Library of Sociology: 274 Volumes
ISBN 0-415-17838-X

Publisher's Note
The publisher has gone to great lengths to ensure the quality of this
reprint but points out that some imperfections in the original
may be apparent

To the memory of

GEORGE MOUZELIS

Contents

vii

Contents

Acknowledgements

This book was originally written as a Ph.D thesis at the London School of Economics. I must first of all express my gratitude to my supervisor Professor D. G. MacRae and to Professor J. H. Smith for all the encouragement and the valuable help they gave me. I want to thank as well Professor W. J. H. Sprott who had the kindness to read the whole manuscript and to make many valuable suggestions. I am also indebted to my colleagues at the University of Leicester, in particular Professor N. Elias, Professor I. Neustadt and E. G. Dunning. The many discussions I had with them helped greatly, especially in the formulation of the last chapter. I am especially obliged to Mrs. R. Bridger for her patient help in correcting the final draft. Finally, my acknowledgements would be incomplete if I did not record the personal debt I owe to Jil McMullen. She helped me in more than one way to carry through this work.

Introduction

It has become a commonplace to emphasise the proliferation of large-scale organisations in modern society. This emphasis is not unjustified. As Etzioni puts it, 'we are born in organisations, educated by organisations, and most of us spend much of our lives working for organisations'.[1] Our society has been called 'bureaucratic' or 'organisational'[2] as, in fact, there are very few crucial problems today which do not pertain more or less directly to its organisational features.

The volume of the literature on this subject and its rate of increase is as impressive as the magnitude of the phenomena which it tries to analyse and explain.[3] Moreover it is not only the sheer volume of studies which is enormous and bewildering but also the multiplicity of points of view from which organisational phenomena have been examined. Contributions to the theory of organisations have come from many sides: psychology, social psychology, sociology, political science, economics, business administration, and so on. Indeed a major characteristic of the literature is the variety of theoretical angles from which organisations are studied. This being the case, the novice in this field has great difficulty to make sense of, or to see some order and connection between studies ranging from the analysis of the bureaucratisation process in western societies to the examination of individual motivation or decision-making in industrial contexts. The present study tries to provide some guidance which may help students to orient themselves with greater ease in the labyrinth of organisational writings. More specifically, it tries to identify and examine critically some of the major approaches to the study of organisations, and the ways in which such approaches are linked with each other.

Thus, on a very general level, two main lines of thought will be propounded.

The first, which is examined in Part One, starts with such

I

theorists as Marx, Weber and Michels who, from a very wide perspective, try to assess the impact of large-scale bureaucracy on the power structure of modern society. The classical writings and especially the Weberian ideal type of bureaucracy (chapter 2) have become the basis of subsequent theories of bureaucracy (chapter 3). These subsequent theories, by limiting their scope, have tried to treat in a more rigorous and empirical manner some of the problems examined by the classical theorists.

The second part of this study examines the other major tradition of organisational writings which starts with Taylor and the movement of scientific management. Here the focus of analysis is not society as a whole but the individual worker, seen as an isolated unit whose activities must be rationalised in the interests of maximum productivity (chapter 4, 1). The Taylorian spirit of rationalisation is extended from the plant level to the firm as a whole by Fayol and other theorists. Such theorists try to elaborate a set of general principles about how to build and manage an efficient organisation (chapter 4, 3). With the introduction of the behavioural sciences into the industrial scene, the managerial tradition moves away from its previous formalism and takes a more empirical and socio-psychological approach. As a matter of fact, both the human relations school (chapter 5) and the decision-making approach to organisations (chapter 6) focus their attention on the impact of an organisation's structure on various aspects of individual behaviour.

Finally in the third part an analysis is made of recent theoretical trends which indicate a certain convergence of the bureaucracy and the managerial line of thought.

In dealing with these three major theoretical orientations and their interconnections, the main purpose is not to present an exhaustive review of the literature or a compilation of the findings which pertain to each one of them. Rather, more emphasis is put on their underlying conceptual framework and on the theoretical problems which they raise. So, in this study, the term 'theory' will not so much have the meaning of a set of interconnected hypotheses about specific organisational problems (which can be validated or rejected by empirical research). It will refer to those conceptualisations which 'map out the problem area and thus prepare the ground for its empirical investigation'.[4] In this sense theory constitutes a more or less useful guide which tells the researcher how to look at organisational reality and what to look for. More precisely, it provides conceptual tools which indicate the level of analysis, the variables to be taken into consideration and the ways in which these variables may be accounted for in a systematic manner.

Of course, there is no clear-cut distinction between these two types of theory. The difference is one of emphasis – whether the main stress lies on the analytic structure or the empirical content of a writing. Thus, no systematic attempt has been made in this study to distinguish in a rigorous way theoretical framework from empirical content, but on the whole, and especially as we move on with our study, the emphasis is increasingly on the former. Of course this does not mean that specific organisational problems, which occupy a central position in each approach, and which are therefore necessary for understanding its conceptual framework, are neglected. Granted that often it is impossible to understand the underlying analytic framework without coming to grips with the concrete problems that it is supposed to tackle, still our aim is not to give a complete solution for each specific problem in the light of all that has been written on it. Our aim is rather to use specific problems and the various controversies around them in so far as they illustrate and make more intelligible the way in which various writers look at organisational reality.

At this point another qualification must be made. This study is not an essay in the sociology of knowledge. In dealing with the development of organisation and bureaucracy theories, no serious attempt has been made to account for such a development by trying to link changes in theory with changes in social structure. Such an enterprise, which certainly constitutes a major research subject in itself, is out of the scope of the present analysis. In our context, when we emphasise the ways in which one approach is linked or develops from another, the assumption is made that in addition to external influences there is an internal dynamic which can partially account for

3

changes in theory. More precisely, the problematics of each approach, its weak points and insufficiencies become potential foci of theoretical change in so far as attempts are made to overcome such difficulties and to provide a more adequate conceptual framework.

For instance, as we will see in detail in Part Two, the psychologistic bias of the early human relations school and its obvious shortcomings are clearly relevant in explaining how organisation theorists, eventually, shifted their focus of analysis from the individual and the group level to the organisation as a whole and to its societal context. Although in accounting for this theoretical development, changes in social structure might be relevant, there is no doubt that for such small-scale changes in theoretical perspectives internal factors (e.g. numerous criticisms against the human relations approach, inconclusiveness of results, strain towards consistency, etc.) play a major role.

Also a word must be said about the definition of the terms 'bureaucracy' and 'organisation'. As it will become apparent in the following chapters, there is no consensus among social scientists as to the adequate meaning of the terms. At present, it will be sufficient to define organisation or formal organisation as a form of social grouping which is established in a more or less deliberate or purposive manner for the attainment of a specific goal.[5] Thus purposiveness and goal-specificity seem to be the two crucial criteria differentiating organisations from other types of social units.[6] For instance a firm, a political party or a voluntary organisation are typical examples of formal organisations. In all these cases men, in a purposive manner co-ordinate their activities and efforts in order to achieve a specific goal. As to the term bureaucracy, for the moment, we may define it as a special type of formal organisation, one which has a number of specific characteristics first identified systematically by Weber (cf. chapter 2).

A final note about the technical design of the book: in order to make the main exposition less cumbersome I have decided to use quite extensive footnotes. Thus much information about the content and implications of specific writings is to be found in the footnote section at the end of the volume.

4

Part One

THE STUDY OF BUREAUCRACY

Chapter One

THE CLASSICAL APPROACH TO THE STUDY OF BUREAUCRACY

Despite the variety of sources from which the classical writings on bureaucracy have sprung, it is possible to identify in all of them a common and recurrent preoccupation around which one can organise all the early literature on the subject: this was to enquire into the impact of the growth of large-scale organisations on the power-structure of society. In what ways does 'big' government or 'big' business influence the political institutions of modern society? Or, on the level of the individual, in what ways are such developments going to affect man's chances for a free and meaningful existence? In a cruder way, the problem is to find out whether bureaucracy, despite its dimensions, is still an administrative apparatus for the implementation of social goals or whether it has lost its instrumental character; whether from a tool in the hands of the legitimate policy-making body, it has become itself the master dictating the general goals to be pursued.

As the problem is formulated, it becomes evident that one can hardly find any student of society who has not dealt directly or indirectly with this subject. Thus, necessarily, the following analysis will be limited in two ways: firstly, we will try to discuss only the theories which deal systematically with bureaucracy or which are crucial for the understanding of the problems and discussions which surround it. Secondly, the main focus in these writings will be on points which are crucial for understanding the basic assumptions and the problematics of the classical approach. From this perspective three major contributions seem to constitute the key elements in the development of the classical literature of bureaucracy: the Marxist, the Weberian and that of Robert Michels.

The Study of Bureaucracy

A. Marx

Although the concept of bureaucracy does not occupy the central position in Marx's thought, his views on bureaucracy and its relation to the power-structure of society is of crucial importance for an understanding of the early controversies about this problem. Indeed the Marxist position constitutes a frame of reference for such students of bureaucracy as Weber and Michels who, although amongst the most prominent critics of Marx, were very much influenced by his thought. Marx studies the phenomenon of bureaucracy and uses this concept in the limited context of the state administration. His ideas on bureaucracy can only be understood in the general framework of his theory of class conflict, the crisis of capitalism and the advent of communism.

Marx elaborates his concepts of bureaucracy by studying and criticising Hegel's philosophy of the state.[1] The Hegelian analysis conceives public administration as a bridge between the state and the civil society. The civil society comprises the professions, the corporations which represent the various particular interests, the state representing the general interest. Between the two, the state bureaucracy is the medium through which this passage from the particular to the general interest becomes possible.

The Marxist analysis accepts this tripartite structure but it radically changes its content. According to Marx this formal and legalist notion of bureaucracy does not represent its true nature; it is simply the false image that the bureaucracy has of itself, an image which derives from law books and administrative regulations. Hegel's bureaucracy takes its meaning from the opposition between the particular interests of the corporations and the common interest of the state. According to Marx, this opposition is meaningless, as the state does not represent the general interest but the particular interests of the dominant class, itself a part of the civil society. From this viewpoint, bureaucracy constitutes a very specific and particular social group. It is not a social class, although its existence is linked with the division of society into classes. More precisely, bureaucracy, as the state itself, is an instrument by which the dominant class exercises its domination over the other social classes.

In this way, to a certain degree, the future and the interests of bureaucracy are closely linked to those of the dominant class and the state. Its justification and existence depends on them. In capitalist society, its real task is to impose on the whole of society an order of things which consolidates and perpetuates class division and domination. At the same time, its other task is to mask this domination by interposing itself as the general interest smoke screen between exploiters and exploited.[2] But on the other hand, as bureaucracy is not an integral part of the capitalist class, it has a certain autonomy which makes conflict with its masters possible. This conflict cannot go beyond certain limits, which are always determined by the existing forces and relations of production.

Briefly, from the above, it follows that bureaucracy does not occupy an organic position in the social structure, as it is not directly linked with the process of production. Its existence and development has a transient and parasitic character. Its main task is to maintain the *status quo* and the privileges of its masters. From this point of view bureaucracy and further bureaucratisation become unavoidable and indispensable in a society divided into classes. Indeed the political system of such a society increasingly requires further and stricter control for the maintenance of the divisions and inequalities among its various groups.[3] This basic position of Marx had a great influence on his disciples as well as on his critics.

Once the problem of bureaucracy is placed in the wider context of the class struggle, we must examine how Marx analyses and explains its main features in terms of the preceding general analysis. In the first place bureaucracy is one specific instance of the general process of alienation. The concept of alienation has a central place in Marxist thought. It is by this process that social forces escape from the control of man, attain an independent existence and finally turn against man, their creator. This philosophic notion of alienation applies

9

admirably in the case of bureaucracy. Indeed, according to Marx, bureaucracy becomes an autonomous and oppressive force which is felt by the majority of the people as a mysterious and distant entity – as something which, although regulating their lives, is beyond their control and comprehension, a sort of divinity in the face of which one feels helpless and bewildered. And, of course, this attitude is reinforced by the bureaucrat's creation of special myths and symbols which sanctify and mystify further his position. It is in this way that bureaucracy becomes a closed world. A sort of caste jealously guards its secrets and prerogatives, presenting to the outside world a united front of silence and hostility.

But the alienation is not only limited to the relation between bureaucrats and outsiders. It is to be found within the bureaucracy itself. Bureaucracy does not only hide its true nature to the non-bureaucrats, it hides it from itself. More often the bureaucrat is not aware of the parasitic and oppressive nature of his job. He thinks of his job as indispensable for the general interest.[4] This self-illusion is consolidated inside the bureaucracy by the strict hierarchy and discipline and the bureaucrat's veneration of authority (another form of alienation).

Incompetence is the other major feature of bureaucracy. Marx has stressed the bureaucrat's lack of initiative and imagination, his fear of taking any kind of responsibility. And this incompetence does not intimidate the bureaucrats who think of themselves as capable of doing everything. Indeed they try continually to extend their functions of domination in order to consolidate their position and their prerogatives. By this bureaucratic imperialism, the bureaucrat tries to persuade himself that he has a useful and salutary function to perform. Moreover, this process of self-aggrandisement is accompanied by what Marx calls the 'sordid materialism' of bureaucracy: the internal struggle for promotion, careerism, the infantile attachment to trivial symbols, status and prestige.[5]

Bureaucracy is the instrument of the capitalist class. Thus, with the proletarian revolution and the advent of a classless society the state and its bureaucracy will wither away. Indeed, according to Marx, in a communist society where no exploitation and social divisions exist bureaucracy becomes redundant. This 'withering away' must be conceived as the gradual absorption of bureaucracy into the society as a whole. Thus instead of having an oppressive structure which is separated from and antagonistic to the rest of society, in the communist state those functions of bureaucracy which are not parasitic will be performed by all social members. The administrative tasks, losing their exploitative character, will consist of the administration of things and not of people, as was the case with bureaucracy.

This radical transformation of the administrative tasks must be seen in conjunction with Marx's general conception of the Communist society, a society in which the division of labour no longer exists and where every man will be free 'to do one thing today and another tomorrow, to hunt in the morning, fish in the afternoon, rear cattle in the evening . . ., without ever becoming hunter, fisherman, shepherd, or critic'.[6] Thus the end of the division of labour marks the end of alienation and the beginning of an era of individual freedom. It is only in such a society that a really democratic administration can exist. The administrative tasks, simplified and demystified, will be the concern of everybody. There will be no more monopoly of the administrative positions. The worker, citizen of a true democracy, will be at the same time elected and elector, administered and administrator. It is only by this kind of 'auto-administration' that the 'public' authority returns finally to its true basis and the state 'withers away'.[7]

B. Lenin

As far as the analysis of bureaucracy is concerned, Lenin follows faithfully the basic position of Marx, elaborating it further in certain respects. For example, going into more detail, Lenin believes that the gradual decline of the bureaucratic apparatus must begin as soon as the dictatorship of the proletariat is established. The struggle against bureaucracy should be one of the first tasks of the revolution.[8] In his *State and Revolution*, he shows by what concrete steps this could be realised. These are as follows:

(*a*) the eligibility and instant revocability of every civil servant

(*b*) the official's salary reduced to the level of ordinary workmen's wages

(*c*) the creation of a state of things in which the 'functions of control and accounting – becoming more and more simple – will be performed by each in turn'.[9]

Lenin's writings about bureaucracy become more interesting after the Revolution of 1917, as from this time on he is obliged to accommodate his master's theory with a bureaucratic reality which does not fit very well into the Marxist scheme. Lenin realises very quickly that the post-revolutionary bureaucratic apparatus not only did not show any sign of decline, but on the contrary, was expanding at a rapid rate.[10] How can a Marxist explain this phenomenon? Lenin explains it as a sign of the 'immaturity of socialism'. The civil war and the ensuing chaotic state of the economy partially account for it. Moreover such factors as the non-socialist relations of production between the workers and the peasants, the still existing small bourgeois and the tsarist bureaucrat with his feudal mentality, constitute a fertile soil for the further strengthening of bureaucracy. But, according to Lenin, the cure for this bureaucratisation will come automatically when economic development is achieved. In the long term, it is increasing industrialisation which will constitute the objective basis for a final victory over bureaucracy.[11]

C. Trotsky

As Trotsky wrote about bureaucracy at a moment when the process of bureaucratisation had reached its peak (with Stalin as dictator), the reconciliation between theory and reality takes a somewhat different form.[12]

According to Trotsky, the increasingly oppressive character of the Soviet bureaucracy and its gradual formation into a closed privileged group, cannot be explained merely by the immaturity of socialism and the inadequate development of

The Classical Approach to the Study of Bureaucracy

the forces of production. The roots of the bureaucratic evil are deeper. They are to be found in the first years after the Revolution. Trotsky believed that socialism in one country, especially in a predominantly agricultural one, is not possible. This is because the substructure of such a country, its weak industrialisation, excludes the development of a political superstructure of the socialist type. This does not mean that the Russian Revolution was premature. It simply means that it had to be continued in other countries, especially the industrialised ones. In this way the Russian Revolution should have been immediately transformed into a world-wide proletarian revolution.[13]

This theory of the 'permanent revolution' was ignored by Lenin as early as 1917 at Brest-Litovsk. According to Trotsky, 'Brest-Litovsk has been the first retreat of the victorious Revolution'. The economic difficulties which followed, the introduction of the new economic policy and all the internal contradictions of the system have their source in the erroneous belief that one can build up socialism in one country. So, under such conditions, it is not suprising that bureaucracy, instead of withering away, fortifies itself. If the danger of counterrevolution has disappeared, the effort to impose a juridical and political régime on an inadequate material basis necessitates a tremendous oppressive force. The party bureaucracy has undertaken this task of oppression.

Indeed Trotsky saw clearly that the problem of bureaucratisation did not only have a quantitative aspect. There was something more than a simple increase in the dimensions of hierarchical administrative structures. There was a qualitative change, as the party bureaucracy began to detach itself from its proletarian basis. If, under Lenin, bureaucracy still kept its character of instrument at the service of the people, with the advent of Stalin this was not any more the case: the distinction between party and state bureaucracy disappeared, the Soviets lost completely their autonomy and all the power was finally displaced from the workers to the party apparatus and ultimately to Stalin.[14]

But in spite of the domination and the caste-like character of bureaucracy, Trotsky does not believe that the Soviet bureaucrats have formed a new social class. On this point he

13

criticises severely all those who look at the Soviet régime as a new form of state capitalism or those like Rizzi and Djilas who speak of the 'new class' characterising a régime completely different from socialism and capitalism (cf. section 3).

Against such theories Trotsky holds to the basic Marxist position: a social class always has its roots in the sphere of production. The domination of one class over another is essentially an economic domination which reflects itself in the legal, political and ideological sphere. If this is so, the Soviet bureaucracy does not constitute a social class, and its domination has a purely political, non-economic character. Indeed the economic roots of the bureaucracy are very weak. If the bureaucrats regulate the distribution of income, they are far from regulating production. Thus the function of the bureaucracy in the productive process is not organic. It disposes of the means of production only by delegation. And this fact makes the situation of the bureaucrat uncertain and his domination precarious.

Finally, as far as the future of bureaucracy is concerned, Trotsky is quite optimistic. Although the economic development of the Soviet Union is accompanied by further bureaucratisation, at the same time this development undermines bureaucracy. And first of all serious contradictions begin to appear within the bureaucracy. Power is displaced from the inferior to the superior echelons and this centralisation creates conflicts which cannot always be suppressed by brutal force. But the greatest hope for a decisive victory over bureaucracy lies again within the oppressed proletariat. The economic and cultural development of the masses will render intolerable the dictatorship of the bureaucrats. The workers must prepare themselves for a second revolution. In this way the theory of the permanent revolution is further enlarged. Before world revolution, it implies a new internal revolution against the Stalinist régime.[15]

Conclusion. Both Lenin and Trotsky have tried to interpret Soviet bureaucracy in a way that could be compatible with Marxism. Being *a priori* committed to such a theoretical enterprise, they were automatically forced to see no other possibility in the historic evolution of society, except the capitalism-socialism alternative.[16] Indeed, had they admitted other possible developments, a great part of Marx's theoretical edifice would have been seriously shaken. Thus their main effort was not to study the phenomenon of bureaucracy in itself, but rather to see how they could accommodate the Soviet reality with their theoretical commitments.

The same remark can be made about Marx's analysis of bureaucracy. As far as it remains on a descriptive level, although partial, it is very vivid and penetrating. Indeed Marx has grasped many of the problems and characteristics which will be elaborated later by Weber and his followers. (The sanctification of the bureaucratic post, the displacement of goals and so on.) But when he tries to explain these characteristics by linking them to the structure of society as a whole, one feels that his observations are forced and distorted in order to fit within his general theoretical framework.

The Marxist debate over the nature of the Soviet bureaucracy does not stop here. If Trotsky and Lenin tried to fit increasing bureaucratisation into the Marxist scheme, as the future course of events was making this intellectual exercise more and more difficult, authors like Rizzi and Burnham tried to fit Marxism into bureaucracy – that is they accepted bureaucratic domination as a central feature of the Soviet system and they tried to find out how a Marxist could analyse a situation which was manifestly not predicted by Marx.

2. WEBER'S POLITICAL SOCIOLOGY

A. Basic concepts

In order to understand Weber's ideas about bureaucracy, we shall have to place them in the more general context of his theory of domination. Weber defines power as the possibility of imposing one's will upon the behaviour of other persons.[17] But he is not so much interested in power generally as in a special type of power relationship, which he calls domination. Domination refers to a power relationship in which the ruler, the person who imposes his will on others, believes that he has a right to the exercise of power; and the ruled consider it their duty to obey his orders. In other words in this kind of established authority one finds always a number of beliefs which legitimise the exercise of power in the eyes of both the leaders and the led. These beliefs about the legitimation of power are very important. They determine the relative stability of systems of domination as well as portray the basic differences between such systems.

The other important element in this approach is the notion of the administrative apparatus. Domination, when exercised over a large number of people, necessitates an administrative staff which will execute commands and which will serve as a bridge between the ruler and the ruled.[18]

Thus the beliefs about legitimation and the administrative apparatus constitute the two main criteria for the Weberian construction of a typology of domination. Weber distinguished three principles of legitimation – each corresponding to a certain type of apparatus – which define three pure types of domination.

Charismatic domination. Charisma means literally 'gift of Grace', an exceptional quality by virtue of which one becomes leader. The charismatic leader – whether a prophet, a hero or a demagogue – justifies his domination by his extraordinary capacities and deeds. His disciples accept his domination because they have faith in his person.

Under such a type of domination, the administrative apparatus – when there are enough followers to necessitate one – is very loose and unstable. The most faithful disciples usually play the role of the intermediary between the leader and the masses.[19]

Traditional domination. In this case, the legitimation of power comes from the belief in the eternal past, in the rightness and appropriateness of the traditional way of doing things. The traditional leader is the Master who commands by virtue of his inherited status. His orders are personal and arbitrary but within the limits fixed by custom. His subjects obey out of personal loyalty to him or out of respect to his traditional

status. When this type of domination, typical in the patri-
archal household, is extended over many people and a wide
territory, the ensuing administrative apparatus can ideally
take two forms.

In the *patrimonial* form of traditional domination, the
officials of the apparatus are personal retainers – servants,
relatives, favourites, etc. – usually dependent on their master
for remuneration. On the other hand the *feudal* apparatus has
a greater degree of autonomy towards the master. The feudal
officials are not personal dependants but allies giving an oath
of fealty to their vassal. By virtue of this kind of contract, they
exercise independent jurisdiction, they usually own their
administrative domain and they are not dependent on their
superior for remuneration and subsistence.[20]

Legal domination. The belief in the rightness of law is the legitimation sustaining this type of domination. In this case the
people obey the laws, not because they are issued by a charismatic or traditional leader, but because they believe that these
rules are enacted by a proper procedure, a procedure considered
by the ruler and the ruled as correct. Moreover the ruler is
considered as a superior who has come to hold a position by
legal procedures (appointment, election, etc.). It is by virtue
of his position that he exercises power within the limits set by
legally sanctioned rules.

The typical administrative apparatus corresponding to the
legal type of domination is called bureaucracy. It is also
characterised by this belief in the rules and the legal order.
The position of the bureaucrat, his relations with the ruler, the
ruled and his colleagues are strictly defined by impersonal
rules. These rules delineate in a rational way the hierarchy
of the apparatus, the rights and duties of every position, the
methods of recruitment and promotion and so on (cf. chapter 2).
In such a type of administration, contrary to the feudal case,
the means of administration (i.e. the resources necessary for
the accomplishment of the administrative tasks) do not belong
to the bureaucrat. They are concentrated at the top. Thus the
position of the official cannot be sold or inherited, it cannot be
appropriated and integrated in his private patrimony. This

strict separation between private and official income and fortune is a specific characteristic of bureaucracy, distinguishing it from the patrimonial and feudal type of administration.[21]

Of course the three types of domination mentioned above are never to be found in pure form. Real systems of domination constitute a mixture of elements pertaining to all three types of domination. But, according to Weber, the typology is useful as an analytic tool helping the student to identify the various combinations of legal, charismatic and traditional elements in a real system of domination, as well as to find the reasons for the discrepancies between ideal type and reality.

B. The increasing bureaucratisation of modern society

Although bureaucratic administrations have existed in the past, it is only with the emergence of the modern state – the closest example of the legal type of domination – that bureaucracy has prevailed on such a large scale.[22] Indeed this process of bureaucratisation is not limited to the state apparatus. Although Weber elaborated his concept of bureaucracy in the context of his political sociology, he uses the term in a more extensive way. It is not only public administration which becomes more bureaucratised. Bureaucracy, as a type of organisation, has gradually penetrated all social institutions.

Whether in the religious, educational or economic domain, Weber observes the proliferation of large-scale organisations, the concentration of the means of administration at the top of the hierarchy and generally the adoption of the bureaucratic type of organisation. The modern army, the church, the university are gradually losing their traditional aspects. They are increasingly administered by impersonal and rational rules aiming at maximum efficiency. The large-scale enterprise is the most striking example in this context. The means of production are no longer in the hands of the producer-worker and the whole structure of the organisation is consciously designed according to rational principles. The discipline at work is assured by a set of rules which tries completely to adjust the worker to the exigencies of maximum productivity.

The Classical Approach to the Study of Bureaucracy

This rationalisation of work is to be seen in its extreme form in the American system of scientific management which 'enjoys the greatest triumphs in the rational conditioning and training of work performances'.[23]

The impact of such an organisational setting on the individual is the extreme limitation of his personal freedom and spontaneity, and his increasing incapacity to understand his own activities in relation to the organisation as a whole. In a more general way, modern bureaucracy, whether in business, government or education, favours a crippled type of personality, the specialist, the technical expert who increasingly replaces the ideal of the cultivated man of past civilisations.[24]

Finally Weber uses the term bureaucratisation in a still wider sense when he refers to ways of acting and thinking which are not only to be found in organisational contexts but which permeate all aspects of social life. From this point of view the term coincides more or less with the concept of rationalisation. Weber distinguishes two notions of rationalism:

(a) 'The methodical attainment of a definitely given and practical end by means of an increasingly precise calculation of means'.[25] Here the focus is on the means, their adequacy or inadequacy to an end, even if this end has a religious or mystical basis. In that sense even Yoga, with its discipline and its systematisation, constitutes a rational activity.

(b) The second meaning of the term refers to 'the kind of rationalisation the systematic thinker performs on the image of the world: an increasing theoretical mastery of reality by means of increasingly precise and abstract concepts'.[26] In a negative sense, this process of rationalisation, of which science is an aspect, leads ultimately to the rejection of all religions, metaphysical or traditional values and explanations of the world, to the demystification of the world.

This brings us to Weber's conception of the historic movement and its trend towards increasing rationalisation: the tension between charisma, representing the creative, spontaneous forces of society and routine, is a theme underlying the whole of Weber's work. In the historic process, the charismatic leader constitutes a revolutionary force. In critical moments, when social institutions become too rigid and unfit to meet new difficult situations, the charisma, a disruptive force, upsets the established order and opens up new ways of life. But the victory of charisma over routine is never definitive. On the contrary, the charisma ends by being routinised, by becoming of the established order of things. Thus, for example, when the charismatic leader dies, the disciples have to resort to a more formal and rigid organisation in order to preserve and propagate his message. In this way the spontaneity and creativity of the master is replaced by rational impersonal rules (bureaucracy) or by a traditional type of organisation, which becomes hostile to any new manifestation of charisma.

Whether the former or the latter form of routinisation prevails depends on the numerous factors of the specific social context. But through this charisma-routine dialectic, Weber perceives an overwhelming tendency towards the increasing rationalisation of the world and the decline of charismatic leadership. In this context bureaucratisation, when not identified with rationalisation, is an important aspect of it.[27]

On the other hand, the increasing bureaucratisation and rationalisation brings with it a basic irrationality: Weber believes that if scientific progress contributed to the 'disenchantment of the world' by destroying the demons and gods who populated the earth for so long, it did not succeed in putting something else in their place. Science has destroyed the values and the meaning of life which religion and tradition were giving to man, without being able to give new values and a new purpose for living. This is because science can only give man knowledge about the phenomenal world. It can help him to conquer nature and acquire tremendous forces, but it can never tell him what to believe, where to direct these forces. In this way modern bureaucratic life becomes more rational and irrational (i.e. aimless) at the same time.[28]

More specifically, it might be useful to emphasise at this point Weber's dialectic or rather ambivalent position towards bureaucracy and bureaucratisation. On the one hand he considers bureaucracy as the most efficient form of organisation invented by man, on the other hand, as we shall see later, Weber is afraid that this very efficiency which results from the

The Classical Approach to the Study of Bureaucracy

increasing bureaucratisation of the modern world constitutes the biggest threat to individual freedom and to the democratic institutions of Western societies.[29]

C. Bureaucracy and the problem of power

The bureaucrat and the politician. In the ideal typical case, the bureaucrat has the attributes of impartiality, expert knowledge and obedience to superiors. His duty is to comply with the rules and with the orders coming from above. In cases where his personal opinions differ from those of his superior, he has to put them aside and do his utmost for the faithful execution of the orders received.

As to the political leader, ideally, he is engaged in a struggle for power. If the bureaucrat must prove himself by impartial performance, the political leader proves himself in the competition for votes during elections and in the legislature. The responsibility of the bureaucrat is limited to the way in which he executes assigned tasks. He is not responsible for the assignment of the task itself (i.e. for the ultimate ends and the larger policy towards which the politician is seriously committed).[30]

Finally, when one looks at the bureaucratic organisation as a whole, this ideal typical formulation of the roles of the bureaucrat and the politician implies that the whole bureaucratic apparatus is a simple tool in the hands of its master, whether this master is a despot, an elected president or a ministerial cabinet.

But of course in reality things never take such a pure form. Weber, after formulating the ideal type of domination, proceeds to the analysis of the problematics of each type, that is of the basic tensions which make social reality diverge from ideal formulations. Thus in the charismatic type of domination the focus of tension and instability is the process of depersonalisation of charisma, as decentralisation is the major problem of traditional domination. In the legal type of domination the power position of the bureaucrat, based on his expert knowledge constitutes the major source of conflict. Indeed specialised knowledge may be used as a powerful weapon of the bureaucrat against his political master, the latter, with the increasing

The Study of Bureaucracy

complexity of bureaucratic tasks, becoming a dilettante in administrative matters. As a matter of fact, the head of a bureaucracy, whether elected or appointed, usually lacks any expert knowledge. Consequently he is not in a position to control the bureaucrat and to see to what extent the latter complies with his orders. This uncomfortable position of the master is further aggravated in a non-democratic régime. In such a régime, very often, the monarch is dependent for information solely upon the bureaucrat. Consequently he might find himself at the complete mercy of his inferiors, as there is no way to find out to what extent his orders were executed or ignored. But even in democratic régimes, where the public served by the bureaucracy can directly reach the political heads of the administration and protest against abuses, the control is difficult. The most important spheres of bureaucratic activity are excluded from public scrutiny, and the label 'official secret' can be extensively applied, even to cases where such secrecy is not really necessary. This persistent bureaucratic tendency towards secrecy, which Marx has so vividly described, can be seen as self-defence against eventual hostile criticism by outsiders. It can also be understood in terms of the natural tendency of every officeholder to consolidate and expand his power position.[31]

But all these tendencies which displace power from its legitimate centres, do not necessarily lead to a complete bureaucratic domination. There are limits, as well as forces, which can counterbalance such tendencies. For instance, as the bureaucrat does not own the material means of administration, he has lost much of the autonomy and power which the feudal official enjoyed. Moreover, the fact that most bureaucrats do not belong to the propertied classes makes them more afraid of losing their jobs and more compliant to the orders of the master. This strategic advantage of the bureaucratic head is reinforced by the internal struggles between bureaucrats. Indeed their intensive competition for promotion enables the master to control a recalcitrant bureaucrat with the help of his antagonistic colleagues.[32]

In conclusion, Weber finds inherent in every bureaucracy

The Classical Approach to the Study of Bureaucracy

tendencies towards an overexpansion of its functions to areas which ideally lie outside its jurisdiction as well as counter tendencies which permit the effective control and direction of the bureaucratic apparatus by its legitimate ruler. Which of these tendencies will prevail and to what degree, is an empirical question which cannot be answered *a priori*. Basically the outcome of this tension depends on the relevant social forces operating in a concrete historic situation.[33]

Bureaucracy and democracy. The above considerations make necessary a more detailed examination of how Weber conceived the relations between increasing bureaucratisation and democracy. Here, although the analysis of the problem of power is shifted to the societal level, one finds a similar basic ambivalence.

On the one hand the method of bureaucratic recruitment, based on diplomas and examinations, brings a certain levelling of social differences. Indeed impersonal and universalistic criteria of recruitment and promotion go against the privileged access to important bureaucratic posts of those who are economically or otherwise powerful. Moreover, the impersonality of bureaucratic rules and authority is in harmony with the democratic ideal of the equality of everyone before the law. But on the other hand, the same conditions might have the contrary results. Thus, insistence on diplomas of higher education indirectly favours all those who have the material means to undertake the long studies that such certificates require. In that sense the development of bureaucracy destroys real equality of opportunity and favours a plutocratic régime.[34]

In a similar way, if impersonal rules protect the individual from the arbitrariness of the official, the popular demands for substantial social justice are easily frustrated by the legal formalism of these rules:

> The propertyless masses especially are not served by a 'formal' equality before the law and a 'calculable' adjudication and administration, as demanded by 'bourgeois' interests. Naturally, in their eyes justice and administration should serve to compensate for their economic and social life opportunities in the face of the propertied classes.[35]

Finally, concerning the democratic aspect of the public administration itself, Weber thinks that in a modern bureaucracy, the democratic principles are necessarily violated. Weber's ideal type of democratic administration has many common elements with the Marxist conception of administration in the future communist society. For instance in such an administration every member of the group is capable of assuming administrative tasks, the power of the official is reduced to a minimum by rotation in office, frequent elections, etc. Weber thinks that such a system of administration can only function in a very small group (e.g. in a small locality), whose members have more or less the same social status and where the administrative tasks are relatively stable and simple.

A century before Weber, De Tocqueville, in his analysis of the democratic institutions in the United States, has described the dysfunctions and the dangers of a too democratic administration. Indeed when the position of the bureaucrat is too unstable and temporary, he is at the complete mercy of local political bosses, corruption and bribery becoming institutionalised practices. But, on the other hand, De Tocqueville was also aware of the totalitarian dangers of the increasing centralisation in the federal government and administration. This centralisation was seen as a threat to the local autonomy and generally to the pluralistic system of American politics.[36]

The tension between extreme democratic decentralisation leading to a kind of anarchy (in which case the administration, invaded by external forces, has no power at all) and a totalitarian system in which bureaucracy has absolute power, was not any more a realistic dilemma at the time when Weber was writing. By this time, with the relative detachment of public administration from politics, the real dilemma was whether this bureaucratic autonomy, so indispensable for the effective functioning of the administration, had not gone too far. In this context, no longer the fear of anarchy, but only the fear of totalitarianism was still relevant.[37] Indeed, according to Weber, as the position of the official has been consolidated and has become less dependent on public opinion, bureaucracy as a whole has acquired a permanency which it is almost impossible to shake. Whatever the political régime and whatever the political and social changes in the modern state, bureaucracy is there to stay.[38]

But this permanence and technical superiority of the bureaucratic apparatus, if it is a threat to the democratic process, does not automatically imply its destruction and the dictatorship of the bureaucrat. The power position of bureaucracy cannot be decided *a priori* by its indispensability or its other characteristics. The slaves in older times were also indispensable for the functioning of society, but this did not make them politically dominant. Moreover, the impersonality of the bureaucratic apparatus, its rational articulation, means that it can equally well function under the most diverse masters and for very different political and economic purposes. As Weber puts it, '. . . the (bureaucratic) mechanism – in contrast to feudal orders based on personal piety – is easily made to function for anybody who knows how to gain control of it'.[39]

Bureaucracy and capitalism. Finally, western capitalism, as an economic system closely linked with the rise of mass democracy in the occident, portrays the same ambivalence in its relations with bureaucracy. On the one hand, increasing bureaucratisation, with its levelling and equalitarian tendencies has greatly contributed to the abolition of local and feudal privileges and has thus helped the development of large-scale commerce and industry. Moreover the efficiency and regularity of bureaucratic administration is a prerequisite of any long term economic calculation.

But on the other hand, the increasing government intervention and regulation of the economy and the development of the welfare state with its armies of pensioners and *rentiers* do not constitute a fertile soil for the further development of capitalism. Under such circumstances the aversion to risk taking and the bureaucratic craving for security spreading to the whole population, undermine the initiative and entrepreneurial spirit which is the driving force of capitalism.

In the socialist movements of his time Weber saw the danger of the increasing domination of the government bureaucracy,

leading ultimately to a totalitarian régime and the abolition
of all individual freedom.[40]

Conclusion. Despite Weber's pessimism as to the long-term
consequences of bureaucratisation and his fears about the
decline of democracy and individual freedom, he was cautious
enough not to draw definite and dogmatic conclusions as to the
future dominance of bureaucracy. Indeed, as we have seen,
in his analysis of the power situation of bureaucracy, Weber
repeatedly stresses that inherent in the bureaucratic type of
organisation are tendencies which both favour and discourage
bureaucratic domination. Thus, whether bureaucracy will
remain a simple tool at the service of its legitimate masters
or whether it will replace them depends on the external forces
operating upon it within a specific social structure. In this
sense, Weber's position is clearly distinct from the writings of
subsequent scholars who have studied bureaucracy as a system
of political dominance.

3. BUREAUCRACY AND OLIGARCHY

The term bureaucracy, especially in political writings, very
often implies an abuse of power, a situation where officials
have more power than is necessary for the performance of their
legitimate tasks. When this abuse of power is implied in the
definition, *a priori*, as we have seen, we have departed from
Weber's definition of bureaucracy. Indeed after Weber many
scholars, overemphasising the oligarchic tendencies of bureaucracy, started to analyse it, not so much as a type of organisation, but more in terms of domination and power.

A. R. Michels: the problem of internal democracy

If Weber was mainly interested in the impact of bureaucratic
organisations on the political structure of society as a whole,
Michels[41] concentrated his analysis on the internal politics of
large-scale organisations. In this field, he saw the most striking
confirmation of the Machiavellian theses[42] about élite domination and the meagre chances of democracy or a classless society
in the modern world.

The Classical Approach to the Study of Bureaucracy

Very briefly, Michels' famous 'iron law of oligarchy' states that modern large scale organisations, by their very structure, are necessarily oligarchic. This is so even if this oligarchy runs against the ideals and intentions of both leaders and led. To prove this, he studied the internal structure of the German Socialist Party, which, more than all other parties, was supposed to be organised along democratic principles. He found out that the system was oligarchic and that democracy was a mere façade to be found only in official regulations and codebooks. By generalising such observations, he concluded that all big organisations tend to develop a bureaucratic structure which rules out the possibility of internal democracy. There are various reasons for this.

First, real democracy, according to Michels, implies that all organisation members should directly participate in the political process of policy making. But such a participation is technically impossible because of the great number of the rank and file. Moreover, the increasing complexity of organisational problems makes them less and less comprehensible to anyone without special knowledge and training.[43]

From the side of the rulers, similar structural tendencies give them the monopoly of power. The hierarchical aspect of the bureaucratic structure and the concentration of the means of communication at the top, make the power position of the leader impregnable. Thus information can be manipulated (distorted or withheld from the members) and the whole communication network can be used against any potential rival. Above all, the leader, by the exercise of his functions, gradually acquires a specialised knowledge and political skills (making speeches, writing articles, etc.) which make him irreplaceable to the organisation.[44]

In this way, both the position of the rulers and the ruled lead to a political system which perpetuates the leadership of the person in power and alienates completely the rank and file from the political process of the organisation. But oligarchy does not necessarily mean exploitation. The oligarch might rule, having always in mind the interests of those who brought him into power. The second step in Michels' argument is to show the *naïveté* of the above contention.

The Study of Bureaucracy

By rising to power, the leaders become an integral part of the élite. As such, their interests do not always coincide with those of the masses. Once in a dominant position, the primary interest of the organisation élite is to maintain its power, even if such a policy were detrimental to the organisation as a whole. Thus for example, the evaporation of the revolutionary ideals and the bureaucratic conservatism of the established socialist parties serve more the interests of the leaders (anxious for the preservation and stability of 'their' organisation and leadership), and less the masses whose interests they are supposed to represent. This behaviour of the organisational leader does not so much depend on his character (e.g. whether or not he is honest, etc.). Rather it must be understood in terms of the structural strains in which he finds himself, in combination with general psychological traits common to all human beings.

From a social psychological point of view, once the leader has achieved prestige and prominence and has been accustomed to a certain way of life, he is most reluctant to give it up. Of course, the fear of losing the privileged position is felt more acutely by a leader who, before achieving power, had a low status job (as in the case of the ex-worker trade union leader). Moreover, with the exercise of power a psychological metamorphosis occurs in the person of the leader. He comes to believe in his own greatness and uniqueness and gradually, in all sincerity, he begins to identify the organisation with himself.

In more general terms, this defensive and conservative policy of the leader can be explained by the general Machiavellian principle postulating that the behaviour of any dominant group, inside or outside organisations, follows a logic of self-interest. In the political and organisational context, self-interest refers not so much to economic gain, but more to power and prestige considerations. In this way, Michels thinks, his position does not contradict the Marxist conception of the economic interest as the major determinant of human action (in a capitalist society); it rather completes it by elaborating the political aspects of this determination.

Finally, Michels, being as aware as Marx and Weber of the

gap between what people say and what they do, examines the various ideologies by which the organisational oligarchy justifies its position. The main stress of such proclamations is usually on the necessity for internal unity and harmony in the face of external dangers and enemies. Under such conditions any emerging opposition becomes a subversive element helping the enemies. Moreover, the democratic myth can always be maintained by the elaboration of a Bonapartist ideology which makes of the democratically elected leader the permanent expression of the collective will.

When Michels shifts his focus from organisational politics to a more general institutional level, his conclusions about the chances of democracy are not less pessimistic. Indeed, the impossibility of internal democracy undermines the democratic institutions of the whole political community. Although he does not identify the exact mechanisms by which organisational oligarchy results in societal oligarchy, Michels has no illusions as to the fate of both the capitalist and the socialist version of democracy. Before the Russian Revolution, he predicted the failure of a socialist democracy and the dictatorial outcome of an eventual socialist victory. Indeed revolution would end as 'a dictatorship in the hands of those leaders who have been sufficiently astute and sufficiently powerful to grasp the sceptre of dominion in the name of – socialism . . .'.[45]

In a more general way, Michels sees the democratic movements in history as successive waves which 'break ever on the same shore' and which 'are ever renewed'.[46] Democratic ideals and movements lose their revolutionary purity as soon as they seem to prevail. When a popular revolution is successful the representatives of the masses take the place and the conservative manners of the old oligarchy. And the same story starts all over again. This cyclical view of history often finds the source of social changes in the emergence of charismatic leaders who are strong enough to break through the institutional and organisation constraints of modern life. It is by such thinking that Michels, towards the end of his life, gave up his socialist convictions (shattered by his law of oligarchy) and found a new faith in the charisma of Benito Mussolini.[47]

B. The problem of external democracy

Michels has mainly dealt with the problem of internal democracy. Following the same line of thought, other writers have examined more systematically the problem of external democracy, i.e. the impact of bureaucratic organisations on the political democratic system as a whole. Indeed, from the beginning of this century, social thinkers have been debating the political consequences of the extraordinary growth of bureaucratic organisations, whether in the political or the economic field.[48]

On the one hand, liberal economists like Ludwig von Mises[49] and Hayek[50] are alarmed at the proportions of the state Leviathan and its increasing interference in economic life. For them, it is the government's bureaucratic expansionism which gradually destroys free enterprise and undermines the democratic institutions of society.

On the other hand, there are those who attribute increasing bureaucratisation and the decline of democracy, not to the state's interference, but to the internal dynamics of the capitalist economic system. According to this view, the technological change under a capitalist system necessitates the formation of huge corporations which dominate the market and destroy any kind of competition. Under such circumstances economic power is concentrated in the hands of a few monopolists who become a 'state within a State'. Thus for instance, Franz Neumann[51] thinks that it was the extreme concentration and monopolisation of the German economy which brought the Nazis to power. In a similar fashion, Robert Brady[52] believes that business concentration favours totalitarianism. And as he finds that economic concentration is as strong in some democratic states (Great Britain, United States) as in totalitarian ones (pre-war Japan, Germany, Italy), he is apprehensive of the chances of democracy in the Anglo-Saxon countries.[53]

The other centre of similar debates has been among Marxist circles examining the relation between Marx's predictions and the political realities of the Soviet régime. In the first section we have left the debate with Lenin and Trotsky, who have

The Classical Approach to the Study of Bureaucracy
tried to accommodate the Marxist optimistic prediction with
the increasing bureaucratisation of the régime. They have
achieved this by viewing the Soviet bureaucracy as a pathological and transient phenomenon, not well rooted in the
economy and bound to decline in the long term.

But if these prominent Marxists could not admit that
bureaucracy had an 'organic' position in the Soviet system,
others thought that it was in its centre and that it defined
more than anything else the very nature of the régime. From
this point of view, bureaucracy is not only a privileged oppressive group, but a real class, a class characterising a new type
of régime which was neither socialist nor capitalist and which
Marx had not foreseen.

Rizzi's bureaucratic collectivism. The first systematic elaboration
of this position was attempted by Bruno Rizzi. (*The Bureaucratisation of the World*, 1939.) For him, the Soviet bureaucracy
constitutes a new class which dominates and exploits the
proletariat as much as capitalists had done. Like every Marxist,
he regards this domination as based on the appropriation of
the means of production. The only difference between this
and the capitalist system is that this appropriation is not
individual but collective. As a matter of fact, in the Soviet
Union the means of production are not socialised but simply
statised. They do not belong to the people but to the state and
ultimately to the bureaucracy who owns the state. In the last
analysis, it is a part of the bureaucracy (the technicians, the
directors, the specialists, etc.) which exploits the proletariat
and steals, in a collective way this time, the surplus value of
work.[54]

These are the main features of this new régime which Rizzi
calls bureaucratic collectivism, a phenomenon, Rizzi thinks,
which is not limited to the Soviet Union, but which is also
manifest in the fascist countries and even in the 'new deal'
type of capitalist democracies. But there is a happy end to this
bureaucratisation of the world. Rizzi believes that the bureaucratic type of exploitation, in which the state is not an instrument of the dominant class but is the dominant class itself, is
the last form of exploitation before a really classless society is

achieved, by a new revolution of the proletariat. So, in the last analysis, the Marxist scheme is not completely abolished but simply enriched by an additional historic stage (bureaucratic collectivism), from which society must pass before the advent of socialism – communism.

The managerial revolution. Whether by coincidence or not, it is evident that Burnham's theory[55] of the managerial revolution is more or less an elaboration of Rizzi's ideas. Indeed, all but the last optimistic theme of the *Bureaucratisation of the World* are taken up again and expressed in a somewhat different manner. Technological progress, the growth of large-scale organisations in the economy as in the political field, render the old ruling class (the bourgeois private owners) incapable of controlling the means of production. Although this declining class in some countries still maintains legal ownership, the effective control of the economy and the ensuing power passes to the managers (i.e. the production executives, the co-ordinators, the administrators of the state apparatus).[56]

On a more advanced level of the historic evolution, the system of the private ownership of the means of production is abolished and state ownership is established. In this manner the control of the means of production comes directly to the managers, the state being to some extent their property. Finally, with the rise of the managerial class, even when not conscious of its worldwide struggle for power, new ideologies are developing which justify its eventual domination. From this point of view, Leninism-Stalinism, fascism-nazism, 'new-dealism' and various technocratic ideologies are all approximations of the new managerial ideology, which has not yet taken its definite form.[57]

4. SOME CRITICAL REMARKS

The classical writings on bureaucracy constitute a coherent body of thought with a well-defined pattern of development, a pattern which reflects the changing character of the problems posed by the increasing spread of large-scale organisations in modern societies. As we have seen, the concepts of bureaucracy and bureaucratisation do not have the same meaning in all these writings. But this is not so much due to a terminological confusion or to a lack of continuity between them. It is explained by the fact that they refer to different problems arising from a swiftly changing organisational reality.

In the Marxist analysis, identified as the first stage of the above theoretical development, the concept of bureaucracy refers strictly to the problems of the state administration, conceived as an oppressive apparatus of the capitalist class. In this context, bureaucratisation means simply the proliferation of government officials or activities, but without any change to the basic power situation of the bureaucrat. He remains an obedient tool at the service of his masters. So the problematics of bureaucracy derive directly from the struggle between classes and its ultimate outcome: the victory of the proletariat, the establishment of a classless society in which bureaucracy gradually disappears. This kind of optimism, as well as the conception of history as a succession of well-defined stages leading towards freedom and human happiness, is a part of the eighteenth- and nineteenth-century humanist faith in the future of man and in the idea of historic progress.

But when the type of organisation which characterised the government administration was gradually prevailing in all social institutions, the Marxist optimistic predictions as to its eventual decline became too unrealistic. Weber, by conceiving bureaucracy as a type of organisation, has stressed the all-pervasiveness of the phenomenon and the *naïveté* of those who hoped for its future disappearance. By widening in this manner the analytical focus, the problems change as well as the meaning of the terminology which expresses them. If, in Marx, the class struggle is at the centre of attention and defines all other problems, with Weber bureaucracy becomes the central concept. From this perspective the problem is not any more if bureaucracy will decline or not; rather, its permanence and technical indispensability taken for granted, one begins to ask about the impact of this type of organisation on the social structure and on the individual personality. What institutional forms are possible within a bureaucratic society? What are the chances of individual freedom in a society of giant bureaucracies interfering in the most intimate aspects of private life?

As the problems and the theoretical perspectives change, the terms which are used change their meanings too. From Weber's point of view bureaucratisation means mainly the increasing prevalence of a rational type of organisation, in all administrative systems, inside or outside the public sector. Used more loosely, it also refers to the increasing rationalisation of human relationships and beliefs, to a certain style of life which is partly the outcome of the process of bureaucratisation in the previous sense.

But, if Marx conceived bureaucracy as an oppressive instrument and Weber as an efficient one, with Michels and those who, impressed by the subsequent rise of totalitarian régimes, shared the Machiavellian pessimism about democracy, bureaucracy ceases to be an instrument and becomes the master. In this third theoretical stage, bureaucracy is studied as a system of political domination which arises from a shift of power from the legitimate source of authority to those office holders (whether in the big corporation or the government) who are in a *de facto* dominant position because of their specialised knowledge. For Weber the political domination of bureaucracy was problematic and depended on the external forces of every particular situation. For Michels and Burnham, it becomes an inevitable outcome, inherent in the internal dynamics of bureaucracy. From this angle the capitalism-socialism alternative is rejected and the main problem becomes the analysis of the exact nature of the new oligarchic society.

As for the philosophy of history underlying most of the theories of Burnham and Michels, it departs clearly from Weber's cautious position and affirms the exact opposite of Marx's thesis. In spite of the apparent change and revolution, basically everything remains the same. The dominance and relative exploitation of the masses by a small élite, bureaucratic or other, is a permanent feature of human history. Any revolution striving for democracy and justice, even when successful, ultimately leads to an oligarchic situation, and the cycle starts all over again. Thus, we could arrange these three instances of the classical theory along an optimism-pessimism continuum.

The Classical Approach to the Study of Bureaucracy

The increasing stress on the pessimistic side, reflects a general disillusionment and loss of faith which partly came as a reaction to the earlier overconfidence in the human reason and the inevitable march of history towards progress.

Now, if we try to identify common elements underlying the classical theories of bureaucracy, the most basic one is the all-inclusiveness of their scope. Their analysis of bureaucracy was not placed, as in many modern studies, in a political and social vacuum. It was systematically linked with the social structure as a whole, with its main tensions and dilemmas. Problems occurring on a societal level were traced back to their organisational implications. Inversely, the impact of bureaucratic organisations on the power-structure of society was systematically examined. Moreover, most of the classical writers had a broad historical perspective. In dealing with the problems of bureaucracy and bureaucratisation, they were fully aware that such problems can only be understood when the societies within which they arise are studied dynamically, in their historical development and change.

Thus, such a wide approach helped the classical writers to see the organisational problems and their consequences in all their fundamental dimensions and to grasp the main issues of our organisational civilisation. Indeed, most of the basic problems which were subsequently re-examined (in a more empirical and systematic way), are to be found in these early writings. For instance, an attitude common to all classical writers (which we find again in modern studies of bureaucracy) was their anti-formalism. Their study of bureaucracy was never based on observations taken from law books, or administrative regulations. They all had an acute awareness of the difference between what people say they do and what they really do; between social relations, as described in law books and actual dealings in terms of power. As a matter of fact, the formal-informal theme was all-pervasive, although it took different forms according to the writer and the problems treated.

Marx criticised Hegel's idealistic conception of a 'general interest' bureaucracy and analysed its relations with the social structure in terms of power and domination. The concept of

35

the displacement of power, so common in the classical literature, indicates as well the gap between those who really have power and those who legitimately should have power. In a similar manner, the phenomenon of goal displacement, which was systematically elaborated by Michels, underlines the difference between reality and ideal, between what is and what ought to be.

Another frequent theme in the classical literature is the preoccupation with the impact of bureaucracy on the individual's freedom and personality. In Marxism, it took the form of man's alienation, his feelings of powerlessness and helplessness in the face of a mysterious and oppressive caste of bureaucratic officials. This preoccupation was also expressed by his analysis of the dehumanisation of the worker's personality in the process of the increasing division of labour.

Weber elaborated and enlarged a similar theme: the Marxist concept of the alienation of the producer from his product and his tools. The concentration of the means of production becomes a special case of the concentration of the means of administration, which takes place, not only in the economic but in the political, religious, educational and military institutions. In all these cases, the individual, occupying an insignificant place in a huge organisation which he cannot control or understand, becomes a simple cog in a machine, a well disciplined and regulated automaton with a specialised technical knowledge and a generalised ignorance and indifference as to his position and purpose in the organisation and in society in general. Finally, Michels placed more emphasis upon the political aspects of the individual's alienation, upon the unavoidable ignorance and hopelessness of the simple organisational member, eternally manipulated and exploited by those who are supposed to promote his interests.

Of course, the broadness of scope and the all-inclusiveness of the classical approach has its shortcomings. Necessarily, by wanting to embrace all the aspects and implications of the bureaucracy problem on a societal level, one's analysis lacks the rigour and precision which is achieved by a more limited and less ambitious investigation. The concepts used by the classical writers are often imprecise and one cannot be sure in what way they are linked with the social reality that they want to express.

Moreover, they seem to formulate oversweeping generalisations which clearly are half-truths (in the sense that they are only valid under certain conditions which remain unspecified by the classical theory). From this point of view, as will be shown in the following chapters, more recent writers preoccupied with similar problems try to refine these generalisations by examining in a more limited and empirical manner the specific conditions under which the classical statements hold true (cf. especially chapter 3).

Chapter Two

THE IDEAL TYPE OF BUREAUCRACY

Weber's ideal type of bureaucracy has been, especially since
the war, the starting point and the main source of inspiration
for many students of organisation. At the same time it has been
the object of criticism and long controversies. As such, it is
important to analyse and criticise it in some detail and to pay
particular attention to the way in which it has been used by
modern students of bureaucracy. The first section of this
chapter comments on the Weberian characteristics of bureaucracy, especially on the way in which they were used in recent
organisation literature. The second section is mainly an assessment of the logical status and the methodological functions of
the ideal type. In the third section, different modern uses of
the term bureaucracy and their links to the ideal type are
briefly discussed.

I. SOME COMMENTS ON THE CHARACTERISTICS OF BUREAUCRACY

The ideal type of bureaucracy is a conceptual construction of
certain empirical elements into a logically precise and consistent form, a form which, in its ideal purity, is never to be
found in concrete reality.[1] The detailed way in which this form
is constructed will be examined in the second section. For the
moment, we shall only be concerned with the empirical
elements which refer to the various characteristics of bureaucracy. Indeed, the characteristics contained in the ideal type,
although transformed and exaggerated in a certain way,
correspond, more or less, to concrete features of existing
organisations. Briefly, the main characteristics of the bureaucratic type of organisation are:

The Ideal Type of Bureaucracy

- High degree of specialisation
- Hierarchical authority structure with limited areas of command and responsibility
- Impersonality of relationships between organisational members
- Recruitment of officials on the basis of ability and technical knowledge
- Differentiation of private and official income and fortune

and so on.

Now, if one tries to see what lies beyond the above characteristics, how they are linked with one another, one finds a common, all-pervasive element; the existence of a system of control based on rational rules, rules which try to regulate the whole organisational structure and process on the basis of technical knowledge and with the aim of maximum efficiency.

> Bureaucratic administration means fundamentally the exercise of control on the basis of knowledge. This is the feature of it which makes it specifically rational.

So from this general point of view, what makes an organisation more or less bureaucratic is not simply the existence of rules, but the quality of these rules. Feudal administration also controlled organisational action through rules.[3] But the decisive difference between it and a bureaucracy is that these rules were not based on technical knowledge and rational thinking but on tradition. The above point must always be kept in mind when one deals with the ideal typical features of bureaucracy. This will become clearer by a brief discussion of the ways in which some of the above characteristics have been used by modern writers.

A. The nature of bureaucratic hierarchy

Modern theorists of bureaucracy, basing their views on Weber, often use the hierarchy characteristics as one of the most decisive criteria for finding out to what degree an organisation is bureaucratised. For example, Stanley Udy Jr., wanting to make this criterion operational, decided that from the hierarchical point of view, an organisation should be labelled bureaucratic if it had three or more levels of authority.[4] Other authors use the term hierarchy in general as a feature of bureaucratic organisation, without specifying in what sense a hierarchy constitutes a bureaucratic characteristic.[5] In this way, they imply that any kind of hierarchy is a bureaucratic characteristic, an implication which is not correct, at least in the Weberian sense.

Actually hierarchy in general (in the sense of levels of authority) is to be found in any administration which has a certain degree of magnitude and complexity. The feudal type of administration had a complicated hierarchical system. 'There is hierarchy of a social rank corresponding to the hierarchy of fiefs through the process of sub-infeudation . . .'[6] But the difference between the two kinds of hierarchies, according to Weber, is to be found in the type of authority relations. In the feudal case the relationship between inferior and superior is personal and the legitimation of authority is based on a belief in the sacredness of tradition. In a bureaucracy, authority is legitimised by a belief in the correctness of the rules and the loyalty of the bureaucrat is oriented to an impersonal order, to a superior position, not to the person who holds it (cf. chapter 2, section 2). So what makes an administration more or less bureaucratic from the hierarchical point of view is not the number of levels of authority, or the size of the span of control; the decisive criterion is whether or not the authority relations have a precise and impersonal character, as a result of the elaboration of rational rules.

B. *Hierarchy and discretion*

Another point for comment on the hierarchical characteristics of Weber's model is the problem of discretion: the relation between initiative and discipline. Monroe Berger,[7] who bases his analysis of the Egyptian bureaucracy on Weber's concept, uses as one of the criteria of bureaucratisation of an organisation the high degree of discretion that an official has in the performance of his duties, discretion being defined as an emphasis upon personal judgement and initiative, acceptance of responsibility and full use of discretionary powers within the rules. It is indeed very problematical if this characteristic can be called bureaucratic in a real or in an ideal sense.

On the one hand it is true that Weber in his discussion about hierarchy in the ideal model, left room for both centralised and decentralised systems of authority.

> Hierarchies defer in respect to whether and in what cases complaints can lead to a ruling from an authority at various points higher in the scale, and as to whether changes are imposed from higher up or the responsibility for such changes is left to the lower office, the conduct of which was the subject of complaint.[8]

Moreover, it is clear that by the strict delineation of the areas of command, the bureaucrat, outside his official role, is much more free and independent of his superior than any other type of official.

But on the other hand, within the area of the office and concerning the ways in which a bureaucrat performs his duties, there is no doubt that for Weber's ideal type his discretion is minimised by strict procedural rules. These rules, aiming at the avoidance of any arbitrary action, imposing strict discipline and control, do not leave much room for initiative and discretion. 'In the great majority of cases he (the bureaucrat) is only a simple cog in an ever-moving mechanism which prescribes to him an essentially fixed route of march.'[9] Moreover, one arrives at the same conclusion if the problem is placed in the larger context of Weber's philosophy of history. The trend towards increasing bureaucratisation in the modern world is very closely linked with a decrease in individual freedom (cf. chapter 2, section 2).

So we must conclude that although he does not explicitly elaborate this point, Weber not only does not include the concept of discretion in his ideal type, but rather he does the contrary. In order to rationalise and make an administrative machine efficient, one has to control and guide administrative behaviour by strict rational rules – thus limiting individual initiative to a minimum.

C. Administration and organisation

Does the ideal type of bureaucracy refer to the organisation as a whole or simply to its administrative apparatus? If one takes into consideration all the characteristics formulated by Weber, it becomes clear that some of them refer only to the administrative apparatus of an organisation. For example such characteristics as insistence on written documents and files could only apply to an office, to the clerical staff of a factory, not to its workers. But when Weber uses the ideal type for the examination of concrete historic cases, he often gives bureaucracy a more inclusive meaning. This is evident, for instance, when he speaks about the bureaucratisation of the factory or of the political party.[10]

The lack of distinction between organisation and administration in Weber's work can be explained by the fact that he formulated his concept of bureaucracy within the context of his political sociology – i.e. having in mind the governmental apparatus. Moreover, in many cases, it is difficult to distinguish organisational members who belong to the administrative staff and those who do not. The same difficulty arises when one tries to delineate the boundaries of an organisation. For instance to what extent the shareholders or the clients of a firm are part of the organisation.[11] In modern literature the term bureaucracy seems to be used in the same indiscriminate manner. Sometimes it refers only to the administrative apparatus of an organisation; at other times it refers to the organisation as a whole.[12]

I think the best conceptual clarification of this problem was given by Parsons who distinguished three levels or subsystems in the hierarchial structure of every organisation: the technical, the managerial and the institutional. The first subsystem is concerned with all those technical activities which contribute directly to the performance of the organisation's goal (e.g. the processing of raw material in a factory, the actual teaching in a school). The managerial system administers the internal affairs of the organisation and mediates between the technical subsystem and its immediate environment by procuring the necessary resources and by finding 'customers' for the disposal of organisational products. Finally the institutional subsystem operates as a link between the technical-managerial subsystem, and the larger society. Thus for instance, in a business organisation the plant would correspond to the technical subsystem, the office or administration to the managerial and the board of directors to the institutional. Parsons thinks that these distinctions are justified by the fact that each subsystem has different functions to perform and consequently different structural arrangements by which it tries to cope with such problems. Therefore at the points of articulation between them 'we find a qualitative break in the simple continuity of "line" authority'.[13]

In the light of the above distinctions it is clear that most of the literature on bureaucracy examines mainly the managerial subsystem of an organisation. It is also clear that such distinctions must be kept in mind in order to broaden the scope of organisational studies and in order to promote comparative research on the similarities and systematic differences between subsystems of various organisational types.

2. THE MODE OF CONSTRUCTION OF THE IDEAL TYPE

Many criticisms of Weber's concept of bureaucracy are rather irrelevant, as they make the assumption that the ideal type has the same logical status as a simple classifactory type, or as an empirical model. For example the ideal type has been criticised for not focusing on other crucial aspects of organisational reality (informal organisation, dysfunctional consequences, etc.).[14] To such a criticism, Weber could reply that it was not his intention to construct a model of bureaucracy which would approach as much as possible to concrete reality. Rather, he tried to identify the administrative characteristics typical of a certain kind of organisation. Thus he was not obliged to use all or the most important organisational aspects, if and in so far as these aspects existed in other types of administration as well. For example, the feudal type of administration also had rules (traditional rules) and as a consequence even in this case, there was an informal organisation deviating from the traditionally prescribed rules. The same could be said about other important aspects of an organisation like decision-making, dysfunctions and so on.

Other critics have pointed out that some of the ideal type's characteristics are not to be found in organisations which are manifestly bureaucratic in Weber's sense; consequently they are not essential and they should not be included in the concept of bureaucracy.[15] Such criticisms consider the ideal type of bureaucracy as a simple logical class which should group under its denomination all concrete organisations having certain specific characteristics. But Weber has explicitly stated that the ideal types cannot 'be defined by *genus proximum* and *differentia specifica*, and concrete cases cannot be subsumed under them as instances'.[16]

The only way to make a valid criticism of Weber's concept of bureaucracy is to consider it as what it was meant to be (an ideal type) and to analyse it on this level. But before such an analysis, because of the numerous misunderstandings and misuses of the concept, it is necessary to point out in some detail what the ideal type is not meant to be:

(a) The term 'type' has been used in various ways and has had many meanings in the social sciences.[17] The first meaning which is most obviously dissociated from Weber's ideal type, is when the term is used in the sense of average. When one speaks of the ideal type of bureaucracy, there is certainly no implication of a typical bureaucracy in the same sense in which we would speak of an average firm or a typical student.

(b) Moreover, as was said above, the ideal type is not a logical class or a simple type. A simple classificatory type, as a logical class, has as a function to group under its heading various concrete phenomena, taking as criteria of classification certain common and specific properties.[18] Thus the ideal type of bureaucracy must not be seen as comprising a fixed number of specific characteristics determining which organisations must be put in the bureaucratic pigeonhole and which must be left outside.

(c) Neither is the ideal model of bureaucracy an 'extreme type'

44

which has as a function the ordering of various concrete phenomena along a qualitative or quantitative continuum. Such types, which are very often used in psychology, and sociology,[19] are constructed by the exaggeration of certain properties of concrete phenomena. They thus constitute extreme poles of a scale and they are useful in so far as they help in the comparison of concrete instances along a continuum.[20]

Although the ideal type of bureaucracy has been used in this sense (cf. section 3), it was not meant by Weber to be simply an extreme type. Weber's construct, more than a classifactory or an ordering type, was meant to be an analytic tool contributing directly to the explanation and interpretation of social phenomena.

(d) But in spite of such claims, Weber does not consider the ideal type as a theoretical model, that is as a set of interconnected hypotheses which can be validated or rejected by empirical research.[21]

In order to see how an ideal type differs from a theory or a model, we must try to analyse in detail the various steps taken for the construction of the former:

– The first step is the selection and conceptualisation of empirical data, this selection being determined by Weber's interest in finding the typical aspects of a certain type of administration. So for example many of the ideal characteristics of bureaucracy, despite their purity, were selected in an inductive way, by taking into consideration real organisations in which such features were more or less present.[22]

– The second step consists in exaggerating such selected features to their logical extreme.[23] For example, in the ideal type of bureaucracy, the hierarchical relations between bureaucrats are one hundred per cent impersonal. In reality this is never the case.

– Finally, the selection and exaggeration of empirical elements and their formation into an ideal type is not done in an arbitrary way. These elements are interconnected in such a way that they form a whole portraying an inner consistency and logic. These interconnections are not theoretical statements

45

making hypotheses about interrelationships between concrete phenomena. Thus their validity cannot be judged by experimentation but by the following criteria:

(a) The criterion of objective possibility requires that the constructed type must be an empirically possible one. In our example, this would mean that, even if the type of bureaucracy is never to be found in its ideal extremism, it must not contradict any of the 'known laws of nature'.[24]

(b) Moreover, the ideal construction must not only be objectively possible, but also 'adequate at the level of meaning'.[25] Very crudely, that means that it must also make sense to us, give us the feeling of consistency and plausibility. It is this kind of intuitive understanding, of empathic knowledge[26] which plays a great role in the construction and comprehension of the ideal type.

In the case of bureaucracy, it is the meaning of rationality, grasped in the above intuitive manner, which links together the various ideal characteristics and which gives consistency and logic to the whole construct. An ideally rational organisation, in the Weberian sense, is an organisation performing its tasks with maximum efficiency. Thus the selection and exaggeration of the various empirical elements and their interconnections were established in such a way, that a perfectly efficient organisation would result if ever such an extreme type existed in reality. In other terms, to the empirical elements which Weber incorporated into his ideal type and to their combination he attached the attribute of rationality. And this evaluative assumption is not a hypothesis to be checked by further research. It is simply the meaning of bureaucracy which is caught when this type of organisation is imagined, in isolation from all alien elements which, in the real world, distort its ideal rationality.

The issue at this point of the discussion is to see to what extent it is possible to construct a conceptual model of a perfectly rational organisation, by specifying in detail and *a priori* (that is without previous empirical research) the characteristics and their combination which, if ever realised, should give the maximum degree of efficiency. Or in other words, to what extent is it possible, assuming the members of an organisation to be acting in the most efficient way in the accomplishment of their tasks, to find out by the imagination only what the structural characteristics of such an organisation should look like? The answer to such a question must be in the negative. Although in different cases an ideal typical formulation may be very useful, in this particular case it does not seem to have been successful. Indeed, the way in which Weber constructed the ideal type of bureaucracy does not satisfy even his own criteria of validity for such a type.

Concerning first the criterion of meaningful adequacy, it does not necessarily make sense to someone that a type of organisation having the Weberian characteristics to an extreme degree should yield maximum efficiency. One could equally well imagine such an organisation as being extremely inefficient. For example, some of these characteristics, even from a common sense point of view, seem to promote administrative inefficiency rather than efficiency (e.g. promotion by seniority).

As to the criterion of objective possibility, in the light of the empirical research done since Weber, one can argue that a perfectly rational-efficient organisation having Weber's ideal characteristics is not objectively possible, in the sense that it runs against the *known laws of nature* – in this case, against recent empirical findings. Such findings rather indicate that the more accentuated some characteristics of the ideal type are, the more inefficient the organisation becomes. In one sense, a great part of the literature on bureaucracy since Weber is a systematic exposition of the dysfunctional aspects and the unintended (mainly undesirable) consequences of strict bureaucratic control (cf. chapter 3). For the moment a few examples will be sufficient. Consider for instance, the problem of the efficiency of rules. Although to a certain degree the elaboration of precise and strict rules avoids indeterminancy and arbitrariness, on the other hand, especially when there is an effort to control by procedural rules even the details of each bureaucratic activity, and thus reduce seriously the initiative of the official, the results are rigidity and inefficiency of the whole organisation.[27]

Moreover, it has been shown that ideal characteristics are not always compatible with each other. Consequently, when present in an organisation, they become the source of friction and inefficiency. Among many writers, Parsons[28] and Gouldner[29] point out an inherent contradiction in the ideal type between hierarchical position and technical knowledge: 'On the one side, it was administration based on expertise: while on the other, it was administration based on discipline'.[30] In the ideal type both hierarchical authority and expert knowledge are present, but the eventual conflict between them is ignored, as it is not compatible with the assumption of ideal rationality.

In consequence it is clear that the characteristics included in the ideal type, when approximated in reality, do not necessarily yield maximum efficiency. Their efficiency or inefficiency is always determined by the specific organisational situation, mainly by the existing technology, the objectives and the societal environment of the organisation. As a consequence, it is radically impossible to construct ideally, outside a concrete context, a type identifying the mechanisms which should bring maximum efficiency.

For Weber the ideal type is a conceptual tool which helps us to understand better social phenomena, by analysing the discrepancy between their ideal form and their concrete state. In our case the problem should be to compare the ideal type of bureaucracy with a real administration, find out the differences, and try to explain them.[31] Even if a conceptual construction of an ideal bureaucracy were possible, in order to make the comparison, we ought to know something about concrete bureaucracy. But to do this, we have to use a non-ideal model, that is a model which attempts to describe, explain and approach, as much as possible, the real situation.

So the ideal type, in any case, cannot be a substitute for theory and model building in the social sciences. Finally, if one should insist on building up a construct approaching the ideal type of bureaucracy, one should begin the other way round. One should construct a realistic model, learn something about actual efficiency or inefficiency of real organisations and then try, on the basis of this knowledge to speculate on the hypothetical form of an entirely rational model. Thus one does not need an ideal type in order to understand reality, but rather one needs some knowledge of reality in order to construct an ideal model (at least in the study of bureaucracy).[32]

But on the other hand, the contradictions of the ideal type have not seriously handicapped Weber's insights and contributions to the study of organisations. This is because Weber has not used the ideal type in the way he said one should use it. As in other instances, there is a discrepancy between Weber's methodological writings and the actual method that he uses in his historical analyses.[33] Martindale has pointed out that Weber does not so much compare ideal to real phenomena in order to establish and investigate their discrepancy – rather, he uses the ideal type as a tool for the historical comparison of two or more real situations. In this context the type helps to isolate 'the factors on which the comparison becomes critical'.[34] Moreover, as Andreski remarks there is nothing very ideal about the way Weber talks about bureaucracy or feudalism. 'He moves on the level of abstraction which is not very far removed from observable reality.'[35]

Thus Weber does not use the concept of bureaucracy for a micro-analysis of the internal structure of an organisation.[36] He uses it in his cross-cultural general analysis, mainly in order to distinguish various types of domination and their corresponding administrative apparatus (cf. chapter 1). On this macroscopic level, where details and minor variations become irrelevant, the concept of bureaucracy, used as an extreme type, is useful and adequate. Even the assumption concerning the rational superiority of the bureaucratic type of administration, when considered as a hypothesis assessing the comparative efficiency of various historical types of administration, is very plausible. Indeed, in spite of all the dysfunctions of the organisational control by rational rules, one could hardly imagine a big modern corporation functioning without such rules. As a matter of fact the complexity and size of modern administrative tasks make the bureaucratic type of organisation, when compared with the feudal or the patrimonial, by far the most efficient.

3. THE MODERN USES OF THE TERM 'BUREAUCRACY'

There is a duality in Weber's ideal type of bureaucracy. On the one hand it contains empirical elements which were formulated in an inductive way, by observing certain characteristics of concrete organisations. On the other hand, it contains assumptions about the attributes of such elements (i.e. about their efficiency), assumptions which were derived intuitively from the alleged ideal meaning of such structures: their rationality. So bureaucracy could mean different things according to which of the two parts of the ideal type one refers to. In modern theory the concept is used in both ways.

A. The uses of the empirical aspects of the ideal type

In this case one can distinguish different subtypes in the literature of bureaucracy:

(a) The simplest approach is to take all the characteristics of the ideal type and disregard all considerations about efficiency. According to this approach an administration is bureaucratic or non-bureaucratic, according to the degree in which its features are similar to the Weberian characteristics.

(b) Very often writers use the empirical characteristics of the ideal type in a more selective way. They add, modify or subtract some of the Weberian characteristics according to their analytical purposes and their conception of bureaucracy.[37]

(c) A more sophisticated use of Weber's concept is to consider the bureaucratic attributes as dimensions, magnitudes, each one varying quantitatively from one organisation to another.[38] In this view there is no assumption of intercorrelation between the different dimensions. Thus it is possible for them to vary simultaneously in opposite directions. In this way one avoids the dichotomy between bureaucratic or non-bureaucratic organisation. An organisation may thus be more bureaucratic in one dimension and less bureaucratic in another. Moreover, as there is no intercorrelation between the different magnitudes, one can directly link and assess the influence of extrabureaucratic factors (like urbanisation, industrialisation) to only one dimension, not to the whole organisational complex. In this way the analysis becomes much more refined and sophisticated.

B. Uses of the evaluative aspects of the ideal type

In this case, the detailed characteristics of the ideal type are neglected and an organisation is called bureaucratic in so far as it displays certain qualities in the performance of its tasks (rationality, efficiency, inefficiency).

(a) In common language, and even in that of social scientists bureaucracy is used with the evaluative connotation of inefficiency or red tape. A behaviour pattern or an administration is called bureaucratic when it displays any of the dysfunctions analysed by the modern students of bureaucracy (formalism, displacement of goals, etc., cf. chapter 3). This usage of the term is, of course, in diametrical antithesis with Weber's concept. This does not mean that Weber has completely neglected the dysfunctional aspects of modern organisations. But he did not give much significance to it as by definition there was no place for such an element in his ideal type.

(b) Another meaning which bureaucracy has been given is that of rationality. The concepts of rationality and efficiency are among the most ambiguous and controversial in organisation theory. In the Weberian sense, rationality implies the appropriateness of means to ends. In the bureaucratic context this means efficiency.[39] An organisation would be rational if the most efficient means are chosen for the implementation of goals. But it is only the collective goals of the organisation, not those of the individual members which are taken into consideration. Thus the fact that an organisation is rational does not imply that its members act rationally as far as their proper goals and aspirations are concerned. On the contrary, the more rational and bureaucratic an organisation becomes, the more the individual members become simple cogs in a machine ignoring the purpose and meaning of their behaviour. This is the sort of rationality that Mannheim calls 'functional'.[40]

More specifically, for Weber, functional rationality is attained by the elaboration (on the basis of scientific knowledge) of rules which try to direct from the top all behaviour towards maximum efficiency. It is this conception of rationality which underlies the theories of scientific management, which aim at discovering and applying the one best way of performing an industrial task (cf. chapter 4).

(c) A different approach to the concepts of rationality and efficiency consists in avoiding the identification of them with the existence of rules or any other bureaucratic feature. According to Blau for example, it is not strict discipline and rule elaboration which brings efficiency, but rather the achievement of conditions favourable to the development of individual initiative and spontaneity. In this positive sense, if the top management intervenes and regulates the official's activities, it is with a completely different intention: the aim of such an intervention is not to tell the official what to do, but rather to destroy the obstacles and to establish the conditions which could help him to cope spontaneously and responsibly with emerging problems.[41] These considerations and findings cause Blau to 'disregard all characteristics and to identify bureaucracy with efficiency: rather than considering it an administrative system with particular characteristics, it may be preferable to follow another lead of Weber's and to conceive of bureaucracy in terms of its purpose. Bureaucracy, then, can be defined as organisation that maximises efficiency in administration, whatever its formal characteristics.'[42]

(d) If one dissociates from the concept of administrative rationality both the idea of efficiency and the existence of rules, one can give to this term a third relative meaning: if as Weber thought, it is evident that modern administrative behaviour has increasingly a rational orientation, looking at the organisation as a whole, one could conceive this trend as a shift from what Sumner calls a 'crescive' type of social organisation (with rules and goals spontaneously emerging in the course of human interaction) towards a type where men try (on the basis of scientific knowledge and rational thinking) deliberately to determine and shape the structure of such

The Ideal Type of Bureaucracy

organisation according to their values and goals. Such rational orientations, although they often aim at an increase of organisational efficiency do not necessarily achieve this goal.[43] This rational determination not to let things go by themselves (the effort toward conscious control of the organisational evolution) is not necessarily accompanied by the existence of strict procedural rules on the individual level, or by an increase in efficiency.

C. Bureaucracy in terms of power

Finally, in order to complete the range of the various uses of the concept of bureaucracy, we should briefly mention a third group of definitions which have an abuse of power connotation (cf. chapter 1, section 3). Such definitions are very common among political scientists and refer mainly to the state administration. Here as well the submeanings are numerous. For example, bureaucracy could imply an abuse in the domain of internal politics (overcentralisation, authoritarian controls, lack of democratic decision-making), or the abuse may refer to the organisation as a whole in its relation to other centres of power ('big' government, excessive power of the executive over the legislative, etc.).[44]

4. FINAL CONSIDERATIONS

The above discussion has shown the confusion and ambiguity in the way bureaucracy is used in modern social theory. This situation is due partly to the inherent contradictions of the ideal type, and partly to the uncritical adoption and transformation of the term by various authors. The ideal type of bureaucracy was mainly constructed in view of a wide historical comparative analysis of administrative systems. Modern writers, although influenced by Weber's construction of bureaucracy, have ignored the problems of development and cross-cultural comparison of organisations. Bureaucratic theory has become 'predominantly ethnocentric, nonhistorical and microscopic in orientation'.[45]

Consequently as the concept of bureaucracy, at least in the

manner formulated by Weber, does not seem adequate for the empirical and detailed investigation of concrete organisations, and as there is no way to judge which of the numerous modern uses of the term is the most successful, its further utilisation could only bring more confusion and ambiguity. Probably the best way out of this difficult terminological situation is to use bureaucracy as Weber did, that is only as an extreme type useful for broad historical comparisons; and for all other purposes to employ the term 'organisation'.

Chapter Three

THE POST-WEBERIAN THEORIES OF BUREAUCRACY

INTRODUCTION

Weber's ideal construction, for reasons we have discussed in the previous chapter, did not claim to be an empirical model or a theory of bureaucracy. It was only taking account of the rational aspects of administrative behaviour. Of course, Weber was aware of the one-sidedness of his type and of the necessity to compare the ideal with the real in order to understand organisational reality. But he did not proceed to the empirical study of the internal structure of bureaucracy and it was left to his followers to carry on the analysis on an empirical basis.

Robert K. Merton was among the first sociologists to point out the other side of the bureaucratic picture: if, as Weber thought, close control by rule favours reliability and predictability of the bureaucrat's behaviour, at the same time it accounts for his lack of flexibility and his tendency to turn means into ends. Indeed the emphasis laid by bureaucracy on conformity and strict observance of the rules induce the individual to internalise such rules. Thus, instead of simple means, procedural regulations become ends in themselves. The instrumental and formalistic aspects of the bureaucratic job become more important than the substantive ones (that is, good service to clients), and the effectiveness of the whole system suffers accordingly. Moreover, these dysfunctional aspects of the system are reinforced when, as a response to the protestation of clients, the bureaucrat defends himself by behaving in a more formalistic and rigid way (hiding behind the rules, etc.).[1]

The Study of Bureaucracy

Thus, when one leaves the level of ideal rationality, when non-rational aspects of behaviour are taken into consideration, the same structural elements (strict control by rules) may have both functional (predictability, etc.) and dysfunctional (rigidity) effects as far as organisational goal achievement is considered. Of course, Merton's theme is not new. The classical writers have dealt extensively with the phenomenon of goal displacement.[2] Moreover, the non-empirical character of Merton's article[3] places it, in a sense, within the writings discussed in our first chapter. But on the other hand, its limited scope and its emphasis on organisational dysfunctions make it the link between classical and modern theories of bureaucracy.[4] Indeed, it has been the starting point of a series of studies which try firstly to complement, make more empirical and realistic Weber's ideal type; and secondly, limiting mainly their scope to the organisational level, to elaborate in a more precise and empirical way some of the problems of the classical literature.

I. THE CONCEPTUAL FRAMEWORK

The study of any social phenomenon requires a choice of those of its concrete aspects which are most relevant to the problem under consideration. This choice, which in a way isolates a part of social reality in order to reduce its complexities of observation, determines the analytical or conceptual framework of a theory: that is, it sets theoretical boundaries, it discriminates between relevant and irrelevant properties, it indicates what is going to be explained and what is going to be considered as given.

A. The level of analysis

As was pointed out in the first chapter, the classical writers have dealt more with the impact of large-scale organisations on the political structure of society than with bureaucracy in itself. The social scientists who, after Weber, continued to examine the problems of bureaucracy, have shifted their attention to the organisational level. Indeed, although they often examine the wider environment of the organisation as well as the individual's problems within it,[5] the main focus of analysis is the organisation as a whole. This narrowing of focus permits the formulation of more precise concepts and of limited hypotheses of a more testable nature.

In this way most studies since Weber have a strong empirical character. The single case study is the usual research pattern. The investigator chooses one organisation for an intensive examination of its internal structure[6] or for the testing of a limited set of interconnected hypotheses.[7] As for data collection, apart from the analysis of organisational documents and charts, both direct observation and various types of interviewing are used. It is on the basis of such data that the various hypotheses put forward are accepted or rejected.

B. The variables taken into consideration

But if empiricism has reduced the scope of analysis, in another way it has made it more comprehensive. Contrary to Weber who has conceived the ideal bureaucrat as a mere administrative tool, the new approach has an all-inclusive character. The instrumental aspects of bureaucratic behaviour constitute now only one dimension of the model. The bureaucrat is, in this case, seen as a whole human being with emotions, beliefs and goals of his own; goals which do not always coincide with the general goals of the organisation. These aspects of his behaviour may influence the structure and functions of the whole organisation. Consequently they cannot be ignored or seen as constant variables which can be safely put aside. When these variables are seriously taken into consideration, the need also arises for appropriate conceptual tools which can account for them. A kind of organising scheme is needed which can relate in a meaningful way the various aspects of organisational reality that are chosen as relevant.

C. The functional approach

Indeed, with the introduction of the non-rational aspects of individual behaviour, on the organisational level, bureaucracy ceases to be merely a formal arrangement of consciously co-ordinated activities. It can be seen as a social system, a system which is partly shaped by purposive design and partly formed spontaneously by forces emerging during the interaction of social beings. The various subgroups, roles, norms and values which thus emerge within the prearranged formal framework, constitute some of the interdependent parts of the social structure.[8]

Functional analysis, as an expository and explanatory tool, is a convenient way for dealing systematically with relations among such parts as well as with the role that each part plays in relation to the whole. The organisation as a system and the various subsystems within it can be conceived as having needs (functional requirements). Any structural part is said to have a function when it contributes to the fulfilment of a need.[9] On the other hand, when the effects of the part hinder this fulfilment one speaks of dysfunctional consequences or of the part as dysfunctional with respect to the above need.[10] From the above it becomes evident that a certain part or social pattern can have both functional and dysfunctional consequences for different needs of the system. In such a case the problem arises of 'assessing the net balance of the aggregate of consequences'[11] in order to find out if the overall effect of a pattern is functional or dysfunctional.

Another fundamental distinction of functionalism is between apparent and latent functions (or dysfunctions) of a social pattern. Every contribution to the fulfilment of a system need is not purposive. When the distinction is made between the subjective purpose of an actor, intentionally establishing a certain pattern, and the objective consequences of this pattern, it becomes evident that very often the two diverge. Certain patterns have unanticipated consequences as to the need fulfilment of the system or its subsystem. Moreover often such consequences are not only unintended but also remain un-recognised even after their occurrence. These are the latent consequences of a social pattern.[12]

Finally, according to the functionalists, it is not enough for the analyst simply to state that a certain structural element has functional or dysfunctional results from the point of view of system needs. Functional analysis has an explanatory capacity only when one tries to identify the precise mechanisms through which a pattern contributes to the reduction or intensification of social needs. In this way, the investigator does not limit his study to a static enumeration of structural features and their functions or dysfunctions; he is constantly reminded to look for processes which ultimately account for movement and change.

2. THE 'DIALECTICS' OF BUREAUCRACY

One of the most distinctive and interesting features of the post-Weberian theories is their dynamic and dialectic character, their emphasis on small-scale social change which is due to certain inherent strains and dilemmas in bureaucratic organisations. Let us examine this central aspect of bureaucracy theories in some detail.

A main point of differentiation between bureaucracy and other social systems is that in the former there is more purposiveness and explicit design in the shaping of its activities and goals. Formal organisations are established for a certain purpose: men, in a more or less conscious way, co-ordinate their activities in order to achieve certain goals. This co-ordination necessitates a system of purposive control. It usually consists of rules which define the tasks and responsibilities of each participant as well as the formal mechanisms which could permit the integration of these tasks. Such rules constitute the formal structure of the organisation.[13]

But as the above rules do not refer simply to inert materials and tools but to people who act as whole human beings, they never succeed in completely controlling the situation and in directing the organisational activities towards their predefined goals. Individuals have goals of their own which do not always coincide with organisational goals. More precisely, from the point of view of individual members, organisational goals are simply the means through which individuals may achieve their private goals[14] (the same can be said about the particular goals of various groupings within the larger organisation). So it becomes evident that individual goals may come

The Study of Bureaucracy

into conflict with the organisational ones, jeopardising their predefined schemes and objectives. Moreover, relationships stipulated by contract are often in discord with actual relations established in the process of face to face contact. Formal rules may be in conflict with informal rules or norms of conduct, which emerge spontaneously in the process of social interaction.

For all these reasons, organisational members do not comply automatically with formal rules. Their compliance is always problematic and unpredictable. It is this fundamental 'recalcitrance of human tools'[15] which accounts for the unanticipated consequences of purposive action and control. The tension between the formal rules, which attempt to control organisational behaviour, and the 'recalcitrance' of such behaviour which defies full control and develops in an unpredicted manner, generates new situations and needs which in their turn bring forth a renewed attempt to control the situation by further rules. Thus in a general schematic way the general pattern underlying most of the models of bureaucracy under consideration seems to be:

Purposive control (rules) → *unanticipated consequences* → *renewed control*

This formal-informal conflict gives to the organisation a dynamic, ever-changing aspect.[16] Contrary to the popular image, bureaucracy is not seen any more as a static and rigid structure, but as a going concern, as a system of continual tension and change. Of course, the basically dialectic pattern which underlies the various bureaucratic models, takes various forms according to the writer and the type of organisational situation that he examines.

Thus Alvin Gouldner in his *Patterns of Industrial Bureaucracy* stresses the dialectic nature of bureaucratic rules. Rule elaboration has the functional and often unintended consequence of decreasing the visibility of power relations between inferior and superior bureaucrats.[17] In a culture with democratic egalitarian norms (like the American one), this simulation of power behind the written law decreases interpersonal tension and favours co-operation. But on the other hand, the imposition of rules has a dysfunctional aspect. Specifically, the detailed definition by rules of unacceptable behaviour increases the

60

The Post-Weberian Theories of Bureaucracy
knowledge of employees about the minimum acceptable behaviour. This last variable, in conjunction with a low level of internalisation of organisational goals incites the bureaucrat to accomplish the minimum work required. Such an attitude of course is detrimental to the productivity performance of the organisation. As a consequence there is an increase in supervisory activity and control and this in turn increases interpersonal conflict and tension.[18]

In his *Wildcat Strike*[19] the dialectic pattern takes a somewhat different form. It is expressed in terms of threats or disorganising patterns, upsetting the equilibrium of the system and increasing tension; and of organisational defence mechanism which are responses to such tensions and which try to bring back the system to a new equilibrium.[20] If in the place of threats or tensions and defence mechanisms we substitute needs and the mechanisms for their satisfactions we have Blau's model of bureaucratic change. In this case rational intervention (rules), in an attempt to cope with emerging needs, brings forth unintended new needs as soon as the old ones are satisfied. In their turn the new needs demand further rational intervention and so on.

Finally, Selznick[21] conceives the central dilemma in bureaucracy as arising out of the need for the delegation of power to organisational subsystems. The increasing complexity of organisational tasks makes decentralisation and the delegation of responsibility to intermediaries inevitable. But such a measure brings forth the organisational paradox of goal displacement, a bifurcation of interests between the central system and its decentralised subunits. There is a tendency for the latter to neglect the main organisational goals in favour of their limited subgoals.[22] In this way subgoals, from simple means, become ends in themselves. This situation makes the need for centralised control stronger and the circle may start all over again.[23]

Of course the circular, self-reinforcing pattern of rationalisation (rules bringing forth the need for more rules) in the bureaucratic models discussed in this chapter, has an analytic character. It simply refers to a tendency which, in concrete cases, can be more or less checked by countervailing forces.

61

Thus, for example, in Gouldner's model such variables as strong internationalisation of common goals, supervisors' attitudes, manipulation of equality norms may act against the rationalisation spiral. Moreover, concerning the utility of the above models, it must be said that they are not so much aimed at providing a detailed prediction of organisational behaviour (they rather stress the unpredictable character of such behaviour). Nor do they give us a ready-made formula for the solution of administrative problems. But they seem very useful as instruments of analysis, as indicators of tendencies and constraints which must be taken into account for a correct assessment of particular organisational situations.[24]

3. THE EMPIRICAL RE-EXAMINATION OF THE CLASSICAL PROBLEMS

As was said above, the main issues which were put forward by the classical theorists have been taken up again and examined in a more systematic and rigorous way. In very general terms, one could say that this empirical re-examination does not modify radically the insights of the earlier writers. It does not prove that they are wrong. Rather it qualifies their statements, shows their sweeping character, points out that things are more complex and that the classical generalisations are rather one-sided, that is, they are valid only under certain conditions (the urgent task of the social scientist being to identify them).

Moreover, the prevailing mood is more optimistic. There is a strong reaction against what Gouldner calls the 'metaphysical pathos'[25] in the literature of bureaucracy – that is, the tendency to dramatise and overstress the inevitability of bureaucratic domination and the undermining of individual freedom and democracy. There is the growing conviction that 'if the world of theory is grey and foredoomed, the world of everyday life is green with possibilities which need to be cultivated'.[26] Indeed what seems to prevail is the belief that in the last analysis, there is no radical incompatibility between the existence of large-scale organisations and the survival of personal initiative and political freedom; that whether bureaucracy is going to remain a tool or become a master depends on a complexity of factors which one should identify and manipulate accordingly.

A. Bureaucracy and individual initiative

Is the structure of large-scale organisations and the requirements of rationality and efficiency hostile to the exercise of initiative on the individual level? Peter Blau in his various writings on bureaucracy[27] speaks of the myth, first implied in Weber's theory, and later adopted by the theorists and practitioners of scientific management (cf. chapter 4), that rationality comes only from the top; that the only way to make someone behave rationally (from the organisational point of view) is to tell him exactly what to do and to deprive him of every initiative. By his research work he has shown how such a policy usually lowers the productivity and morale of employees. Blau thinks that there are other types of non-authoritarian, decentralised control which permit the conscious direction of bureaucratic activities and the exercise of individual initiative. For example, appropriate recruitment and training procedures can assure that each individual would be able to exercise responsibility and take important decisions without the frustrating guidance of rules or orders coming from the top. By such indirect controls reliability and organisational planning might cease to imply the regimentation of the individual. They might, on the contrary, refer to a conscious effort from the top to remove systematically any obstacle to the exercise of initiative and responsibility.[28]

Gouldner's research in a gypsum plant has a similar optimistic and anti-authoritarian attitude. In his effort to by-pass some of the limitations of Weber's theory of bureaucracy – which he takes as his starting-point – he distinguished between rules having a punishment character and representative rules. The former are enforced and legitimised unilaterally without the full consent of all the parties concerned, the latter are democratically established and have the joint support of both management and the workers.[29] According to Gouldner, in a bureaucracy where representative rules predominate, overt conflict is avoided and deviation from the rules is attributed to ignorance or well-intentioned carelessness. As a consequence, the stress is not so much on punishment but on education as the means for reducing deviant behaviour.

By such distinctions the above authors do not want to deny the frustrating effects of bureaucratic structures on the individual personality; rather, they point out that when one looks closely at the functioning of bureaucratic organisations, one perceives possibilities and alternatives which are often blurred by armchair theorising referring to bureaucracy, democracy, and freedom, in an abstract and general way. Moreover, they point out that authoritarian control, instead of being a stimulus, in most cases is an obstacle to high productivity.[30] Finally, many other empirical researches in various organisational settings point out a persistent trend in modern organisations towards a decentralised and more flexible structure of authority.[31] Even in military bureaucracies, whose authoritarian structure is always taken for granted, Janowitz identifies a similar trend towards the use of less strict and rigid methods of control (control by persuasion, etc.).[32] Moreover, in industrial organisations, the introduction of automation is thought to have similar results, as it replaces the strict regimentation of the assembly line system.[33]

B. Bureaucracy and the problem of oligarchy

Michels' law of oligarchy is another main issue which was empirically re-examined by modern students of bureaucracy. As has been stated in the previous section, the chief result of such an empirical reassessment was not the total rejection of the general hypothesis but rather its further elaboration and refinement. Indeed, although nobody seriously questions the existence of structural elements facilitating oligarchy in modern bureaucracies, the over-deterministic aspect of Michels' generalisations is rejected. There is an increasing awareness that it is impossible to study bureaucracy and to find its laws without specifying under what conditions a certain generalisation holds true. And it is evident that Michels did not pay systematic attention to organisational and social conditions

The Post-Weberian Theories of Bureaucracy
which would qualify and delimit the area of applicability of his statements.

This part of the task was most successfully tackled by Lipset, Trow and Coleman. In an intensive case study of the International Typographical Union[34], whose democratic system defies the iron law of oligarchy, they tried to identify the structural and historical conditions which accounted for the initiation and maintenance of the union's two-party system. They found as relevant and examined extensively how the internal political system was affected by such factors as the relative autonomy and decentralisation of the local subunits,[35] the status of the union leaders,[36] the degree of participation and interest of the rank and file in union politics,[37] the general value system of the organisation[38] and so on.

The above analysis raises some doubts as to the inevitability of oligarchy in all large-scale organisations. More than anything else, this empirical study makes the student sensitive to the lack of monolithic uniformity and to the existence of alternative possibilities in organisations; it incites him to look out for the factors which make organisations vary in their structure and functioning. As the authors put it, this study has 'shown that there is much more variation in the internal organization of associations than the notion of an iron law of oligarchy would imply'.[39] Moreover, such political scientists as Maurice Duverger and Sigmund Newmann[40], by stressing the extreme variability of party political structures have shown the inadequacies of Michels' formulations.[41]

But, in order to put the above criticisms of the law of oligarchy in their right perspective, we must not exaggerate their optimistic message (as to the chance of democratic institutions inside organisations). Thus, for example, the authors of *Union Democracy*, by pointing out the high contingency of the combination of historic events and structural peculiarities which made ITU's internal democracy possible, show how difficult and rare it is for such a political system to arise. Indeed ITU's two-party system is a unique exception among American trade unions. Moreover, many other recent studies have shown the widespread validity of Michels' hypothesis: in the trade union field, most studies point out the oligarchic aspects

65

of their structure.[42] The phenomenon is not limited to union bureaucracies, it is common to all sorts of voluntary organisations (co-operatives, medical associations, churches, etc.).[43]

But in spite of the undeniable fact that most large-scale voluntary organisations have a one-party political system, many modern writers refuse, because of this fact, to accept Michels' pessimistic conclusions (as to the manipulation of the rank and file by a permanent organisational élite, and as to the meagre chances of democracy in the modern world). The debate on this crucial subject is far from being ended.[44] In closing this section, we must emphasise that the above considerations of some of the problems in modern theories of bureaucracy was not meant to be exhaustive or to give definite answers to these problems. Rather it was intended to show in which way some of the central problems created by our organisational civilisation, and analysed by the classical theorists, have been re-examined by more recent writers.

4. CRITICAL REMARKS

A. Methodological problems of the one-case studies

The most representative writings on bureaucracy since Weber are based on intensive research in a single organisational setting. It has become a commonplace to speak of the case study – survey dilemma in organisational literature: on the one hand the one-case study is alleged to give many insights and fruitful hypotheses about the functioning of a particular organisation but to provide no possibility of testing such hypotheses. On the other hand, by a survey study of many organisations, there is the possibility for generalised and methodologically more valid findings – but of a superficial or trivial character. This superficiality is due to the fact that by the survey of numerous organisations one tries to relate in a highly abstract manner a few organisational variables without taking seriously into consideration the larger environment within which such variables are embedded. Thus a choice seems inevitable between theoretical substance and methodological sophistication.

The Post-Weberian Theories of Bureaucracy

Although such a dilemma exists in the study of organisations (and in the social sciences in general), most often it is not as clear-cut as it is suggested. Its 'either . . . or' character is more apparent than real. Thus, concerning first the methodological weakness of the one-case study, although it is not certain if its findings have a wider application, they are certainly not mere impressionistic insights or simple descriptions of non-general relevance. A one-case study can have either a particularistic or a generalising character. In the first instance, the student is more interested in the description of the particular case itself than in its theoretical implications. Although he might use theoretical generalisations in order to describe and explain the case under observation, theory is for him simply a tool, the analysis of the particular situation being his main purpose. On the other hand, in a generalising case study, one is interested in the particular aspects of an organisation only in so far as they are theoretically relevant.

The studies of bureaucracy under consideration are clearly of the generalising type. The writers, usually sociologists, in undertaking such investigations, have in their minds certain hypotheses, certain theoretical problems which influence the method of observation and the kind of data which are collected. Moreover, whenever historical data are introduced in the explanation of the organisational structure, the same generalising perspective is followed.[45]

If the one-case study does not necessarily imply a descriptive, particularistic study, neither does it imply a purely impressionistic statement without any kind of supporting evidence. Most of the hypotheses advanced in such writings are formulated in more or less operational terms and have a fairly testable character. For example, Francis and Stone's *Service and Procedure in Bureaucracy* is a long attempt to test by various devices whether impersonality of relationships and the procedural orientation of employees (i.e. insistence on the formal aspect of rules) is a necessary feature of a bureaucratic organisation. Moreover, although by definition in the one-case study one cannot test the relationship between two variables by the comparative method (that is by examining their variation in other organisations), yet, a certain comparison and variation

67

is possible within one organisation. This can be done, for instance, by examining relations between variables through time. Thus Lipset has tried to test the relationship between high occupational stratification and intense political cleavage in a democratic union, by examining whether in the past the existence of greater heterogeneity of interests between occupational groups was accompanied by an intensification of political conflict within the union.[46]

Of course, the above considerations in defence of the one-case study are not intended to conceal its evident limitations and the usefulness of the comparative study of many organisations. It is obvious that however ingenious the testing of hypotheses within one organisation, we can never be sure of their generalised validity. On the contrary, we can be almost certain that such hypotheses are only valid under certain conditions and for certain types of organisations. This being the case, the only way to find out which are these conditions is by the appropriate comparison of more than one case.[47]

But comparative study does not automatically mean survey study. The conflict between methodological rigour and deep insight is not as insurmountable as we often like to think it is. We are not necessarily forced to a sweeping and superficial examination of hundreds of cases once we abandon the intensive one-case study. By strategically choosing a few cases (say two to five), it is possible to combine intensity of study with comparative variations of significant variables. Indeed it is not necessary to study an unmanageable number of organisations in order to identify some of the important conditions under which a certain hypothesis, formulated within the context of a one-case intensive study, is valid. By the intensive study of one or two cases and by appropriately choosing a few others for a less intensive treatment, one may avoid the disadvantages of both the survey and the one-case study. Actually in *Union Democracy*, the authors followed a similar method in their effort to find out the conditions under which the iron law of oligarchy is valid and those under which it is not. Instead of sending a written questionnaire in a haphazard way to dozens of organisations, they chose a significant case (significant in the sense that Michels' generalisation did not apply to it)

68

for comparison. So, in a way, their work is a completion of Michels and both studies seen together provide a good illustration of what fruitful results a limited comparative study may yield. Indeed it is by such a method that one can gradually build up limited generalisations which are both well founded and theoretically important. And it is mainly this type of study, conspicuously lacking in the literature, which seems to me to provide the most promising approach in this context.

Of course, the above argument does not intend to minimise the great utility of survey studies for providing useful information about organisations. Such information (usually in the form of correlations between organisational variables) delineates the distributional aspects of the organisational structure.[48] But such surveys are not of great help when we want to study the structure of an organisation as a whole social system in terms of its environment, groups, rules, values and their interrelationships.[49] Indeed, I do not think that in the present state of our knowledge, the survey studies (especially those which try to establish correlations valid to all sorts of organisations) can be very successful. The factors involved in each organisational situation are so complex and intermingled that, by abstracting a few variables from their context in order to establish their relationships on a wide range, the ensuing results are likely to be trivial or inconclusive.[50]

Could it, for example, be really meaningful to study the relationship between close supervision and productivity, or the problem of internal democracy by taking a big sample of organisational cases comprising political parties, automobile associations, churches and firms? Of course, the example is very crude, but it makes the point clearly. At the present moment, research should rather concentrate on organisation areas within which bureaucracies portray a high degree of similarity in their aims, in their crucial problems and in their other characteristics. And by the 'intensive-comparative' approach of a few similar cases, generalisations can be built up, valid in well circumscribed and narrow organisation contexts. It is in this way that systematic knowledge, having a cumulative character, can be developed. Moreover, such limited knowledge could become a sound basis for the formulation of organisational typologies; typologies which are not arbitrarily constructed, but which are closely tuned to research findings and the requirements of theory.[51] It is by such tactics that ultimately we may achieve wider generalisations cutting across bureaucracies with the most various aims and within the most various cultures.

B. The functional approach

After falling into disrepute, as a consequence of its early organicist bias, functional analysis has been rehabilitated and adopted by many modern sociologists.[52] But if functionalism occupies a central position in modern sociological theory, it has also become the centre of numerous criticisms. As this method is widely used in organisation literature,[53] it is important to discuss some of its most controversial problems, especially those which are the most relevant to the study of bureaucracy.

Functional analysis and the formal-informal dichotomy. The formal-informal notion, which is so widespread in writings on bureaucracy, is both useful and confusing. On the one hand it is a very convenient tool, as it draws the attention of the student of bureaucracy to the inherent and continuous tension between rational co-ordination of activities and the spontaneous pattern formation of interpersonal relationships and unofficial values and beliefs. Moreover, as we have seen, such a concept gives a dynamic and dialectic aspect to organisational analysis and provides a useful starting point for the study of organisational change.

But on the other hand, when we want to use the formal-informal concepts in a more precise way, many difficulties arise. For example, when one enters a concrete organisation in order to observe closely the behaviour of its members, it becomes extremely difficult to distinguish what is formal and what is informal in their actions. These two aspects, in concrete cases, are so inextricably mixed together, that any systematic attempt at their differentiation is bound to fail. Thus, as we shall see in a later chapter, at least for a micro-level

The Post-Weberian Theories of Bureaucracy

analysis of organisational behaviour, the utility of the formal-informal distinction is rather doubtful.[54] Moreover, a great insistence on the formal-informal dichotomy might distract our attention from the systematic study of the organisation as a whole social system (in which the formal structure is one of its many aspects). As a matter of fact, although bureaucracy theorists speak so often of the functional approach and of the organisation as a social system, as we shall see below, they have paid more attention to the formal-informal dialectics than to the systematic analysis of its structure and functions.

Latent functions and the unintended consequences of action. As with the formal-informal distinction, the concepts of unintended and latent consequences of action (which are closely linked with the former) both facilitate and present dilemmas to the student of bureaucracy. On the one hand, they are very useful methodological tools, as far as they sensitise the researcher to look for problems which are not obvious or socially acknowledged. As a matter of fact, it is this systematic attention to the unobtrusive, to the unexpected which yielded many illuminating insights and has given to the writings on bureaucracy certain vitality and interest which is often lacking from more recent organisational studies (cf. chapter 5).

But on the other hand, the use of such concepts gives rise to methodological difficulties. Thus, for Merton, a latent function is one whose consequences are not intended or recognised by the actors in the relevant situation.[55] The difficulties arise when one tries to apply such a concept in an empirical research. Operationally, how can we determine if a consequence is intended or unintended, recognised or latent? What if some actors recognise such consequences and others do not? Should we decide, in such a case, according to the state of awareness of the majority, or of the leaders or of some actors? In an attempt to solve such problems, Gouldner has proposed a somewhat modified definition of manifest and latent functions. Manifest functions should refer to those consequences of a social action which are culturally prescribed for it, latent functions referring to consequences which are not 'culturally prescribed or preferred'.[56] By this redefinition one avoids the often

The Study of Bureaucracy

impossible task of finding out the state of awareness of each
social actor and pays attention to the culture of the organisation
or the group (that is to all the common patterns of beliefs
and values which usually define the recognised consequences of
a social pattern).

Of course, even with this modification, the problem is not
entirely solved. It might be equally difficult to determine what
is prescribed and preferred in a culture and what is not.
Moreover, certain consequences may be more or less culturally
prescribed. Thus in certain cases, for research purposes, it
might be useful, instead of the manifest-latent dichotomy, to
use a scale on which manifest and latent should be the two
poles of a continuum. In this way, we could speak of degrees
of unpredictability or latency of the consequences of social
action.

Functional analysis and 'self-maintaining' systems. But one may ask
to what extent are we entitled to speak of latent functions
and dysfunctions. Why should we not simply speak of the
effects or consequences of action on a certain structure or
property of the organisational system. According to the
critics of functionalism, one can see the justification for
differentiating effect from function in the case of purposive
action, when a social pattern was purposively established in
order to meet certain consciously felt social needs.[57] It is only
in such cases that one is justified in using function instead of
effect, the former term having an excess meaning (i.e. the
implication of a purposive agent). But when such a purposive
action is not behind a social pattern, every *function* statement
can be paraphrased into an *effect* statement without any loss
of meaning.[58] Moreover, according to the critics, by speaking
of latent functions, we ran the risk of reifying social reality;
of conceiving it as something separate from the actors who are
its basis. Indeed if by latent or unintended we mean the
absence of purposive action, and if by function we mean
more than effect, then we commit a teleological bias. We
implicitly introduce into the analysis a sort of mysterious
entity regulating the needs of the social system behind the
backs of its members.[59]

72

The Post-Weberian Theories of Bureaucracy

This serious objection is met in a satisfactory way, once it is made clear that whenever one speaks of a latent function which meets organisational needs or contributes to the maintenance of a system property (e.g. its cohesion), one makes the implicit assumption that the system in question is self-maintaining (or directively organised) in relation to the above property. That is to say that the system variables which are causally relevant to the above property are so related that a variation in one of them will affect the others in such a way that the system will stay within certain predefined limits (as far as the specific property is concerned). In other words this means that built into the system, there is at least one 'negative feed-back' mechanism which tends to maintain a certain state or property of the system constant (or within certain limits).[60]

If the above is accepted, then speaking of functions does not necessarily imply the existence of a goal-seeking agent;[61] neither the concept of latent or unintended functions implies a mysterious social consciousness regulating the social system. It simply implies a special type of relationship between some variables of the system.[62] In other words, it implies that the variable or social pattern which has a latent function is directly or indirectly a part of a self-maintaining whole. And it is precisely this implication (this excess meaning) which makes the difference between effect and function statements. If this implication is not made, if a system is not considered self-maintaining, then there is no reason why we should prefer the term function to the term effect. Indeed, if there are no feed-back mechanisms regulating system needs, if there is no guarantee that at least one property (or need) of the system will be kept within certain limits, it makes no sense to speak of latent or unintended functions or dysfunctions of a system.[63]

Functional analysis and the multiplicity of the frames of reference. Another important criticism of the functional method refers to its vagueness. To say that a certain social pattern is functional because in a general way it contributes to the maintenance of the system as a whole, is almost a tautology – in the sense that by definition all parts of a system, being more or less

73

interdependent, contribute somehow to the whole. But even if such a statement is not tautological, if the functional explanation stops at this point, it does not tell us anything interesting or illuminating. This criticism is justified as far as it refers to the superfluous way in which many organisation analysts use the functional method. But it is not at all justified when it refers to functionalism *per se*. If a rigorous application of functional analysis is very difficult in practice, it is not impossible. In other words, vagueness is not an inherent and insurmountable weakness of the method.

The first thing to be said in this respect is that a system can be goal directed towards many of its properties or needs. Thus all parts of the global system are not necessarily relevant to a certain need. Some system parts may be causally relevant to one or more properties and irrelevant to other self-maintaining properties of the same system.[64] Moreover, the existence of subsystems with their own properties (departments, groups, individuals) makes the problem more complicated. Indeed a social pattern may be simultaneously relevant to the general system and to one or more subsystems. Thus a certain management policy (close supervision) may have functional effects with respect to the productivity of the whole organisation; dysfunctional effects as far as the productivity of a special group is concerned (e.g. the group norms are hostile to authoritarian supervision); and non-functional effects on certain individuals (we can imagine, in this case, the mode of supervision as being irrelevant to their productivity rates). Furthermore, it is not enough to specify the property with respect to which a variable is functional or dysfunctional. One must also identify the other variables which are causally relevant to the maintenance of the above property. For example, it is not enough to say that close supervision is dysfunctional as far as productivity is concerned. The mode of supervision is not sufficient by itself to explain why productivity is at a certain level. A complete account of the phenomenon in functional terms should include all the other variables which are positively or negatively relevant to a certain level of productivity (e.g. professional values, norms about the proper amount of work, technological variables, etc.). It should also include the way in which these variables are related to each other and to the above property (that is productivity); for example, in what way are informal norms, which are against competition and high productivity, related to professional values or to a certain type of supervision?[65]

When the above specifications are taken seriously into consideration, one sees clearly the insufficiency of talking in a vague way about the organisation as a self-maintaining system of interdependent parts, and of social patterns as being functional to the organisation as a whole. Indeed neither the interdependence of parts, nor the self-maintaining aspect of an organisation should be taken for granted. There are various degrees and types of interdependence and their identification is a matter of empirical research, not of *a priori* speculation. The same holds true for the self-maintaining aspects of the organisation. It is not enough to speak of the organisation in general as a self-maintaining whole. One should try to find out the various properties towards which the system is self-maintaining, and this again is a problem of empirical investigation.

Part Two

THE MANAGERIAL TRADITION

Chapter Four

TAYLORISM AND FORMAL
THEORIES OF ADMINISTRATION

INTRODUCTION

The second line of thought which has contributed to our knowledge about organisations has Frederic W. Taylor as its starting point. Taylor, in contradistinction to the classical writers on bureaucracy, is not so much interested in the organisational problems of society's power-structure, but in the practical problem of efficiency. His main unit of analysis is not society as a whole, but the individual at the workplace. Although Taylor is more concerned with the worker as an isolated unit rather than as an organisational member, a brief analysis of his approach and its organisational implications is important for understanding subsequent theoretical developments which try to complement or to refute the Taylorian system.

Taylorism, as a movement of ideas and practical realisations in industry, constitutes a very complex but, at the same time, cohesive system; although Taylor's initial teaching was modified by his disciples, its main character and its basic elements remain more or less the same. This movement must be seen in the general context of the changing structure of capitalism at the end of the nineteenth century. At that period important technological and economic developments in the industrialised world contributed to the proliferation and relative dominance of large-scale economic units.

> At that time were founded the great horizontal and vertical combinations, the 'pools' and 'corners', the mergers of businesses, the cartels and trusts, the 'holding companies', and in France the 'comptoirs'. From the 1890s the reign of the 'Titans' begins in the United States ...[1]

79

The Managerial Tradition

The growing size and complexity of the enterprise and the accentuation of the division of labour created acute problems of co-ordination. The internal organisation of the vast material and human resources could not any more be regulated by the traditional methods of management. Thus there was an increasing need for the rationalisation of man to machine and man to man relationships in industry. This need was felt more acutely by a group of men which was more directly involved in the day to day problems arising at the workshop level: the mechanical engineers. With mechanisation of production, the mechanical engineers came to acquire a strategic position in the social structure of enterprise. The foundation in 1880 of the American Society of Mechanical Engineers was an indication of the growing importance of this profession.[2] The ASME was the parent organisation of the numerous management societies which developed subsequently. Indeed many early publications and papers read in the ASME were dealing with ways of applying engineering principles (which were proved so successful in solving technical problems) in the administration and organisation of the workshop.

Besides the mechanical engineers, in the United States discussions on management problems were also frequent, especially after the civil war, among entrepreneurs who were at the head of big enterprises. As it was in the railroad business that problems of large-scale organisation were more acute, the railroad journals were the forum for such early discussions. Finally the reform movement in cost accounting – which was promulgating new ideas about cost measuring and control – was a third centre of debate on the problems of management.[3]

Taylor, who, after starting as a simple worker became chief engineer in the Midvale Iron Works, was initially a member of the ASME. But he soon initiated a system of his own which, in a way, was a synthesis of the ideas which arose from the various sources mentioned above. As a matter of fact, Taylor's originality did not consist so much in the invention of any one of his particular techniques of scientific management,[4] but rather in the fact that he succeeded in integrating into a cohesive system various techniques and ideas

Taylorism and Formal Theories of Administration
about management which had existed before his time but had
never been systematised.

I. THE MAIN FEATURES OF TAYLORISM

A. The fundamental approach

The basic aim of Taylorism is the increase of organisational
productivity, especially on the workshop level. In order to
realise this goal, Taylor advocated the empirical and experimental approach to the problems of workshop management.
He believed that for every process, every task in industry,
there is one best way of performance; in order to discover
this unique way, one has to examine this part of organisational
reality in a scientific way. Industrial organisation, like any
other part of reality is governed by definite regularities,
laws which can be discovered by observation and experiment.
Once these laws are known, they can be applied in the working
situation to regulate the various activities and other factors
of production in such a way, that maximum productivity is
achieved. Thus, scientific knowledge replaces intuition and
the rule of thumb method in organisational behaviour.

Once this new, rational attitude towards industrial problems
is emphasised, the second fundamental principle of scientific
management indicates the general procedure by which the
newly acquired scientific knowledge about work shall be
implemented. Management must bear the main responsibility
for this radical transformation. Instead of leaving the worker
alone to solve the operative problems by which he is confronted
in his work, managers should try to train him to perform his
task in the one best way. This implies a radical separation
between the planning and the performance of the work. Only
the latter activity must constitute the worker's job. Finally,
as a complementary measure, the selection of the worker
cannot be left to chance, but must also be regulated in such
a way that for every task the man with the most relevant
aptitudes is chosen.[5]

B. The main tools

As Taylor states, time study, job analysis and other techniques with which scientific management is usually associated, are simply tools which either help the scientific analysis of the industrial organisation or facilitate its rationalisation. The starting point in Taylor's investigations was his efforts, as a foreman, after he had failed to make the workers increase their rhythm of work by traditional methods, to find an objective way by which he could measure the proper time in which a specific job should be completed. This was the time and motion studies which involve the following processes: by detailed analysis and registration of the movements of a specific task, the whole working process is broken down to simple operations, each operation being timed. Then, by systematic analysis of the data thus obtained, the unnecessary movements are eliminated and the work process is reconstructed in a simplified, rational way. Finally, the standard time of the new way of doing the work is calculated by adding up the time units of each operation and the necessary idle times (rest and other unavoidable delays).[6]

According to Taylor, a standard method and time for a task established by the time study, cannot be applied unless the other factors entering the working situation are standardised as well (machine speeds, tools, supply of raw materials, etc.). The analysis of the management engineer shifts from the individual worker to wider organisational problems: relations between the various workplaces, rational regulation of the work-flow, 'routing', storing and accounting techniques, methods of supervision, functional foremanship and so on. Thus by the logic of the situation, the effort towards rationalisation cannot be limited to the individual worker; it spreads outwards and upwards, until ultimately, it covers and controls the whole organisation.

If the main burden for implementing rational methods in the enterprise lies with the management, the worker must be willing to accept the new system of work. This, according to Taylor, can be realised by the construction of the proper wage-incentive system, which will stimulate the worker to keep up with the standards set by the management engineer. Such a construction was constantly a central preoccupation of Taylorism. Taylor's incentive system (the differential piece-rate system), being rather complicated and disadvantageous to the mediocre worker, was not widely applied;[7] many disciples have tried to correct the shortcomings of the piece-rate method by constructing more flexible and simpler systems.

C. The underlying philosophy

Co-operation, the last and most fundamental principle of Taylorism, is the essential pre-condition for the implementation of scientific management. According to Taylor, if the co-operation of workers and managers is not achieved, all the other principles and techniques are useless. Scientific management has not only as its goal the increase of output; it also attempts to provide a definite solution to the class conflict, to the continual and wasteful antagonism between workers and management. How can co-operation be substituted for conflict? Science, according to Taylor, gives us the solution. Taylor believed that once the natural laws governing work and production are discovered, the determination of the proper time for doing a job and the proper amount of pay can be determined in an objective, scientific way. Consequently if everybody adheres to the laws of the situation, there is no place for bargaining and quarrel; one cannot bargain about scientific facts.[8]

Of course, under such conditions, it follows that trade unions become obsolete. Taylor was systematically hostile to trade unionism, despite occasional declarations about his willingness to tolerate them. According to his opinion, the role of the trade unions was not only negative to the economy as a whole, but it was against the real interests of the workers. The workers, dealt with individually and not herded into groups, would be better able to pursue their own individual ambitions. Collective bargaining was vastly inferior to his own plan of 'stimulating each workman's ambition by paying him according to his individual worth, and without limiting him to the rate of work or pay of the average of his class'.[9] Taylor's attitude towards industrial conflict and the trade unions was not followed by all his disciples. After his death and under the influence of various social factors which forced the trade unions radically to change their attitude towards scientific management, the position of Taylorism on the labour problem was reversed. The advocates of scientific management gradually realised that the implementation of their methods in industry could not be realised against, but only with the support and collaboration of the unions.[10]

But although the optimism of the Taylorites about the possibility of a scientific solution of the labour problems gradually lessened, yet, as the movement gained momentum and Taylor's ideas were accepted and partially applied all over the industrialised world, the visions and ambitions of some of his followers took fantastic dimensions. This development of the system is well illustrated by an excerpt from the records of the International Congresses for Scientific Management.

> It (the Scientific Management movement) will give people better understanding and co-operation, and realize a new policy, the policy of a human world. . . . A world organization of scientific management could form a right basis for the foundation of world co-operative production and organized sales, removing the economic causes of war. . . . The new philosophy of scientific management must help to bring about the Christian philosophy of love and welfare among all nations . . . it is absolutely beyond question that a knowledge of the principle of scientific management is fundamental for the success of everybody . . .[11]

2. CRITICISM

For Taylorism, it is the individual worker which constitutes the main unit of analysis. Within this narrow focus, as has been said before, the emphasis is on the detailed study of the physical operations which are relevant to the performance of a task. Every theory of organisation operates and is based on an implicit or explicit model of human behaviour – of a certain conception of how people behave in organisational contexts.

84

Taylorism and Formal Theories of Administration

The Taylorian model, as Simon has pointed out is clearly a machine model: Taylor and most of his followers, being engineers, approached the organisation from a mechanistic frame of reference. Systematically, in analysing the organisation member at work, and in building up standard ways of procedure, they concentrated on the instrumental aspects of human behaviour.

Indeed the organisation member was conceived as an instrument of production which can be handled as easily as any other tool (provided that one knows the laws of scientific management). In such a conception there is no consideration of the feelings, attitudes and private goals of the individual; neither is there any realisation that the worker is a social being influenced in his behaviour and attitudes by his colleagues by the social structure and culture of the groups within which he finds himself. Briefly, Taylorism neglected the psychological and sociological variables of organisational behaviour. Of course, Taylor was not completely unaware that workers had feelings and that they associated with other workers in the factory. But he simply assumed that these aspects of behaviour were more or less irrelevant to the problems of productivity. For example, in job analysis, the movements chosen as the most appropriate for reconstructing the standard, best way of doing a task, are chosen according to the mechanistic criteria of speed and output (choice of the shortest and swiftest movement); the psychological aspects of the worker, his needs as a whole being are systematically ignored.

The development of industrial psychology has shown clearly the one-sidedness of this approach. According to Otto Lipmann

> we cannot abstractly cut out from it (i.e. the individual) the working units and isolate them from the needs of the personality considered as a bio-psychological whole. The movements supposedly 'useless' for a well-defined task may actually not be useless from the point of view of the total individual. Obviously, if they are suppressed, a certain amount of physical energy is saved. But by the very inhibition of this movement, the expenditure of mental energy may be increased and consequently also the worker's inner tension.[12]

Moreover, as Myers[13] has pointed out, when one considers the

85

whole individual personality, one realises that what might be the best way of working for one individual might be the worst for another having a different psychological make-up. Imposing a uniform manner of work, does not only destroy individuality but it might cause other psychological disturbances to the worker. Finally, the way by which Taylorism tries to cope with the problem of morale and productivity (i.e. exclusively by economic reward and punishment), illustrates well the lack of sociological insight in its approach. Very briefly, scientific management did not provide a satisfactory solution to the incentive-productivity problem as it systematically conceived the worker as an isolated individual, outside his social context, thus neglecting the most relevant variables of the problem (informal organisation, conflict of interests, etc.).

Taylor has tried to apply the methods of engineering in order to analyse phenomena and solve problems which pertain to a more complex reality. Today, it becomes more and more clear that a multi-dimensional approach is indispensable, whenever a scientific treatment of human problems, inside or outside industry, is attempted. In this respect Taylorism has failed. It is not that all his findings about man at work are false or unscientific, as Friedmann suggests.[14] A partial approach, even a mechanistic one, to the problems of work is not necessarily false. The fact that the quickest way of performing a job may not be the best way, does not invalidate the findings about the speed characteristics of the human organism. In the same way, if Taylor's pro-management ideology and values determined his approach to the problems of work, these values do not necessarily discount the correctness or scientific value of some of his findings.[15]

Rather one can criticise Taylor for a technicist[16] bias – that is for having ignored the partiality and limitations of his approach; for trying to apply his method in order to solve problems, the handling of which demand a more inclusive conceptual framework.

If technicism refers to a methodologically illegitimate expansion of the technological approach in irrelevant areas of research, scientism in a similar manner, implies an over-estimation of the possibilities of science as far as value-judgements and their validation are concerned. Both fallacies are present in Taylorism.

Indeed Taylor, by his insistence that the proper amount of wages and the labour problem in general can be solved in an objective-scientific manner, did not only show his inability to place the worker-management conflict in its wider institutional context; he showed, as well, a misconception of the nature of scientific method. For if it is scientifically possible to determine the length of time in which a certain job could be done (assuming that relevant characteristics about the worker and his tools are given), there is no scientific way of determining the time in which a certain job ought to be done. And this is because in the latter case the solution of the problem will depend on one's value-judgements – that is on explicit or implicit statements about values which cannot be validated or rejected by empirical research. Thus in Taylor's case, it is not very difficult to identify behind his pseudo-scientific solution of the industrial conflict his pro-managerial attitudes and his general conservative orientation (unreserved acceptance of the *status quo*).

3. FORMAL THEORIES OF ADMINISTRATION

Although the methods of scientific management were supposed to apply to all the aspects of the organisation, their focus of analysis remained basically the workshop (whenever the Taylorites turned their efforts towards rationalisation outside the production department they were more concerned with technical and procedural problems and methods of control, than with the administrative function of the top management and the various analytical problems of structure and process). From this point of view the body of theory to be discussed now is complementary to Taylorism; it shifts the concern for rationalisation from the workplace to the whole structure of the industrial organisation.[17]

Of course Taylor was preoccupied with the problems of the foreman, his marginal position between administration and workshop.[18] In a way such preoccupations constitute the link between the management theories studied in the first part of this chapter and the theories that we are going to examine now.

Henri Fayol[19] is usually considered the father of this development and his approach has greatly determined the way in which subsequent authors have analysed the problems of management. Although since Fayol's time the formal thinking about management has changed, it is possible to identify the general pattern and common features underlying the theories of authors[20] who have tried to build up a discipline of administration based on this tradition. They constitute what is usually called, the classical or universalist school of management.[21] Moreover, as there are basic similarities and a continual interchange of ideas and practices between the study of business and public administration,[22] many problems and methods of analysis have been common to both disciplines; so the label universalist or classic is often used in writings on public administration to identify similar approaches to organisation problems.[23]

4. THE GENERAL FRAMEWORK OF THE 'UNIVERSALIST' THEORIES

The main aim of these theories is the discovery of a body of principles which would enable the manager to build up the formal structure as well as to administer his organisation in a rational way. There is the basic assumption that in spite of the great variety of goals and environments in which organisations operate, it is possible to identify basic similarities in structure and process which can be conceptually analysed and made explicit. Upon this common ground, a number of universal principles (i.e. applicable to any kind of organisation) can be discovered, which will replace the traditional intuitive rules of administrative action. Let us examine briefly the concepts and methods of this approach as they are applied in the analysis of the organisational structure and process.

A. *The structure*

The focus is on the formal aspect of the organisational structure. The theory makes a clear distinction between the position (the office) and the person who occupies it. The responsibilities of different positions and the relations among them can be defined and delineated independently from the persons who will assume them.[24] From this point of view, the central problem of the classical theory can be formulated as follows: given the general purpose of an organisation, we can identify the basic functions necessary for the realisation of this purpose (e.g. productive, financial, commercial, etc.). When this is done, the problem consists in breaking down these broad activity-categories into specific subcategories, arriving finally at individual tasks; these tasks must be grouped in such a way that we should have the maximum productivity and efficiency with the minimum cost.[25]

The solution of this problem, according to the theory, lies in the discovery of a set of principles, which, when correctly applied to the particular situation will prove invaluable guides to the construction of a rational-efficient framework for management. Now, in order to discover such principles, a basic precondition is a clear idea of the structural features common to all existing organisations. In other words, the formation of principles is preceded by a descriptive and conceptual analysis of how an organisation is structured.[26]

For such an analysis the main concepts generally used are those of authority and function. Vertically, the organisation structure is conceived as a hierarchy which is created by the delegation of authority and responsibility from the top to the bottom of the organisation.[27] Horizontally, the differentiation is analysed in terms of functions[28] (and it is in this context that the controversial 'staff and line' concept can be placed). Finally on the basis of such a type of analysis, combined often with personal experience as administrators, the authors of this school elaborate principles, the number and content of which vary according to the writer.[29] (Typical principles referring to structure: unity of command, specialisation, small span of control, etc.)

B. *The process*

The literature of management is not only concerned with how

to build a formal framework. A manager does not only co-
ordinate jobs but the real activities of people as well. So the
other main preoccupation of the universalist school is the
examination of the process of management. This is usually
defined as 'a process of getting things done by people who
operate in organized groups'.[30] As in the case of structure,
there is the assumption that the basic characteristics of this
process are to be found in any organisation and in varying
degrees, at all the levels of the hierarchy. Moreover, by
analysing this process, by building a conceptual framework for
it and by formulating on this ground a number of principles, a
theory of management can be built up, a useful body of
knowledge which can be taught and learned in the same way
as any other professional skill.[31]

More precisely, the analysis of the process of management
goes on in terms of the basic activities or functions of the
manager (planning, co-ordinating, controlling etc.)[32] and the
more detailed and specific techniques in which the management
process is based (budgeting, financial control, stock control,
etc.).

<h3 style="text-align:center">5. SOME CRITICAL REMARKS</h3>

A. The general character of the classical theory

The universalist school concentrates its analysis on the formal
aspects of the organisation: the organisational structure is
mainly viewed in terms of patterns of responsibilities, and
prescribed relationships among them. The stress is not on
behaviour and motivation but on design and rules to be
recorded in an organisational chart or manual.

As to the process of management, here as well, the approach
has a formalistic character. It does not deal with actual behaviour but with ideal typical ways of acting which are exclusively
related to the formal goals and functions of the organisation.
For example, when examining the control aspect of management, the traditional theorist will try to give a definition of
what managerial control is, or should be;[33] he may also give
a lengthy analysis and description of various types and tech-

niques of control or formulate some new principles for the more efficient practice of control.[34] Finally he may examine the relations of control to the other parts of the organisational structure[35] (e.g. should the quality control responsibility be discharged by a specialist or should it be a part of the foreman's job). But the traditional theorist will not try to examine concretely, behaviourally the process of control, and much less will he try to explain it (i.e. why control takes a particular form in a concrete situation, how it is linked with other aspects – not only formal – of the organisation and with its cultural context; what is the impact of the application of such a control technique on the controller or the controllees etc.).

So, basically, the classic approach to management by the definition and elaboration of a conceptual framework of the organisational structure and process helps the student to get a clear general idea of the formal aspects of the enterprise, of its various activities and techniques and their rational inter-relations. But its limitations are obvious: because of its non-empirical character, it can only describe and, as best, give a clear image of formal arrangements; it cannot explain such arrangements or link them with other aspects of the organisa-tion (its power-structure for instance).

Of course, the usual reply to such a criticism is that modern universalists do not ignore the partiality and the limitations of their approach; they know very well that people have feelings and private goals and that a real organisation is very different from the way it is supposed to be on an organisation chart. But these considerations do not dispense with the necessity to design a formal structure. Moreover, a theory must not be criticised for its partiality, for what it leaves outside its scope, as every approach to reality, if it is to be of any use, has to be partial; as Koontz puts it, 'we should not attempt to cover the entire cultural, biological and physical universe when we deal with management'.[36] Although this argument is plausible, we can still ask to what extent a theory of management, concentrating exclusively on the formal aspect, on the mechanics of the organisation, can stand apart from the various behavioural sciences now invading it; what should the potentialities of such an autonomous discipline be in relation

to the accomplishment of its major objective, the establishment
of a growing body of principles, as reliable guides to sound
management?

B. *The principles*

Before we try to give an answer to the above problem we must
say a few things about the principles which the classical
theorists try to formulate. The principles, which occupy a
central position in the classical theories of both public and
business administration, have given rise to interminable
controversies concerning their nature and validity. Part of the
confusion is terminological; very often the authors do not
specify what they mean by principle;[37] or when they do, they
may not use the term in the way previously specified.[38] Anyway,
one can distinguish three main ways in which classical theorists
use the term:

- Sometimes it has a descriptive connotation; it simply
  states the existence of a certain organisational feature (e.g.
  the hierarchy principle).[39]
- More rarely, it can express a relation between organisation
  variables.[40]
- Finally, and in its most current use, the term has a normative character: it is a guide to management action.[41]

Moreover, there is no agreement between the universalists
as to the nature and validity of these principles. Some writers
consider them as equivalent to scientific laws, universally valid
in all cases;[42] others view them as mere rules which may help
the practitioner in some, but not all, cases.[43]

The long controversy over the scientific character of the
principles and of the discipline of management in general,
has usually stumbled on the definition of the term 'science';
I think a more constructuve criticism of the principles should
avoid any judgement about their scientific status and examine
their usefulness and limitations: to what extent do they
contribute to the improvement of the practice of or the increase
of our knowledge about management; to what extent do they
impede such a development?

Taylorism and Formal Theories of Administration

Often, the quarrel over the principles has the following pattern:

Formulation of a principle in general terms without great precision in the definition or any specification of the conditions under which it is valid (e.g. Taylor's principle of correspondence between authority and responsibility: that the two should always co-vary).

Criticism. The imprecision in the definition of terms, makes the principle very vulnerable of course, and its critics are quick to find cases where it does not apply (e.g. how does the principle of responsibility apply to a staff member, who, according to the same theory, has no authority? If we strictly apply the principle we must conclude that he has no responsibility at all).[44]

Defence. The principle is still valid if its terms are correctly defined and interpreted (e.g. in the case of responsibility, the principle should simply mean that a man should not be held responsible for something which is not in his powers to command – and vice versa).[45]

Criticism. In this case the principle is true but platitudinous.[46]

Defence. 'Some refer to principles as platitudes, forgetting that a platitude is still a truism and a truth does not become worthless because it is familiar.'[47]

Criticism. Of course at this point, if principles are no more than platitudes, their number could be increased *ad infinitum* by anyone who had the patience to undertake such an exercise in common sense.

Other criticisms stress the contradictions involved between various principles. (For instance, the principle of a small span of control contradicts the principle recommending a flat pyramidal structure – that is few hierarchical levels – as a means to better communication.)[48] Furthermore, whenever the principles are not contradictory or evident, they are so general as to be of little use as guides to concrete situations. For example, the principle of specialisation,[49] as it is usually

The Managerial Tradition

formulated, not only does not indicate to what degree or under what conditions one should specialise, but it also distracts one from the real problem: the striking of a balance between the gains obtained by increased specialisation and the costs resulting from the necessity of increased co-ordination. So in general terms, it seems that the problem is not one of following consistently certain principles, but rather of measuring and weighing the advantages and disadvantages of various courses of action, usually recommended by contradictory principles.

One may argue that as the principles were very often proposed by thoughtful men with long experience in administration, they may be of some help to the manager. Mainly, they can help him to look critically at his organisation and perceive problems there which might have passed unnoticed otherwise (in this sense they serve more as tools of analysis and observation and less as direct guides to action). But to what degree have the principles, and in general the whole traditional literature, provided the manager with a knowledge which could not be acquired by his common sense and experience? This is an open question. Any judgement about the efficiency of the principles is difficult, as we do not have precise enough tools to measure and compare the results before and after their application. (Moreover, any failure of the principles can always be attributed to their wrong application.)

To terminate this argument, we may say that if the principles have a degree of usefulness and if a practical theory of management is methodologically justified, the shortcomings of the principles, as they are formulated by the classical school, are not less evident. There is no consensus of opinion, even among universalists, on any single principle of management. The principles and the classical literature of management in general, do not give the impression of a body of knowledge having a cumulative character; they rather give the image of a mosaic of principles, of definitions and redefinitions which does not seem very much to increase our knowledge about organisations. So, if really valid principles have not yet emerged, the question is whether such principles will gradually be elaborated simply by the pursuit of the same abstract and formal methods of analysis, or whether, if such principles do exist (which is also doubtful), they should be sought on an entirely different ground.[50] This problem brings us back to the fundamental question asked above about the possibility of an autonomous discipline of management, with a content different from that of the behavioural sciences.

6. CONCLUSION

Some modern writers of the universalist school, although they acknowledge the behavioural approach to management, think that the two approaches are complementary, and that somehow they could be developed in a parallel way, without being integrated and fused into a single discipline. Thus many recent textbooks on business administration continue in the universalist tradition, although their authors are aware of and well acquainted with the behavioural developments in the study of management.[51] The problem is whether or not this position is justified.

Considering first the discipline of management in its analytic and descriptive aspects, it becomes clear that the classical approach, as far as it abstains from empirical research and observation, can do no more than elaborate and clarify still further its vocabulary. It can really make no substantive contribution to our knowledge of the way in which organisations function. On the other hand, as far as its normative aspects are concerned, the only domain in which the non-empirical, abstract approach seems to have great possibility of development is in the elaboration and improvement of such management techniques as forecasting, quality control, planning and so on (especially in view of the recent application of mathematical and statistical techniques to the problems of rational decision-making – cf. chapter 6).

But outside this domain, any attempt to elaborate principles of sound management in a common sense manner is bound to be unsuccessful in so far as it is based on a formal model of organisational structure – that is in so far as it does not take into account and try to find out empirically about the feelings, beliefs and actual modes of behaviour of people, about the ways in which they are actually related to each other. As we shall see in the next chapter, it is the Human Relations School which started to take systematically into account these aspects of the organisation.

Chapter Five

THE HUMAN RELATIONS APPROACH
TO THE ORGANISATION

INTRODUCTION

As was mentioned in the last chapter, one of the fundamental principles of Taylorism was the scientific selection of the worker so that there should be correspondence between his aptitudes and the requirements of the job. Already such propositions indicated what direction the movement of rationalisation of work would take. As a matter of fact very soon the industrial psychologist appeared on the scene and joined the efficiency engineer in the workshop. There are many factors which account for this development. The most important seem to be the rapid development of experimental psychology at the beginning of this century[1] and the hostile reaction of the workers to the early attempts to put into practice the mechanistic principles of scientific management.[2]

The industrial psychologist tried to investigate such problems as 'how to devise tests to select the best man for a given job, how to find whether he is working at full efficiency, how far his performance is affected by the temperature, lighting, humidity, and noise in the workshop . . . what are the effects of boredom, doing repetitive work and so on'.[3] Such problems although in a way they continue in the Taylorian tradition as they take into account more than the physiological aspects of the individual, have modified the machine model of organisational behaviour. These theoretical developments in conjunction with the increasing power of the trade unions had a considerable impact on the attitudes of employers and their staff. Managers started to emphasise the importance of the human factor in enterprise, questionnaires were compiled with the aim of finding out about the feelings and attitudes of workers and personnel men in firms. Thus started the slogan that the 'human element is the most important element in business'.[4]

It is in this ideological climate that the Human Relations School took roots. The label 'human relations' has had different uses in the social sciences.[5] The one which interests us here refers to some of the studies which try to examine empirically human behaviour in organisational settings (mainly industrial). The lack of specificity in the above definition is inevitable, as what is usually called the Human Relations School is a highly diversified and changing movement of thought, covering under its umbrella writers with very different views on organisation. Thus, as it is difficult to delineate the precise boundaries of the school, and in order to do justice to its diversity, we shall have to pay some attention to its major subschools and its general evolution through time. It is only after such an analysis that a more precise image of the field will emerge, enabling us to identify the shortcomings of the human relations theory and its contributions to the study of organisations.

I. HAWTHORNE AND THE EVOLUTION OF EMPIRICAL RESEARCH IN INDUSTRY

The famous studies undertaken at Western Electric's Hawthorne plant, under the direction of Elton Mayo, are considered the starting point and the main source of inspiration of all subsequent studies in the human relations field.[6] These studies are not only important for the breakthrough which they realised in the analysis of industrial organisations; the various phases of this long research summarise and illustrate in a clear way the successive stages through which the empirical study of man at work has passed. It is on this evolutionary aspect of the Hawthorne studies that we will concentrate in this section, as this evolution shows the bridge by which the human relations approach is linked with the earlier studies of the scientific management movement.

The chief aim of the Hawthorne research is to examine working conditions as they are related to output and generally to classify the numerous problems arising in the working situation.

The 'Human Relations' Approach to the Organisation

At the early stage of the research, the approach does not differ much from Taylor's. The investigators want to relate the worker's performance to such variables as illumination, fatigue and so on. In their methodology, they try to imitate the exact sciences. The test room method consists of the variation of an independent variable (e.g. illumination) and the examination of its impact on the dependent variable (output), all other relevant variables being kept constant. [7]

The results are inconclusive and confusing and the investigators, after two years of research, turn their attention to the psychological and sociopsychological factors determining organisational behaviour. They gradually realise that such variables as illumination or humidity cannot be treated separately from the meaning which individuals assign to them, their attitude towards them and their preoccupations about them. As a consequence of this realisation, the methodology changes. The search for causal variables in the physical environment is replaced by the interview as a more suitable tool for the exploration of a complex situation in which one has to consider not only *external* facts but also attitudes towards and feelings about those facts. By interviewing employees on a plant-wide basis, the research team tries firstly to explore their morale, their satisfactions and dissatisfactions in their job and the organisation, and secondly to explore these attitudes by means of the interviewee's personal history and background. [8]

As the results of the massive interviews are elaborated the investigators realise more and more that one must search for the explanation of workers' attitude and behaviour, not so much in personality characteristics, socially acquired in the past and outside the plant (social psychological approach), but rather in the social organisation inside the plant. The focus here shifts and the determinants of working behaviour are sought in the structure and culture of the group, which is spontaneously formed by the interactions of individuals working together. Thus the worker is not any longer perceived as an isolated psychological being but as a group member, whose behaviour is greatly controlled by group norms and values. As the approach becomes more sociological, the methods of investigation change for a third time. The researchers realise the complexity of the situation and the arbitrariness of taking an individual outside his real social situation in order to interview him. Thus the interview method is complemented with the direct observation of the group at work.[9]

This shift of focus from physiological and psychological to socio-psychological and finally to sociological variables clearly reflects the general trend of empirical research in industrial organisations during the past decades.[10] But before identifying any further general trends, we have to analyse in a more systematic way the type of approach to organisation which is revealed in the late phase of the Hawthorne research as well as in subsequent studies of the orthodox group of Mayo's disciples.

2. THE VARIOUS SUBSCHOOLS

A. *Mayo and the orthodox school*[11]

The conceptual framework

The Mayoites concentrated their attention on the behavioural variables of the organisaton.

> To put it oversimply, we would try to do this by drawing an arbitrary and imaginary line around an organisation and treating the actual behaviour that went on inside as the phenomena to be first observed and in time to be explained.[12]

The formal variables (i.e. rules and activities required by the organisation) and the different values and patterns of behaviour which the organisation members have acquired outside the plant, constitute the boundary conditions, the limiting context into which will be found the activity to be studied. Thus, those two sets of variables, though acknowledged as important determinants of behaviour, are considered as givens, outside the line of demarcation. They are not to be explained or studied in themselves; rather they are going to be taken into consideration only as they enter into the individual's definition of the situation.

Now that the relevant phenomena to be observed have

been determined, we must examine the conceptual devices with the help of which the Mayoites tried to classify and relate those phenomena. The common patterns of behaviour, the values and beliefs which emerge through the interaction of individuals working together, can be seen as constituting a social system: a whole of interdependent parts. Moreover, this interdependence is of such a nature that any change in one part of the system brings such changes to the other parts, that the system tends towards its original state. This is the concept of equilibrium which in our social system is concretised by the mechanisms of social control, that is to say, by a system of rewards and punishments which achieves a certain degree of conformity among the group members.[13] In this conceptualisation, the search for cause and effect relationships between the various parts of the system becomes a very inadequate method. Indeed the parts being mutually dependent, it is impossible to distinguish cause from effect. Thus the situation has necessarily to be examined as a whole, even if this comprehensive approach makes the precise measurement of variables very difficult.

Another closely related device of the orthodox school is the analytical distinction between formal and informal organisation – (a distinction which was adopted by many bureaucracy writers – cf. chapter 3). As it has already been stated the informal organisation refers mainly to values and to patterns of behaviour which are not instigated by formal rules and policies but arise naturally from the interaction of people working together. On the other hand the formal organisation refers to official rules and to behaviour stipulated by them. According to the Mayoites, the way in which the formal organisation is related to the informal is an empirical question to be determined by practical research. As to the relation between social system and informal organisation, when those two concepts are applied on the group level, they seem to be identical, the formal organisation becoming one of the external variables of the system.[14] However, when they are used on the organisational level, both the informal and the formal organisation become internal variables of the social system of the firm as a whole.[15]

The empirical content of the theory. With such analytical framework and tools, the orthodox school tried to explore such aspects of organisational behaviour as motivation, morale, group cohesion and their relations to productivity. The result was the discovery of the impact of group life on workers' behaviour. That cliques and friendship groups exist in a plant was well known long before Mayo. But they were always considered as phenomena unrelated to the problem of productivity and morale. The real discovery of the school was the realisation of the extent to which the shared values of the group determined the behaviour of its members.

When this fundamental fact was taken into consideration, it became clear that the worker does not always behave and react to management rules and orders according to the logics of the economic man. The *logics of sentiments*,[16] the group norms, were different, even opposed, to the *logics of management*. The restriction of output syndrome illustrates this difference: group rules determine the proper amount of a day's work (not too much or too little). The group member cannot disregard these rules without suffering the ensuing unofficial sanctions. By such rules the internal strife and competition between the workers is avoided and group solidarity is increased. Thus, one of the main functions of these informal norms is to allow group members to increase their control over the environment, to be less dependent on management and to be better able to resist any external changes threatening their social and economic position. Moreover, group life becomes a source of social satisfaction and emotional stability for the individual. In that sense it increases workers' satisfaction and lowers turnover and absenteeism.[17]

Finally, management's neglect to take into consideration the informal organisation and its values, results in the breakdown of communications between the top and the bottom of the hierarchy. Communications downwards are impaired as management's orders are based on the *hommo economicus* assumption about workers' behaviour; communications upwards suffer even more as no information about the informal organisation of the plant is transmitted. In conclusion, in order to restore good communications, management must not try to destroy the informal organisation of the plant; it must rather take it into consideration and make sure (mainly through supervisors trained in human relations) that the informal norms in harmony with organisation goals. When this is achieved, the informal organisation, instead of proving an obstacle is transformed into the main driving force for the achievement of the firm's objectives.

It is on the basis of such conclusions that Mayo (influenced also by Durkheim and Pareto) developed his general philosophy about the problems of our industrial civilisation.[18] Briefly, these problems arise chiefly from the social disorganisation caused by industrialisation (weakening of the family and other primary groups, atomisation of the individual, anxiety, loneliness, etc.). The solution is a new society in which the plant, a harmonious unit, with formal and informal organisation well integrated, will become the centre of the individual's life, providing him with the emotional security and the social satisfactions that he can no longer find in the family or in other decaying institutions outside the plant. Finally, the way to achieve this new kind of corporatism is through science. When the gap between technological and social knowledge of the organisation is filled (by the development of human relations), the appropriate methods will be discovered for putting an end to industrial strife and establishing a new industrial order based on co-operation and harmony. Although these views are not shared by all the members of the school, they give some hints about the general intellectual atmosphere and preoccupations which determined, to a certain degree, the main problem to be studied; that is, how a 'harmonious and efficient' organisation could be achieved.

B. *Warner and the Chicago school*

In explaining organisational behaviour, the orthodox school has not paid systematic attention to its determinants outside the plant. To some degree, this gap has been filled by a distinct development in the field which started with W. L. Warner and the committee of Human Relations in Industry at the

University of Chicago.[19] Warner, an anthropologist and late participant in the Hawthorne studies,[20] has concentrated his attention on community and social stratification problems. Before Hawthorne, the studies dealing with relations between community and industry were mainly concerned with tracing the impact of technological changes and innovations on the community structure. From this point of view industry meant mainly technology. There was no interest in analysing how the technological aspect of the organisation was linked with its human aspects. There was no awareness that sociological concepts used in community studies (e.g. status, role, culture) could be applied inside the plant as well, thus establishing more accurate linkages between the two.

It is in this sense that Warner's *The Social System of the Modern Factory*[21] is a major contribution to the community-industry studies. Indeed, in this book, although the author accepts and uses the basic approach developed at Hawthorne, he carries the analysis a step further. He is not only content to see how extraorganisational variables enter into the individual's definition of the situation; he also tries to examine these environmental factors in themselves. For example, Warner shows how the break in the hierarchy of opportunities had an impact on the workers' status and their definition of the situation – all these leading to a strike. Mayo and the authors of *Management and the Worker*, would have stopped the analysis at this point. Warner goes on to explain this change in status by a systematic examination of changes in technology, in the size of markets and firms and their impact on the community and so on. In this way, not only does he account for the environment of the organisation, but by showing how big environmental changes link precisely with individual behaviour, he provides a more complete picture of the mechanisms of change.[22]

Subsequently, many of Warner's students spent a great deal of time in demonstrating that such factors as social class, religion, race, family upbringing, must be taken into consideration in the study of organisational behaviour.[23] One of the environmental factors which received special attention from this school is the trade union. The orthodox school has, in the main, neglected the problem.[24] The Chicago school, having a broader conceptual focus, elaborated a more sophisticated attitude towards the union. Instead of being ignored, it is accepted and becomes an integral part of the social system of the plant.[25] Management must stop resisting union interference; it must assume a more positive role, by taking the initiative and persuading the union to collaborate and participate in the solution of plant problems.

The human relations techniques enter the scene when it is emphasised that in order to achieve such collaboration contractual agreements and formal mechanisms facilitating contacts and consultation are not enough; the most important factor is the atmosphere in which the negotiations take place. When mistrust and hostility prevail, communications become difficult and agreement impossible. The favourable context for collaboration is when confidence and two-way communications are fully established, not only between negotiating leaders, but also between the top and the bottom of each hierarchy and between all levels of business and union organisation.[26]

C. The interactionist approach

The interactionists, although influenced by Mayo and the Hawthorne studies, constitute a distinct group using specific tools and methods. The theory of interaction was first elaborated by Chapple and Arensberg at Harvard. Among human relations writers who use interactionist concepts, W. F. Whyte, G. Homans, L. Sayles are the best known. Although there are important differences[27] between the major representatives of the school, they all agree that in organisational studies, more attention has been given to what people feel and think (sentiments) than to what they do (activities) and to the manner in which they contact each other (interactions). Thus they want to rely as much as possible on observations of concrete measurable behaviour and for this purpose they insist on the use of operational concepts (i.e. concepts referring to phenomena which can be identified by an operation or a measuring technique).

The social system and the interactional structure of the organisation.

The interactionists have further elaborated the concept of the solid system. Interactions, activities and sentiments, the three parts of the system, are related in such a way that a change in one of them would influence the other two. The formal organisation, technology and various environmental factors (economic, legal) although directly influencing the system, are outside its boundaries.[28] Most interactionists regard the patterns of interaction as playing the preponderant role among the internal variables. Indeed, in analysing the organisation, the first and most important task of the interactionist is to identify the interactional structure of the system, that is:

- the identification of the interacting persons
- the registration of the order of the interacting events (who initiated interaction, for whom, etc.)
- the measurement of the duration and the frequency of interactions.[29]

When such measurements are attempted, the determining role of the technological structure and process on the patterns of interaction becomes evident. The sequence, frequency and duration of interactions depend in great part on the work flow, on the way materials are processed from one workpost to the other in time. Thus, we have come back to Taylor, to the examination of the physical and technological context in which interactions take place. The difference, of course, is that the interactionist flow charts[30] emphasise those aspects of the work process which involve or are relevant to contacts among people.

In a similar way such important concepts of classical management theory as line authority, line and staff relations, are redefined in an operational, non-formalistic way, namely in terms of concrete interactions, initiations and responses among the various members of the organisation. When this is done, the famous informal organisation of the orthodox school becomes a residual category of relationships defined as 'those events of interpersonal stimulation among members of the flow of work outside the order of the other relationships'.[31] Thus, as both formal and informal aspects of the organisation are defined in concrete relationships, the distinction between the two takes a different form;[32] or this much discussed formal-informal dichotomy is completely discarded.[33]

The change of attitudes. In consequence of the importance attributed to the interactional patterns and their technological basis, they become the strategic points of change. According to Chapple one cannot change workers' attitudes on a large scale by teaching the supervisor human relations skills. It is only by changing the technological and interactional structure of the organisation that new attitudes and better performance can be achieved. The other aspect of such a change should involve the study of the interactional pattern of an individual's personality, in order to place him in an organisational position which would suit his character. This can be achieved by micro-interaction analysis and the use of the interaction chronograph.[34] By such methods it becomes possible to define both organisational structure and personality in the same quantitative terms, thus facilitating the problem of personnel placement. Finally, these techniques are very similar to the various sociometric devices, elaborated by Moreno and his school, for adjusting the individual to the group or the organisation.[35]

The same critical importance of the interactional pattern is seen when the exact process of social change is examined. Arensberg, in analysing all cases in the literature on human relations where successful changes took place, identifies in all these studies an identical process having three temporal phases. First there is always a change in basic social relationships (in the patterning of interaction). Then follows a change in attitudes. Finally as a result (a by-product) of the above transformations, the activities of the organisation members change (more co-operation, increased productivity, etc.).[36] This 'processual' character of the interactionist analysis is another main characteristic of the school. As a reaction to the excessive use of factorial analysis in studies in human relations (i.e. correlating, weighing of factors), the interactionists, by introducing the time variable, try to examine dynamically the various organisational processes. In this sphere their chief effort is towards the further refinement of their tools in order to achieve ultimately a strictly quantitative analysis of the process of change.

In conclusion, although some interactionists have exaggerated the causal importance of the interactional aspect of the organisation, their emphasis on the technological structure has filled a certain gap in the Mayoite movement, which, by overemphasising the informal organisation, had neglected the formal. Moreover, their methods, stressing observation and measurement, although sterile when strictly applied, had a salutary effect in a field where most of the studies were based on questionnaire data.

3. THE EVOLUTION OF THE HUMAN RELATIONS SCHOOL AS A WHOLE

Our examination of the various subdivisions in the human relations movement has been static and, in a way, artificial. For the sake of clarity, we have overstressed conceptual differences and we have presented the various subschools with well delineated and established boundaries. In reality the boundaries are very fluid and the degree of interpenetration and cross-fertilisation high.[37] Thus from their rapid development, especially after the 1940s, a general common pattern of evolution seems to emerge. In this section we shall try to identify the main stages of this evolution.

A. The comprehensive approach

In the study of a concrete organisation one can choose between abstracting some aspects of it and trying to treat the ensuing problems in a rigorous way or trying to give a full picture by taking into consideration, in a less systematic and intensive way, as many aspects and problems of the situation as possible. This second approach was adopted at Hawthorne. Using a very flexible methodology (unstructured interview and observation), the investigators wanted to account for events as they appeared in the working situation. Moreover, they wanted to break down the artificial and overlapping barriers erected by the various social sciences and to create an interdisciplinary approach accounting for the situation as a whole. Indeed by avoiding any preconceived elaborated theory, which might limit their scope, they tried to take into consideration all the forces influencing behaviour in the plant.

As these forces are ultimately summed up and balanced on the level of the individual, a convenient way to examine them is to see how they impinge on the individual's definition of the situation. Thus, the focus of attention is not so much on the structure of the organisation or the group but on the impact of this structure on the individual. This psychological bias is a common characteristic of the comprehensive type of studies.[38] The risk of such an approach is that when we take into consideration the social environment not in itself but as it is perceived by the individual, we may learn much about the individual but very little about the environment. But there is nothing incompatible in stressing both the individual and the environment. Indeed this stress on the individual's perception of the situation has not prevented the authors of *Management and the Worker* from examining the social structure of the group.[39] (It was only the organisational and environmental factors that they neglected to examine systematically.) Moreover, Warner and the interactionists have further enriched the Hawthorne approach by paying special attention both to the environment and to the technological structure of the organisation.

B. *The abstractive phase*

In the years subsequent to Hawthorne, most research in human relations abandoned the comprehensive approach and concentrated on the rigorous treatment of a few problems.[40] It was hoped that what would be lost by abandoning the exhaustive analysis of one case would be gained by considering, in a more restricted way, many cases, thus arriving at valid generalisations. Moreover, influenced by small group theory, the researchers examined mainly psychological and socio-psychological variables by questionnaire methods. Indeed, a large part of the literature during this phase, consisted of correlations between attitudes and such factors as the characteristics of the respondent (sex, age, social background), the reported behaviour of respondent and indices of performance, productivity, turnover.

To illustrate this kind of approach, let us briefly examine the extensive research on leadership and supervision which occupies the central place in human relations literature. Studies of leadership in industrial settings have been dominated by the work of Mayo at Hawthorne[41] and by Lewin's famous Iowa experiments on styles of leadership in groups of children.[42] Stimulated by such studies and by the extensive treatment of leadership in small group theory, students of human relations began systematically to study problems of first level supervision and the relation of the supervisor's leadership style to workers' attitude and performance.

Very briefly, it was found that the style of supervision played a major determining role in shaping the attitude and behaviour of subordinates. More precisely, a supervisor with permissive or supportive style of leadership (being people-minded rather than job-minded, trying to understand the problems and needs of his subordinates, etc.) was found to create a co-operative group atmosphere and to increase workers' satisfaction and performance. On the other hand, authoritarian leadership and close supervision was repeatedly found to be positively correlated with poor productivity and morale.[43] As a result of such findings, permissive supervision was considered in management textbooks to be the remedy to all industrial ills, and supervisory training programmes for the development of social skills became very fashionable among progressive managers.[44]

C. Return to a more inclusive approach

As it became evident that such training programmes had little effect in changing morale and productivity on a large scale,[45] further research began to show the ambiguity of the leadership – morale – productivity relationships, which were hastily established in a general and abstract manner (i.e. without taking into consideration the specific organisational contexts in which such phenomena occurred).

Taking again the problem of leadership, new studies have

shown no significant correlation between leadership and morale.[46] Thus the inconclusiveness of such results, as well as numerous criticisms about the triviality of human relations findings,[47] has directed research into a more inclusive approach. It was gradually realised that relationships between leadership, productivity and morale were only valid under certain conditions and that the task of further research should be to specify these conditional variables.[48] Thus it was found, for example, that the personality distribution of the group[49] or the type of job[50] may condition which leadership style will be more effective (e.g. when the majority of group members have an authoritarian personality or when the task is repetitive, directive strict supervision seems more effective). Moreover, the critical influence of technology on group structure and leadership was amply demonstrated by Sayles.[51]

This broadening of scope was not limited to the consideration of more group variables; it was extended to the organisation structure as a whole. Thus Donald Pelz, after some unsuccessful attempts to relate supervisory practices to employee attitudes in a general way, has found that these attitudes do not depend only on the style of supervision but also on the supervisor's position in the organisational hierarchy.[52] Other similar studies have shown that the supervisor's ability to exert an influence upwards in the hierarchy does not only affect morale and motivation but productivity as well.[53] In a more general way, it was realised that problems of supervision arise on all levels of the organisation and that from that angle they are similar to the problem of authority with which Weber and other theorists have dealt long ago.[54] Thus by the gradual shifting of focus from the group to the organisation level, many neglected problems, first considered at Hawthorne, come back to the surface and the gap between human relations and bureaucracy students becomes narrower.[55]

Finally, in the practical field of management, these theoretical developments are reflected by the displacement of attention from supervisory skills to the problems at the higher levels of management and to the questions of organisational authority and structure. It is emphasised more and more that many organisational problems cannot be solved by human relations skills as they do not arise from difficulties in face-to-face relations; rather one should look for their solution in structural changes on the organisational level. Thus emphasis is laid upon the diffusion of authority, the participation of employees in the decision-making, and the improvement of two-way communications between the top and the bottom of the organisation.[56]

On the individual level, changes in the formal and technological structure of the organisation should aim at giving more freedom and initiative to the employee by making his job more challenging and satisfying (recommendations for a flat hierarchy with a big span of control, job rotation and enlargement).[57] In this way, the formal and technological factors which were so important to the classical school of management and so neglected by the two previous phases of human relations research come back on the scene. But the new principles of structure-building are the exact opposite of the classical ones.

4. CRITICISM

The long arguments about the methods and findings of the human relations school have confused rather than clarified things. This is because many critics, neglecting the diversity and changing character of the school, attack it as a whole, when their criticisms are only valid for a certain subschool or a certain phase in its development.[58] Thus, for example, the frequent criticism about the school's neglect of the formal and technological structure is more or less valid for the orthodox subschool but it does not apply to the interactionists and to the latest phase of research in human relations. In a similar manner although most of the other criticisms expressed have a degree of validity, they can be met without changing the basic framework of the human relations approach.[59]

A. The narrow focus of analysis and its consequences

I think the only weakness which seems fundamental and common to the school as a whole, is that human relations theory

The 'Human Relations' Approach to the Organisation

has tried to solve the major organisational problems in drawing attention to the individual and group level, and not paying much attention to the organisation as a whole. Indeed even when human relations students take into consideration organisational variables (as in the third phase of the school's evolution), the main focus of analysis remains the group or the individual. The organisational factors, even when specified, remain the external variables of the system; they are not studied in themselves but only as they impinge on the individual's perceived situation or on the social system of the group.[60] As this point is very important, we must analyse it and its consequences in some detail.

Human relations students want to study and find some remedies for the human problems created by industrialisation and the development of big organisations. But in opposition to their predecessors, they want to avoid all inclusive and vague theorising. They decide to study the problems of the worker by observing and interviewing real workers in concrete plants. They try as much as possible to use quantitative data and operational definitions; upon such foundations, they hope to build a body of propositions about organisational behaviour, which, although modest in scope, could be a solid starting point for the future construction of a more general theory.

Thus if their humanistic orientation determined the problems which they studied, their methodological preoccupations with rigour and precision (rather than the nature of the problem) determined the way in which they tackled them. Necessarily they had to pay a price for choosing precision instead of comprehensiveness. Because they narrowed their scope to the individual and the group level, the basic controversies and problems which can be asked and answered on the societal and organisational level, became mere assumptions (usually implicit), outside their limited model. Thus what was gained in precision was lost in fruitfulness and substance.

Of course, no theory can combine all advantages and avoid all shortcomings. As Roethlisberger says, 'one cannot look and talk about everything at the same time'.[61] Any conceptual scheme will have to 'slice the cake' of reality in a certain way, in an attempt to explain certain things and leaving others unexplained. And as the 'ways of slicing cakes for certain investigatory and explanatory purposes have nothing God-given about them', there is no methodological objection to choosing a narrow scope.[62]

Although we can always 'slice the cake' as we like, we can be more or less successful in the slicing: when we choose to explain a certain whole and consider outside factors as givens, it all depends on how autonomous or self-contained this system is (in reference to the system properties that one chooses to analyse and explain). For example, we may want to explain group productivity in terms of group variables (cohesion, supervision, etc.). If these variables have a small degree of autonomy, if the boundaries of the group are very permeable to external forces (e.g. institutionalised intergroup conflict), the explanation in intragroup terms will be meaningless. Of course, groups very often have a high degree of self-contain-ment and they really control and determine organisational behaviour. At other times they do not. The degrees of group autonomy is an empirical question, and in order to identify this degree we have to place it in its organisational context. It is not enough to learn about this context by simply examining how the individual perceives it. We have to focus our attention on it as a whole. When we neglect to do this, we run the risk of obtaining results which, even if positive (e.g. like the correlations between supervision and morale), are not 'general-isable'. (They cannot be generalised by simply studying more and more groups without considering their context.)

In order that such positive correlations become valid generalisations, one has to specify the conditions under which they hold true; and this leads sooner or later to the study of the organisation as a whole. In the third phase of the school's development this process has clearly started but in a very limited way. Indeed, it is not enough to specify certain organisa-tional variables (e.g. the supervisor's position in the hierarchy, cf. p. 111) acting as conditioning variables for the appearance of positive correlations between attitudes. This, although useful, does not solve the problem. Why is it, for example, that in many studies the correlations between supervision and productivity were positive irrespective of the supervisor's hierarchical position? In other terms, when do such conditioning variables determine the group situation and when do they not? Once more, in order to answer such questions, one has to shift one's attention to the organisation as a whole and examine the relations between the whole and its parts. If this is done systematically, much effort can be saved and more meaningful and strategic questions can be asked about the individual and the group within organisations.

B. Levels of analysis and the problem of power

Of course, it is only in one way that human relations students have neglected the organisation. In another way they always speak about it. Indeed very often they use their findings about the individual and the group in order to solve problems which occur in the wider organisational context. This jumping from one level to the other is clearly seen when we examine the way in which the problem of conflict and power is treated.

Human relations students are often criticised for emphasising harmony and neglecting organisational conflict because of their pro-management values, or because they use such conservative biased concepts as functional whole, equilibrium and so on.[63] Although there is some truth in such criticisms, what really prevented them from examining the power-structure of the organisation, was their limited scope and their insistence on methodological rigour. By studying the problem of conflict on the individual and group level, human relations theory has stressed its psychological aspects. It conceptualised it as bad interpersonal relations or misunderstanding arising from the fact that the one party does not understand the problems and feelings of the other. In this way conflict becomes a pathological case, to be cured by better communications or similar devices. In this way the theory fails to make the fundamental distinction between interpersonal frictions and social conflict which has its basis in the structure of the organisation and the society in which groups and individuals are embedded.

Thus, during the second phase of the school's evolution, when the social skills of the supervisor were found to influence group morale, not only were such findings considered applicable to all groups, but also to the organisation as a whole. So, by hastily moving from one level to another, textbooks on management heralded good human relations as the universal remedy for our industrial ills. Of course, the irrelevancy of such acrobatic jumps from one level to another reaches its peak in Mayo's and Whitehead's philosophical writings. There, all the problems of our industrial civilisation are solved on the basis of informal group findings.

What is here ignored is that when we move to the organisational level and consider the power-structure as a whole, there are conflicts which are not due to bad communications or bad interpersonal relations, but to differences in interests – differences in the sense that what one group may gain, the other will lose, and vice versa.

Of course, the fact that all conflicts cannot be reduced to communication problems, does not deny the usefulness of communication theory and its application in organisations. But it implies that future research must specify and distinguish the conditions under which communication findings are applicable, and the conditions where communications are not at fault, but where interest groups pursue in a rational and self-conscious way antagonistic strategies. For instance, it is quite evident that certain types of organisations have a social structure which entails less conflictual situations than others. In such cases communication theory may be more frequently relevant. From this point of view, the narrow scope of human relations students causes them to forget that a firm is not any organisation but an economic[64] organisation with specific problems – and, at least in our society, with a power-structure which makes social conflict, due to divergent interests, unavoidable.

Moreover, if human relations students would view groups in terms of strategy and bargaining, they would realise the utopian character of their preachings about internal democracy and participation in the firm. Indeed when, basing their knowledge on group findings, they advise participation of the employees on the organisational level, they are immediately confronted with the dilemma that they either propose a pseudo-democracy, where employees are given the opportunity to participate only in decisions which do not hurt management; or they propose real participation, which, in the last analysis implies that the manager should voluntarily cede a part of his power and prerogatives to his employees. Of course, when participation reaches that point, it becomes clear that no manager, except the eccentric philanthropist, will sacrifice his own interests for altruistic purposes.

The classical answer to such an argument is that ultimately and in the long run the interests of all organisational groups are the same; or that when, by participation, the workers' control increases, this does not mean that management's control and power decrease.[65] It is evident that both statements are true in some cases and not in others. A concrete example provides the best answer to such arguments; in all human relations literature, there is always the recommendation that when technological changes become necessary in the plant, instead of imposing it on the workers, the best way is to make them participate in the decision of change instead of their having it imposed upon them. In this way they invariably imply that the workers, when consulted or invited to participate, will be so enchanted that they will finally accept the change. But what if they decide against the change (because e.g. further mechanisation might destroy their skills), and what if external competition makes the change imperative? Indeed real participation on a large scale would imply nothing less than the radical transformation of the politico-economic institutions of our society. Here it becomes clear that human relations students have nothing like that in mind. Their mistake, at this point, is that they want to revolutionise the organisation without revolution, without touching its societal foundations.

Of course, the above argument does not imply that human relations techniques are insignificant tools for management. They can be useful but in a much more limited way. From this perspective the task of the social analyst is not to adopt them hastily as the solution to all problems, but rather to identify the conditions under which such practices are effective and the conditions under which they are not. Once again, in order to do this, one must shift the focus from the individual and the group to the organisation and its power-structure as a whole. In fact, the excessive optimism about participation or permissive leadership can only be explained by the neglect of the power-structure of the firm and the often repeated assumption that as workers and managers are interdependent, a community of interest exists in the organisation. Of course, theorists with such views forget the truism, expressed by Simmel long ago, that interdependence does not only imply collaboration, but conflict as well – especially if the interdependent parties, for one reason or another, are not on an equal footing but hierarchically stituated.

C. Conclusion

The argument is not that grand theories about organisation and society are preferable to highly empirical ones. Rather, it is widely accepted that both have strong and weak points and that both are necessary. But if we choose the latter, we pay a lesser price and we reduce our shortsightedness by realising firstly the limits and the implicit assumptions that we make when we reduce our scope; secondly that we cannot apply the considerable findings of small group theory to organisational groups automatically, without taking seriously into consideration their organisational context; thirdly that even when we arrive at valid findings on the group level, the findings do not apply necessarily on the organisational level.[66] Because, although the group as a unit and the whole organisation as another unit are interdependent systems in a firm, at the same time the latter has a varying degree of autonomy from the former (cf. chapter 7). And fourthly we realise that by taking more systematically into consideration the organisation and its power structure as a whole we can study the individual and the group in it in a more fruitful and intelligent manner.

Finally, in order to put the above criticisms into their right perspective, one must stress that, although human relations students, because of their values and methodology, have not given definite answers to the problems they posed (as far as normative management theory is concerned), this fact does not diminish the importance of their contribution to the study of the firm and of organisations in general.

They not only revolutionised the classical theory of management by breaking through its formalistic approach and opening up the whole problem area of human behaviour in the firm; they also filled a great gap in the study of bureaucracy, in being the first to show by what precise mechanisms social phenomena on the societal and organisational level are linked with concrete behaviour on the group and the individual level.

For example, when Kerr and Siegel (two prominent critics of the narrow scope of human relations) show by their method how the interindustry propensity to strike is a result not of interpersonal relations, but of various extraorganisational factors (community structure, etc.);[67] they do not show us, as Warner has done, exactly how those general impersonal forces reach the organisation member, enter into his situation and push him to strike. Moreover, their pattern of analysis cannot account for internal differences between organisations. It cannot explain why similar types of organisations exposed to the same environmental pressures can have different frequencies of strikes. Thus, it becomes increasingly clear that the macro and micro-level approach are complementary, and that any advance on the one is a valuable aid for the other.

Chapter Six

ORGANISATION THEORY: DECISION-MAKING IN ORGANISATIONAL CONTEXTS

INTRODUCTION

Organisation theory,[1] as a distinct approach to the study of formal organisations, has come as a reaction to the shortcomings and opposing positions of previous approaches. It claims to have an integrative character,[2] to bring together under a coherent theoretical scheme all those aspects of organisational behaviour which were treated one-sidedly by the human relations school, the classical management theory and the economic theory of the firm. Whether or not its claim to synthesis is fully justified, this new approach will be better understood if we show in which ways this integration is sought. Thus, whenever possible, during the present exposition, frequent comparisons and references to previous schools will be made.

As we have already seen, the human relations school (and the bureaucracy theorists to a lesser extent), focuses its attention on the informal aspects of the organisational structure, on all those patterns of behaviour and norms which arise spontaneously in the process of social interaction. Thus, human behaviour is predominantly explained in terms of sentiments, motivations and personal values and goals which are often in conflict with formal regulations and organisational objectives. But this emphasis on sentiments minimises the importance of rational problem solving activities in the organisation. It neglects the problems of planning and co-ordination, the fact that an organisation is predominantly a system of consciously co-ordinated activities[3] geared towards the achievement of collective goals. It relegates the formal structure, with its problems of design, to the background by treating it as an external variable of the informal system, not to be studied in itself. Finally, on the individual level, this informal bias is translated by a tendency, traceable back to Freud, to reduce all cognitive problems to matters of affect.[4] Starting with Mayo's criticism of the alleged logic of workers' behaviour,[5] there is a persistent attempt to show that man is not as rational as we normally think he is.

On the other hand, those social disciplines which take into consideration the rational aspects of human behaviour, organisational or not, go to the other extreme. They give us an ideal, non-empirical picture of a human actor totally rational, with no bounds whatsoever to his capacities for computation and problem solving. The classical model of rational choice in economics is a good example of this type of approach. The economic man, when he makes a choice in pursuit of a goal, is supposed:

(a) to know in an omniscient way all the possible alternatives of action

(b) to foresee the set of consequences which will ensue from the eventual choice of each alternative (or the probabilities of the appearance of each consequence)

(c) to have a complete and consistent system of preferences (a utility function), enabling him to rank all consequences, from the most to the least preferred, thus making an optimal choice.

Of course, it is evident that what is modelled above is not the way in which people actually decide, but the way in which they should decide if they were one hundred per cent rational and if their computational capacities were unlimited.[6] As to the classical management theory, rational elements are analysed in a similar fashion. Whether the universalists consider structure designing or other management problems (budgeting, planning, etc.), they are not preoccupied with finding out how the manager really takes decisions. They are rather preoccupied with how the manager ought to take decisions if he wants optimal results.[7]

Finally another common element of economics and management theory is their conception of the agent of rationality. In the theory of the firm, the whole business organisation is seen as a unit. As the emphasis is on the relationship between such a unit and the market, intraorganisational relationships are not considered.[8] It is only the entrepreneur, representing the firm as a whole, who behaves rationally. The theory makes no room for other organisational members to have an individual frame of reference, to make choices or solve problems. Such members, under the label 'labour' become simply a factor of production that the entrepreneur must rationally combine with other factors in order to maximise his profits. Thus, as in Taylorism and in the classical management theory, rationality is concentrated at the top. Organisational participants at the lower levels are mere pawns in the entrepreneurial or managerial game.

Through this brief review of various approaches to organisational behaviour a sort of polarisation is evident. At the empirical pole, the social psychologist of the Human Relations School neglects the rational aspects of behaviour. At the normative pole, the economist and the management theorist take into consideration rational elements. But, as they are not empirically minded, they do not only confine rationality to the top of the organisational hierarchy, but they also neglect the non-rational elements of behaviour which drastically limit ideal rationality.

Organisation theory, especially as it appears in the writings of Herbert A. Simon, its most illustrious representative, can be seen as an attempt to fill the gap between those two extremes and to bring to an end this schizophrenic situation of the social sciences.[9] Simon, in his effort to account for both rational and non-rational aspects of organisational behaviour, tried to construct a model of rational choice combining realism and analytic rigour, a conceptual framework which could refer to 'the actual properties of human beings, and at the same time retain some of the formal clarity of the economic model'.[10]

Organisation Theory:

Behaviour in formal organisations is not completely emotive or aimless. On the contrary, it is primarily purposive.[11] People become organised in order to pursue a common objective. In doing so, they have to co-ordinate their activities in a conscious way. It is precisely this purposiveness, this conscious co-ordination of relationships, which mainly distinguishes formal organisations from other kinds of social groupings (cf. Introduction). This being the case, the concept of decision-making should be central to any theory of administration. When people co-ordinate their activities for the attainment of a certain goal, they have continuously to take decisions, to choose among alternatives of action. Consequently, in administrative studies, the emphasis must be on the rational aspects of human behaviour. A member of an organisation, more than an instrument or an autonomous agent of drives and emotions, is a decision-maker and problem solver.

But the way in which he actually solves problems is very different from the one described in the economic model. In concrete reality there is no such thing as perfectly rational behaviour. Rationality is always limited. And it is precisely by the serious consideration of such limits that the link between the rational and the non-rational, between the economic and the Freudian man, can be achieved. Indeed the environment of the decision-maker can be seen as a set of premises upon which his decisions will be based. Simon distinguishes two kinds of decision premises. There are factual premises subject to empirical testing for the establishment of their validity, and value premises which are not subject to such tests.[12] Roughly speaking, the latter have to do with the choice of the ends of action, the former with the choice of means.[13] From this point of view a rational decision can be seen as the right conclusion reached from these two kinds of premises.[14]

In the economic model of perfect rationality, the decision-maker is supposed to have *a priori* a full repertory of all the factual premises (complete knowledge of alternatives and consequences) and the value premises (utility function or preference ordering) which are relevant to his problem. In reality these premises are not given. The decision-maker has to search for them. In the process of this search, there are all sorts of limitations which reduce the quality and quantity of the premises on which he has to base his decisions. For Simon such limitations fall into three categories:

(a) The skills, habits and reflexes which are more or less unconscious and which determine automatically an individual's performance and the decisions which precede it.[15] It is precisely this type of limitations, most evident on the operative level of an organisation, with which Taylorism was preoccupied. The various techniques of early scientific management can be seen as efforts to increase productivity by widening the boundaries of rational behaviour on the workshop level.

(b) A second group of constraints to rationality derive from the motivations, values and loyalties of the individual. In an organisational context for example, an individual's strong identification with a certain group whose values diverge from organisational values, might limit the individual's rational behaviour (when rationality is judged by organisational standard and goals). Of course, this sort of limitation was the main preoccupation of the human relations school.

(c) Finally, rational behaviour or rational decision-making is limited by the amount of basic knowledge and information available. It is precisely this third class of limitations which have been most neglected in the study of organisations and which come to the centre of attention in *organisation theory*.

All the above limitations put boundaries to or delineate in some way the area in which rationality can be exercised. They determine which alternatives, of all the possible ones, can realistically be considered, to what extent the consequences of such alternatives can be predicted, and how accurately the evaluation and ranking of the predicted consequences can be effected.[16]

Now, if we shift our attention from the decisional environment and look at the same problem of limitations from the inside, that is from the decision-maker's point of view, we may say that his choice is always exercised with respect to a limited, approximate and simplified model of reality. His behaviour is rational or irrational not in an absolute sense, but according to his definition of the situation. Indeed his subjective frame of reference allows him the consideration of only a few of the decision premises. In turn, these limited premises perceived by the individual are themselves the outcome of psychological and sociological processes, which a student of decision-making would have to identify and analyse. Finally, on the basis of such premises, the decision-maker does not search for the optimal decision in the economic sense, but simply for a satisfactory one. He is not the *maximising* man of economics but the satisfying man: that is to say, as soon as he finds an alternative which will lead him to the attainment of his main goal and which, at the same time satisfies a number of auxiliary requirements (or side constraints), he will choose it, thus abandoning the search for the best alternative.[17]

2. THE SOCIAL PSYCHOLOGY OF ORGANISATIONAL DECISION-MAKING

Now that we have considered the process of decision-making in a general way, we must examine in greater detail the decision-maker in the organisational context.

From this point of view, the first things to examine is how the individual becomes a member of the organisation and for what reasons, once he has become a member, he continues to participate in it. Simon accounts for individual participation by elaborating further Barnard's conception of an inducement-contribution equilibrium.[18] Briefly, according to this view, when someone joins an organisation, a transaction takes place by which he receives inducements (money or any other kind of reward) in return for the contribution he makes to the organisation. Moreover, he will continue his participation in the organisation as long as the inducements offered to him are equal to or greater than the contributions which he has to offer. Of course, the above makes sense only if we use a subjective criterion for measuring inducements and contributions. The personal satisfaction of the participant can be used as such a measure in so far as contributions and inducements are assessed in terms of his values – his utilities – and also in terms of the alternatives that he perceives to exist elsewhere.

Thus, when a participant is dissatisfied with the inducement-contribution exchange, if the extraorganisational alternatives perceived by him are few or non-existent, his aspiration level will be gradually reduced and, in the long term, his dissatisfaction will decrease (in other terms, if he cannot find a better job elsewhere, he will finish up by being content with his present situation).[19] One can reason similarly when looking at the organisation as a whole: the contributions of some participants become the inducements of other participants[20] and a general equilibrium on this aggregate level is necessary for the long-term survival of the organisation.

We must now proceed to show what happens to the individual after he has decided to participate in and remain in the organisation. For the individual, joining the organisation means a considerable restriction of his decisional autonomy. It means that he permits the organisation to influence his decisions to a certain degree – this influence being indispensable for the co-ordination of the decisions and activities of all participant members. Thus in this section we must briefly see by which mechanisms the organisation influences the decisions of the individual member, how it integrates him into its overall plan by structuring his decision-making environment.

The division of work is the most fundamental device by which the organisation sets limits to the decisional environment of the individual. By assigning him a certain task, it directs and limits his attention only to the problems which are relevant to this task. Moreover, the way in which some of the above problems must be tackled is, to a certain extent, determined by standard procedures which stipulate in detail the steps to be taken for their solution, thus sparing the individual from the effort of producing the solution by himself.

Authority is another crucial factor for the understanding of organisational decision-making. One way by which the organisation transmits decisions downwards is through its authority system. The broad and crucial policy decisions are taken at the top of the hierarchy. They are subsequently transmitted to the lower echelons and become the guiding criteria on the basis of which the inferior decision-maker will take decisions of a more detailed and procedural character. By this process the organisations can be viewed as a means-end chain, on each level of which, the superior's decisions constitute the major value premises in the decisional environment of the inferior (the latter's decision-making consisting simply in finding the means for achieving the imposed goal).[21]

A fourth important factor influencing the decision-maker is the communication system. It is through the communication channels, running in all directions, that the information indispensable for establishing the factual premises of a decision, is transmitted. Finally, training and indoctrination are powerful devices for influencing individual decision-making. By this method knowledge, values and decision rules are internalised. They therefore become the best guarantee that the individual will take decisions in accordance with the overall organisational objectives.

Thus division of labour, standard procedures, authority, communications and training are important organisational features setting limits to and shaping the decisional environment of the individual. They do not necessarily deprive him of all initiative; rather they determine some of the value and factual premises of his environment in a way which assures that his decisions will be co-ordinated with the decisions of others.

3. DECISION-MAKING AND ORGANISATIONAL STRUCTURE

When the focus of analysis shifts from the organisational member to the organisation as a whole, what is the picture of the latter in decision-making terms?

A. *The organisation as a decision-making unit*

One way to look at the problem is to consider the total organisation as a unit which solves problems and takes decisions,[22] thus concentrating the analysis on the decision-making process as a whole: that is to study the major decisions taken by the organisation (e.g. price and output determination) and then to try to build empirical models accounting for the organisational processes which generate such decisions. This kind of approach has been mainly developed in the context of the various attempts to bring organisation theory and the economic theory of the firm closer together.[23]

The argument for such a weaving together of organisational and economic ideas is that the way in which firms do take major decisions is very different from the way in which they are supposed to decide in the ideal rationality models of microeconomics. However, such decisions are not taken by the individual entrepreneur of the firm theory. They are primarily organisational decisions. The entrepreneur abstraction, although convenient for some purposes, blurs the fact that the firm is a formal organisation and as such, its decisions are not only influenced by market considerations but by its internal structure as well.

Thus the main purpose of the behavioural approach to the theory of the firm is to give a more empirical and realistic account of its decision-making processes by taking more systematically into consideration its organisational aspects. Although some of the decision-making models constructed in this way try to link organisational variables to specific problems or decisions (e.g. price determination),[24] there are also attempts at the construction of a broader framework referring to an organisation's decision-making process in general. Cyert and March have tentatively provided such a framework.[25] It is based on four fundamental concepts which refer to the major aspects of an organisation's decision-making process.

Quasi-resolution of conflict. From March and Cyert's perspective the organisation is viewed as a coalition of participants whose values and individual goals are often conflicting. This minimum common ground of agreement, which is what we call organisational goals, is a result of bargaining and learning processes. Such processes do not stop as soon as the coalition is formed and the organisational goals determined. They are continuously operating as conflict resolution is never complete and as organisational goals are not fixed and agreed upon once and for all but change and are contested according to the circumstances. Thus, when one looks closely at a concrete organisation, instead of an overriding organisational goal, one finds a series of more or less independent goals or subgoals in actual or potential conflict.

Uncertainty avoidance. Partially because of their limited predictive and computational capacities, organisations are continuously confronted with uncertainty. Whenever possible they try to avoid it. In a negative way, this is achieved by avoiding the anticipation of long term events. In a positive way, the organisation will try to reduce uncertainty by regulating and stabilising its environment.[27]

Problemistic search. If goals and uncertainty considerations show us what sort of ends are sought by the organisation, the theory of search tries to examine how the organisation endeavours to find the means for the accomplishment of these ends. The basic assumption here is that organisational search is motivated and simple-minded. It is motivated in the sense that it is always stimulated by a specific problem (problemistic search). It is simple-minded in that it avoids the complex requirements of ideal rationality and accepts more simplified rules of procedure.[28]

Organisational learning. Finally, organisations are adaptive. Whenever problems arise which cannot be dealt with by traditional procedures, changes occur which enable the organisation to cope with the new difficulties.[29]

The general framework. Thus, according to March and Cyert, quasi-resolution of conflict, uncertainty avoidance, problemistic search and learning are the main building blocks for a general theory of organisational decision-making.

If one starts the analysis at the moment when the organisation (or a subunit) evaluates its performance in relation to a certain goal, the decision-making process can be seen as a series of conditional steps having the following pattern.

If the performance is judged satisfactory, the organisation learns that the decision rules, used for arriving at the satisfactory results, were effective and such rules are reinforced and used again in the future (uncertainty avoidance). If the performance is judged unsatisfactory, there is a search for a better alternative. If the search is successful, current search rules are reinforced. If the search is not successful, search rules may be changed and new rules or even new, less ambitious goals may have to be learned.

B. The organisation as a communication, self-controlled system. The second major framework for representing the organisation as a whole shifts the focus of attention onto its internal structure. The organisation is not so much seen as a decision-making unit but as a decision-making system. In the unit model the internal structure of the organisation is not considered in a systematic way, the emphasis being rather on the aggregate decisional behaviour of the firm towards its environment. In the present context more attention is given to decision centres and their interconnections through communication channels.[30] Indeed communication networks and the information transmitted through them are the basis of organisational decision-making and control. This being so, it is not suprising that the main concepts of this model are taken from communication engineering and cybernetics. Very briefly, cybernetics is usually defined as the study of communication and control phenomena in every kind of system.[31] A cybernetic or control feedback network is a system which is self-steered (or self-controlled) with respect to one or more of its properties, states or goals. This self-government is achieved by the fact that information about the system's behaviour is fed-back to the system, the latter readjusting its behaviour in the light of the new information received.

The minimum components of a cybernetic system are:

– *the detector or censor* who receives information concerning the state of the variable or goal to be controlled.

– *the governor or selector* who takes decisions about the steering of the system on the basis of the information received from the

Organisation Theory:

censor and on the basis of his preference ordering. (Often, as an extension of the governor's brain, an information processor which stores, classifies and processes information is considered as a distinct component of the system).[32]

– *the effector* who executes the governor's decisions or orders.

Thus, in a cybernetic system, whenever a disturbance or error occurs which produces a difference between the desired and the actual state or goal, the detector senses the difference and transmits the message to the governor. The governor, on the basis of the new information received, decides on the corrective action to be taken and gives the appropriate orders to the effector who acts in a redressive way.

Of course, the above description reminds one very much of the concept of social equilibrium and control already discussed in the context of the human relations school (chapter 5, section 2). But there are important differences between the two approaches. The most basic one concerns the problem of change. The concept of social equilibrium, as used by the human relationists, hardly allows for any change of the system; whenever a disturbance occurs (e.g. deviant behaviour), the social control mechanism (e.g. sanctions) operate in a way which brings back the system to its previous state of equilibrium (the deviant finally complies to the norm or is ostracised). But what if the norms change, if the deviant behaviour of yesterday becomes the accepted behaviour of today? There is no vocabulary to account for such structural changes in the social control approach. The only alternative to a static equilibrium is the breakdown of the social system.

In the present context, the concept of a learning feedback system meets the requirements of change more successfully. A learning system has the capacity to rearrange its internal structure and elicit new self-controlled behaviour in its attempt to adapt to a changing environment.[33] In such a system the goals and the governor's preferences are not rigid, they change and become adapted to new circumstances.[34] Moreover, in the social control approach the goal is somehow internal to the system. The feedback mechanisms operate in order to maintain a state or property of the system (usually cohesion).

The Managerial Tradition

In this way, not much attention is given to the organisation or the group as a purposive problem-solving system pursuing various and changing goals. The cybernetic model, on the other hand, can deal with systems having feedback mechanisms in relation to problem goals, the achievement of which might necessitate overcoming obstacles, achieving intermediate sub-goals and so on (one might give as an example a firm wanting to achieve a certain quota of sales – the main goal – and changing market strategies according to the moves of its competitors).

Finally, the concepts used in the cybernetic model are set out in much more detail than the concepts of social equilibrium used by the human relationists. They permit a more intensive analysis of feedback phenomena and they direct attention to quantitative measurement. Thus, there is a host of technical concepts sensitising the researcher to such things as the range of oscillation of the controlled variable, the dampers of a system (the forces which reduce oscillation), the lag (the time that the system takes to respond to a disturbance) and so on.[35]

The difference between the social system approach as used by bureaucracy and human relations theorists and the present approach becomes more evident when one looks at the whole organisation as a cybernetic system. Indeed although both approaches view the organisation as a system of interconnected parts, the parts are seen by each one of them from a very different angle. The emphasis in the present approach is not any more on values, roles and their interconnections, but on information processing and decision centres.

More precisely, the overall control system of the organisation can be seen as an information processing, decision-making network steering the organisation towards its general goals. At this level the big decisions about ultimate goals are made and broad strategies for their achievements are set. As these strategies are applied, information about their effectiveness is fed-back through censor and information-processing centres (e.g. staff or intelligence departments) to the governor or decision making centres (managers, board of directors) and new decisions are taken, strategies or goals are modified and so on. Now similar self-steering processes and networks (*loops*) can be imagined at lower organisation levels, within subunits (e.g. departments) which have to take decisions and readapt their policies in order to achieve their narrower subgoals. Thus, the whole organisation can be seen as a system of loops within loops; or rather as a hierarchy of interlocking loops at the bottom of which the loops become smaller and more numerous.[36]

4. EMPIRICAL CONTENT AND METHODOLOGY

How are the various conceptual tools which have been examined in the previous section, used; to what kind of problems do they direct the attention of the student, what sort of insight and guidance do they provide for the manager?

Of course, as it has been often said above, they all emphasise the overriding importance of decision-making in organisations. The main task of the organisation theorist becomes the empirical study of decision-making in organisational settings. From a social psychological point of view this means finding out in a detailed way what sort of decisions are taken in each part of the organisation, what the premises are on which such decisions are taken and how these premises are influenced by other decision centres and by the organisational structure as a whole.

On a more aggregate level, according to Simon one should try to identify the general pattern of distribution of decision-making functions among the various subunits. Such a study of the *anatomy* of organisational decision-making should go far beyond the classical organisation chart method of mapping out the authority relations between offices. It should try to find out where the important decisions are taken in the organisation and why; in what respects the patterns of allocation of decision-making functions differ from one organisation to another and how such differences might be explained. As to the *physiology* of organisational decision-making, the models examined in the previous section suggest numerous problems regarding the flow and processing of information, the various types of feedback control systems and the way they function, the conditions under which a certain type of communication network prevails in an organisation and so on.[37]

What is the relevance of such research reorientation for the practical science of management? What can the manager learn from all this? The basic postulate in this context is that a practical theory of management cannot be divorced any longer from the empirical research into organisational behaviour. Before saying how an organisation should be, one must try to understand better how an organisation actually is. Consequently as the classical principles of management or proverbs of administration are not based on empirical research they are not taken seriously. The whole problem of principles (as guiding rules for the design and management of an organisation) has been put on a very different basis.

For instance, the important question of structure design is not seen any more as a problem of finding a set of valid principles which would tell one how to draw the most efficient organisation chart. Rather, structure design is seen as a particular decision-making problem. As in every other decisional situation, there are many alternatives (i.e. many possible design schemes) from which the decision-maker should choose the one which would meet in a satisfactory way certain specifications imposed by the major problems and goals of the organisation. Thus the problem of design depends entirely on the kind of problems and goals an organisation would like to pursue.[38] Finally, when one considers design problems from the point of view of the individual decision-maker, the structure of the organisation should be constructed in such a way as to facilitate his task as much as possible. That is to say, it should provide him with all the necessary information at the right time and in the correct order, thus enabling him to base his decisions on adequate premises.

New research methods. For the investigation of all the problems discussed above, two new research techniques have been developed and are currently used by organisation theorists together with the older laboratory and field methods.

The experimental simulation technique tries to reproduce as faithfully as possible, under quasi-laboratory conditions, a 'real life' organisation in order to study some of its decision-making features and problems.[39] The various business games which have become so fashionable in management training programmes, are a good example of the simulation technique. Although such experiments may vary in degree of realism or complexity, in all of them individuals are placed in decision-making situations more or less prearranged by the experimenter, and the way in which they reach and try to solve problems is examined. The main difference between experimental simulation and the older laboratory methods used by small group and communication theorists, is that in the former case the experiment has a more continuous, less artificial character.[40]

Computer simulation is another technique for the modelling of organisations.[41] Although computers may be used in the experimental simulation, in the computer simulation all humans disappear and all the variables of the organisation (even such characteristics of its participants as values, conformity pressures, output, etc.) are formulated into the computer. In other words, such attempts represent the organisation as a known closed system whose components and their interrelationships can be measured and expressed in mathematical terms. Of course, although one may always doubt the assumptions used in the simulation of human behaviour, one way to test the realism of the computer model is by seeing to what extent a real life organisation and its computer replica would solve a specific problem (i.e. would decide) in the same way.[42]

5. CRITICISM

A. The empirical reassessment of the rational aspects of organisational behaviour

Although the various writings discussed in this chapter are not uniform in scope and level of analysis, they portray some basic similarities which justify seeing them as a distinct approach to the study of organisations.[43] The common denominator in all of them is the emphasis on the importance of the rational aspects of organisational behaviour and the elaboration of a vocabulary which can account for them in an empirical way. In such a vocabulary, the concept of decision-making occupies the central place as it directs the attention of the student to such vital organisational processes as information-processing, communications and problem solving.

Thus, the formal structure, which was the main concern of classical theories of management and which was so neglected by the human relations school, has been re-examined and its considerable impact on individual behaviour has been reassessed. This reassessment has definitely been a healthy reaction against those psychologists and social psychologists who were treating the most distinctive characteristic of a formal organisation (i.e. its purposiveness) as having very little relevance to the explanation of behaviour. It was finally realised that the formal structure is not simply an organisation chart or codebook forgotten in an office drawer, but an institutional system which must be studied carefully and in detail.[44]

At the same time the emphasis on the empirical study of organisational behaviour opens new perspectives to the classical theory of management. Indeed, although in the latter the critical importance of the problem solving aspects of administration was given full emphasis, its armchair theorising and its predominantly normative character has reduced the study of the formal structure to the elaboration of principles and to the design of neatly drawn organisation charts. Organisation theory has shown how small and inadequate our knowledge of the rational aspects of organisational behaviour is, and how urgent is the need to study the formal structure as it really is before we formulate principles about how it should be.

B. The attempt at integration

Another major feature of *organisation theory* is its claim to have an integrative character, to provide a general framework which can account for both rational and non-rational aspects of behaviour and into which one can fit all important empirical findings about organisations. Has this been achieved?

As far as individual decision-making is concerned, this claim has a certain degree of validity. The idea of human rationality being limited by all kinds of constraints clearly allows for the examination of such phenomena as group norms and pressures, extraorganisational loyalties, emotional drives and any other elements as far as they present themselves in the individual's frame of reference.

But this integration stops on the level of the individual decision-maker. When one moves from the individual level to the consideration of the organisation as a whole, the integrative character of the theory disappears. Indeed, as we shall see below, when one considers the whole organisation as a network of decision centres or as an information processing system, it is very difficult to account for its culture, for its status system, and for all those organisational features traditionally treated under the informal organisation label. Thus the result is either an approach which is integrative but short-sighted (focusing on the individual) or one which is less integrative (more one-sided) but of a broader scope.

The individual level of analysis. To start with the former, it is very evident that Simon's major framework tends to reduce all theory about organisations to the social psychology of decision making. In his book *Organizations* he is quite explicit about the nature of his approach:

> As social scientists we are interested in explaining human behaviour. Taking the viewpoint of the *social psychologist*, we are interested in what influences impinge upon the individual human being from his environment and how he responds to these influences.

But is it enough to focus on the way in which environmental (organisational) factors impinge upon the individual and his reactions to them in order to explain and predict organisational phenomena? What about the interrelationships between such environmental factors as groups? Are they to be studied only through the perceptions and motivations of the individual decision-maker? Reducing the study of organisations to the social psychology of decision-making is restricting its scope in an unnecessary and even misleading way.

Consider for instance Simon's contribution-inducement theory. A man's decision to remain in the organisation depends on his satisfaction level, the latter being partially determined by the alternatives that he perceives elsewhere. Thus, if he is dissatisfied and he can perceive other opportunities outside the organisation, he quits. If he cannot see any other place to go to, he remains, and his temporary dissatisfaction disappears gradually as his aspiration level lowers. But what if we broaden our scope a bit, if we take into consideration that the decision-maker is really a group and organisation member? What if one considers not only *his* dissatisfaction but *their* dissatisfaction? What if they, as a group, do not leave the organisation, but do not become less frustrated and discontented because of that? What if their dissatisfaction does not decrease but is intensified by the formation of special cliques and alliances? What if their discontent is institutionalised, built into the culture of the group and does not change by the perception of meagre alternatives? What if group norms as to the legitimate and proper aspiration level of each member are even imposed on those who might be willing to reduce their aspiration level and be satisfied with lesser inducements?

Such suppositions, suggesting collective conflict, do not fit very well into the contribution-inducement scheme. They are certainly not taken into consideration when Simon jumps from the individual to the organisation level and uses exactly the same vocabulary in order to portray the whole organisation as an equilibrium between the aggregate of contributions and inducements of all the participants. In such an equilibrium there is only room for temporary disturbances and dissatisfactions which are settled either by the departure of the malcontents or by the decrease of their aspiration levels. Thus, lack of permanent dissatisfaction becomes an implicit assumption embedded in the very definition of the organisation as an inducement-contribution balance.[46] Such reasoning simply assumes that what holds true for the individual decision-makers holds for all decision-makers when one looks at the organisation as a whole. In this way inadequate attention is given to the interdependence and interaction of social actors from which new social patterns emerge which cannot be explained in individual terms. In other terms, unless we accept the reduction of the organisation to a simple agglomeration of decision-makers, we do not have the right to generalise about the organisation as a whole on the basis of concepts constructed for an analysis on the individual level.

From this perspective decision-making theory does not differ much from human relations theory. The same psychological and reductionist bias is evident in both of them. They both concentrate on the social psychological aspects of the organisation and they both try to camouflage their narrow scope by formulating generalisations on the organisation as a whole, without having an adequate conceptual equipment for such an enterprise.[47]

Organisation theory and the other approaches. The psychological bias of Simon's approach is one of the reasons why the attempt in *Organisations* to bring together the 'scattered and diverse body of writings about organisations into a coherent whole'[48] has not been very successful. This book is supposed to provide a general framework for integrating the insights and findings of Taylorism and the theories of classical management, human relations and bureaucracy theories. This is done by reformulating some of the hypotheses of the previous theories in a testable and operational manner, and by fitting them into the decision-making framework. The whole book is an extraordinary accumulation of testable or partially tested propositions about organisational behaviour. Such propositions and the tests which prove their validity or falseness constitute the groundwork for a positive science of organisation – a discipline solidly based on empirical evidence.

But as the whole book is a systematic account of how various organisational and extraorganisational variables impinge upon the individual decision-maker, the claim of integration can hardly be justified – at least in so far as previous approaches, especially bureaucracy theories, were built within a broader, sociological framework. Reformulating the hypotheses of such theories into operational prepositions, reducing and squeezing them into the decisional frame of reference definitely does not do them much justice.

A reductionist treatment is given and a similar injustice is done when Simon criticises economic theory and its unrealistic assumptions about human rationality. He considers these assumptions as propositions about concrete reality which the conscientious student of human behaviour must put to the test of facts. But in economics, such assumptions have mainly an analytic character. They are not meant to constitute a realistic account of how an entrepreneur behaves or how he is really making decisions. Rather, they are logical constructions which are used as means for generating implications and explanations about broader market phenomena. Their purpose is not to answer the question 'How does the entrepreneur really decide?' but rather, 'If we assume that he takes such a decision – for example, to maximise – what are the implications of such an assumption on the aggregate level? Does, for instance, such an assumption help us to understand the allocation of resources in the market or the distribution of income?'

Thus it happens that assumptions which may be considered gross simplifications by the behavioural student of the firm are good enough for explaining and predicting broader phenomena and for suggesting new problems and hypotheses on the macro-level. The test of such assumptions should not be how realistic they are but how well they can cope with the problems which they were meant to explain. Thus, Simon's criticisms of the assumptions of rationality in economic theory are somewhat misplaced. His concepts of satisfying or administrative man have not replaced the model of economic or maximising man in economics. Rather these two models indicate two different approaches, two different ways of studying economic phenomena. Thus the behavioural theory of the firm does not destroy the bases of existing economic theory, it simply fills a conspicuous gap in our knowledge of economic and organisational phenomena.[49]

In a more general way, the above discussion suggests that one cannot detach a part of a theory and test it in isolation from its theoretical context. One cannot take a proposition to see how well it fits with the facts without seriously taking into consideration how such a proposition is linked with the other propositions of the theory, and what are the main problems with which the whole theory is supposed to deal. So, if for the discovery of the validity or falseness of propositions, the empirical confrontation with the facts is indispensable,

Organisation Theory:

equally indispensable is the careful consideration of the broader theoretical framework in which these propositions are embedded. It is only inside such a framework that a proposition takes its real meaning and the style of its verification becomes clear.[50]

Analysis at the organisational level. Of course we have included in *organisation theory* writings which use a broader framework (cf. section 4), and do not limit their attention to the individual decision-maker. But whenever such a framework does not consist in the mere transfer of the individual decision-making vocabulary to the organisation level, it does not have the inclusive character of the socio-psychological approach. Thus, for instance, those writers who have tried to elaborate a broader framework on the basis of communication and cybernetic concepts can hardly fit into it such things as value and status systems, group struggles and so on. Indeed, although the organisation is treated as a system, the specifically social aspects of the system are more or less neglected. It is only the aspects common to all sorts of self-controlled systems (thermostats, human bodies and what not) which are emphasised.

Such an approach may be fruitful in so far as one does not accept in an uncritical manner analogies between self-controlled machines, organisms and organisations, and in so far as one does not forget its partiality and limitations. Otherwise it might lead to gross misinterpretations. For instance, there is a tendency among communication theorists (especially in industrial contexts) to reduce all difficulties and troubles in an organisation to communication problems, which could be solved by improving communication channels, reducing *noise* or making messages redundant. Although such techniques may be very successful in some cases, they are not effective whenever the real trouble does not lie in bad communication engineering but elsewhere – for instance, in antagonistic groups fighting for power or scarce resources. In such a case, the eventual breakdown in communications is a simple result, not the real cause of the trouble. Such a breakdown might be an intentional strategic move – the one party not wanting to reveal to the other its real problems and weaknesses. Under such circumstances the solution of the conflict (if there is a solution) is not a technical problem in communication engineering, it is primarily a political one. It is the political solution of the problem which will improve communications, rather than the other way round. Consequently, if we want to find out the organisational conditions under which communication engineering is effective, and those under which it is irrelevant, we certainly need an organisational model which is more inclusive than the cybernetic one.

Part Three

CONVERGING TRENDS

Chapter Seven

TOWARDS A BROADENING OF SCOPE

INTRODUCTION

During the last decade significant theoretical developments have occurred in organisation literature which have gone some way to meet, more or less successfully, the various criticisms about the inadequacies of organisational studies. As more and more social scientists become interested in organisation problems and as they freely choose their conceptual tools from a variety of sources, boundaries between schools become increasingly uncertain and an interchange of ideas and methods constitutes a dominant feature of recent organisation theory. At present, if one can judge by the impressive volume and variety of contributions, the whole field seems to be in a state of accelerated growth,[1] although it is yet too early to give a definite judgement about the direction of change and the theoretical importance of all this intense intellectual activity.

Thus, in this last chapter, we have no intention of delineating a new school; rather we shall try to take a critical look at some significant developments in the recent literature, which indicate a gradual convergence of the various approaches, as examined in the previous chapters. The most important theoretical trend seems to be a broadening of scope which definitely shifts the focus of attention from the individual and the group, to the structure of the organisation as a whole. If we speak about the organisation as a whole, the question arises of exactly how one sees this whole, of the conceptual tools by which one tries to account systematically for its structure and problems. From this point of view, as in general sociological theory,[2] one can identify two theoretical tendencies:

some writers put more emphasis on the system and integrative aspects of the organisation, while others emphasise more its aspects of conflict and division.[3]

Of course, the first framework in the tradition of the human relations studies which also emphasise the co-operative aspects of organisational behaviour. But in the present context one is not so interested in the social system of the group, or in how the individual perceives the organisation and its environment; rather, one tends more to conceive of the whole organisation as a social system whose structure should be studied in itself.[4] This shifting of emphasis from a socio-psychological to a sociological approach has the effect of bringing closer together organisation theory and general sociological theory.[5]

On the other hand, with this broadening of scope, there was an increasing realisation that all conflicts and antagonisms in organisations could not be relegated to the sphere of inter-personal frictions; that for understanding them, more attention should be given to their basis in the organisational and societal structure. Indeed, the most recent and interesting trend in organisation literature is a growing preoccupation with the problems of social power and conflict. If nothing else, the numerous criticisms about the conservative bias of the human relations school have certainly had some influence on organisation writers. Whether they succeed or not, most of them are anxious to show their emancipation from the pro-management Mayoite ideology by paying more attention to organisational conflict. Thus, although the outstanding studies on this subject are not numerous, and although we are very far from an elaborated theory of organisational conflict, there is an increasing realisation of its crucial importance for the comprehension of organisational problems.

I. THEORETICAL CONVERGENCE

Before we try to examine in a more detailed and critical way these major trends, some attention must be given to the patterns of transition and convergence, that is to the ways in which recent developments in the various approaches examined previously have gradually come together to emphasise the necessity of a broader and more inclusive approach to the study of organisations.

It has already been indicated how, in the third phase of the human relations school, its earlier shortcomings were partially overcome, as increasing attention was given to the larger structural features of the organisation.[6] With this broadening of scope more systematic attention was given to intergroup relations, to interest groups, and, to a very limited degree, to problems of power and conflict.[7] Moreover, under the influence of decision-making theory, the formal features of the organisational structure were also taken into consideration. Thus human relations theorists have finished by being concerned with the problems of structure and authority, long the major preoccupation of Weber's disciples.[8]

However, if the human relations school, by abandoning its narrow scope, has gradually lost its original identity, a similar development can be seen in bureaucracy writings. Indeed, the formal-informal dichotomy which was the underlying framework of the major bureaucratic theories, is gradually losing its appeal. This framework has been used in so many different ways, that its usefulness has become very doubtful. Broadly speaking, one can group the various meanings which the formal-informal concepts have taken into four categories.

Informal as deviation from expectations. In this sense informal designates a behaviour which deviates from the expectations of those hierarchically superior. The difficulty with this use of the term arises when one looks more closely at organisational reality and realises that there is a variety of expectations, not always congruent, which the individual takes into consideration before acting: for instance the expectations of the top hierarchy, of his immediate superior, of his colleagues, his family and of many other reference groups. Thus in such cases, where conflicting expectations claim the attention of the actor, most often there is not a clear-cut decision to follow one set of expectations at the expense of all others; rather, the ensuing behaviour is the result of a compromise or fusion of the various expectancies in the mind of the actor.[9] Consequently, under such circumstances, to label certain behaviour as formal or informal, not only does not do justice to organisational complexities, but might also lead to confusion and misunderstandings.

Informal as irrelevant to organisational goals. In this case the emphasis is not so much on illegitimacy or deviation from expectations, but rather on the relevancy of behaviour as far as organisational goals are concerned.[10] Thus some activities of bureaucrats (e.g. gossiping) whether legitimate or illegitimate are called informal inso far as they are not directly relevant to the work process.

Informal as unanticipated. Here the term informal refers to the unanticipated consequences of social action (irrespective of the legitimacy or goal relevancy of this action); to the simple fact that during the implementation of policy there are always discrepancies between the policy-maker's intentions and the concrete results.

Informal as real or concrete. Finally the formal-informal dichotomy was used to distinguish between defunct or inapplicable rules on the one hand and concrete behaviour or what really goes on in the organisation on the other hand. The often-cited distinction between the organisational codebook which has become defunct and the informal structure of the organisation (i.e. its social structure) implies this last meaning of the term.[11]

From the above enumeration it becomes evident that the formal-informal concepts are not adequate to deal with the complexities of organisational behaviour and structure. A more elaborated framework is needed which could not only account for all these various aspects of the organisation now covered under the simple formal-informal formula, but which could also link systematically the one with the other and with the organisation as a whole.

As a matter of fact, many writers have tried to supersede the formal-informal dichotomy, either by providing some additional concepts (thus considering the formal or informal aspect as one among other dimensions of the organisational structure),[12] or by discarding the formal-informal idea altogether.[13] Such theoretical attempts point out the necessity for the development of a more general theory of organisation which could account more systematically and thoroughly for the whole organisational system. From this point of view the most significant contribution towards such a theory has come from Talcott Parsons. Although he has written only a few articles on the subject,[14] and although he manifestly is not well acquainted with all organisation literature, his systematic conceptualisation of the entire organisation as a social system constitutes the most elaborate attempt to provide a really sociological framework for organisation analysis. As such, it reflects most appropriately this trend towards a broader approach which has already been discussed.

2. THE ORGANISATION AS A SOCIAL SYSTEM

Parsons sees the organisation as a social system composed of various subsystems (groups, departments, etc.) and embedded within wider social systems (community, society). At this point it is important to emphasise the system within system character of Parsons' approach. Parsons conceptualises social reality as a complex of interlocking systems ranging from the individual personality and small groups to whole societies. There are two things to be said about this way of thinking.

Firstly, when the focus of analysis is on a system referent (say the organisation), its immediate subsystems (groups) are treated as undifferentiated units. From the system referent point of view we are not interested in the internal structure and properties of the subsystem, but only in their interaction and its relevance to the larger system.

Secondly, as one passes from one system level to another, each higher level (i.e. referring to more inclusive systems) cannot be reduced to the properties of the lower ones because, although there is relative interdependence and interpenetration between a system and its subsystems, there is also relative autonomy between them. For instance, moving from the individual to the group level of analysis, in spite of the evident interdependence between the individual as a group member and the group as a whole, at the group level new phenomena emerge which cannot be explained in terms of the individual personalities involved. The same reasoning is applicable when one considers the passage from the group to the organisation level and so on.[15]

Parsons analyses the organisational system from the cultural-institutional point of view. That is to say, the point of departure and the main emphasis is put on values and their institutionalisation in differentiated functional contexts. Primarily, organisational values (which must be in harmony with wider societal values) legitimise the goals of the organisation by emphasising the system's contribution to the functional requirements of the larger system. This legitimation enables the organisation to assert the primacy of its goals over the goals of its various subsystems, as well as to claim a place and rights in society when faced with outside rivals competing for resources and public support.

At a lower level of generality, as these broad values are differentiated into more specific normative patterns, they regulate the various processes through which the functional requirements of the organisational system are met.[16] As is well known, Parsons has identified four basic functional requirements or problems that every system must solve in order to survive. Two of them – adaptation and goal achievement – have a task or instrumental character. They refer mainly to the relation of the system to its environment. The other two – the integration and latency problems – have to do with conditions internal to the system.[17]

The adaptation requirement is mainly the problem of procuring all the human and material resources which are necessary for the achievement of organisational goals. More specifically, it refers to those normative patterns regulating the processes of financing, of personal recruitment, of land procurement and of the acquisition of entrepreneurial skills.

The problem of goal achievement has to do with the mobilisation of organisational resources (made available by the adaptive processes), for the accomplishment of the organisation's goals. This is basically the problem of fitting means to ends. Consequently it is in this problem area that Parsons places the decision-making processes of the organisation and the various norms which regulate them.[18] In other words, the problem of resource mobilisation for goal attainment and the decisions which this necessitates, is the problem of organisational power. Indeed Parsons defines power as the 'capacity to mobilise resources in the interest of the attainment of a system goal'.[19] Thus the goal achievement sector of the organisation refers to its political aspects in the same way as that of the polity, on a higher system level, contributes to the goal achievement sector of the whole society.

The problems of integration and latency are not treated systematically in Parsons' organisation writings (probably because he was more interested in the relationships between the organisation and its environment). Briefly, the problem of integration deals with interunit relationships. It refers to the processes which ensure an adequate level of solidarity and cohesion between subsystems.[20] As to the problem of latency, it deals with intraunit conditions and their relevance to the larger system (in contradistinction to the integration problem which has to do with interunit relationships). It refers to the twin functional requirements of pattern maintenance and tension management. On the level of the individual, the former requirement concerns the question of compatibility of the participant's organisational role with his various obligations and roles in other collectivities (family, church, etc.). Thus arises the necessity for mechanisms effecting a relative harmony between organisational and extraorganisational expectancies. Moreover, there must be processes which ensure that the motivational commitment of the individual is sufficient for the adequate performance of his organisational task (tension management problems).

Here one should mention Parsons' classification of organisational types which is based again on his four functional problems scheme. According to Parsons organisations vary according to the type of goal function that they perform towards the wider societal system. From this point of view one can distinguish organisations primarily oriented to economic production (thus contributing to the solution of the adaptation problem of society), organisations oriented to political goals (contribution to the goal achievement problem), integrative organisations and pattern-maintenance organisations.[21]

Finally, a few words must be said about the pattern variables, the other major tool by which Parsons analyses and compares social systems. How do the pattern variables fit with the four functional problems? The famous pattern variables[22] are so constructed that they refer simultaneously to the actor's orientation of the situation (individual or unit level), to role relationships (social structure, system level) and to the values (cultural level) which shape roles and guide, through them, individual action.[23] Basically the pattern variables, from the social system point of view, define the role relationships which prevail in each of the four problem areas or phases.[24]

Thus, for instance, in the goal achievement or adaptive context, the organisational participants are usually expected to be neutrally oriented to each other (i.e. not to use their relationship for gratification) and to take into account only that aspect of their colleague's personality which is directly relevant to the job situation (specificity). Moreover, every member is judged according to his contribution to the organisation (performance). The criteria for such a judgement are universalistic, that is they do not take into consideration the status or the specific relationship of the judge and the judged outside of the job context. On the other hand, in the integrative and in the latency contexts the opposite role expectations seem to prevail (affectivity, diffuseness, quality and particularism).[25] In cruder terms, these distinctions highlight the widely shared belief (in our culture) that different attitudes are appropriate in a business context and in a play or socialising context.

Of course, the above differentiation of role expectations is not valid in all organisational cases. For instance, the social worker-client relationship in a welfare organisation, differs from the salesman-client relationship in a department store. Although both relationships belong to the task sectors, the social worker is expected to take a less specific, more diffuse attitude to the person of his client. As to the fifth pattern variable (self *v.* collectivity orientation), it is analytically different from the other four. In the system-unit context, it refers to whether the unit acts on behalf of itself (self-orienta-tion) or on behalf of the larger system (collectivity-orientation).[26]

Thus the five pattern variables, by pointing out the systematic differences between various types of organisation, constitute a useful conceptual tool, complementary to the four problem scheme. Indeed, if the four functional requirements refer to problems common to all sorts of organisations, such problems are solved differently by different kinds of organisations, and different solutions mean different structural arrangements by which each organisational type tries to cope with its environ-ment and its internal subsystems.[27]

Criticism. There is no doubt that Parsons' attempt to apply his general theoretical scheme to formal organisations has been a very important contribution to organisation theory. In spite of the confusing and casual manner of presentation and of its obvious inadequacies, Parsons' attempt has at least shown what a general theory of organisations should look like. It has shown that it is not enough to formulate in a more or less arbitrary way dimensions or aspects of the organisation (the formal, the informal, the technological, the human, etc.) without a serious effort to link in a logical and thorough way such concepts to each other, and to concepts referring to the environment of the organisation and its subsystems.

More precisely, in three respects Parsons' framework seems to me particularly instructive.

(a) I find of great value its capacity to account for different levels of analysis (individual, group, organisational, societal) and to point out the intricate problems of interdependence and autonomy between these levels. Much energy and money has been wasted in organisational research precisely because no due attention has been given to the above problems (cf. chapter 5).

(b) Parsons takes seriously into consideration the fact that a general theory of organisations should apply to all types of organisations, not only to governmental agencies and industrial enterprises. This, although obvious, is quite important as most of the concepts and theories about organisations, despite their claim to generality, are narrowly conceived and applicable to a very limited range of organisational contexts.[28] Thus there is a tendency to overspecialisation and to the proliferation of exclusive jargons which create unnecessary barriers and operate as blinkers to the underlying similarities and to the systematic differences between organisational types.

(c) Finally, Parsons' analysis emphasises the need for closer links between organisational and general sociological theory. Not only should the organisation theorist formulate concepts applicable to all types of organisations, but he should also investigate the similarities and differences as well as the interrelationships between the organisation as a social system and other social systems (families, communities, etc.).[29] This means that one should try as much as possible to show the general sociological relevance of organisational concepts and problems and vice versa. If Parsons' inadequate acquaintance with organisation literature has not permitted him such a translation of concepts, he has at least indicated the need for it.

There is no doubt that more attention to general developments in sociology cou.d illuminate many problems and theoretical difficulties in the organisational field. For instance the terminological confusion which surrounds the formal-informal dichotomy could be partly clarified if more general sociological concepts and theories were sought to account for the various meanings and insights covered by the formal-informal formula.

Thus, when informal is used in its deviation from expectancies meaning (cf. previous section), it might be useful to link it to the general theory of social control. In a similar manner, when formal-informal refers to the relevancy of behaviour towards organisational goals, the Bales-Parsons distinction between behaviour relevant to the task-oriented or to the socio-emotional problem areas, seems to be more useful (mainly because the above distinction is logically deduced from a broader theoretical scheme).[30] As to the meaning of informal as unanticipated, the latter term seems preferable as it is better integrated into general sociological thinking. Finally when formal-informal connotes the contrast between rules *qua* rules (whether applicable or not) and concrete behaviour, the

various sociological and anthropological discussions about the
social structure – culture distinction might be useful.[31] All the
above suggestions certainly do not have a systematic character.
They are simply given as illustrations of the potentialities of a
serious rapprochement between organisational and general
sociological thinking.

It is now time to say a few words about the inadequacies
of the Parsonian theory. When reading Parsons' articles one
cannot avoid the impression that despite the broadness of his
outlook something very important has been left out: that
somehow he gives us only half the organisational picture. As
he talks over and over again about the importance of values
for legitimising goals, for integrating the organisation into the
larger society, for regulating the various processes which deal
with the organisation's needs, one gets the impression of values
as being mysterious entities regulating and arranging everything.

Of course Parsons is not so naïve as to commit such a gross
sin of reification. But he does overemphasise the importance
of values and their contribution to organisation functioning.
On the other hand, he does not seem to be much preoccupied
with what lies behind such values. He does not explain how
organisational values came about and whose interests they
serve. Values seem to appear as a *deus ex machina* assuring in a
providential way the smooth operation of the system. In this
respect the Parsonian view of organisations is not false but
very partial. Indeed the emphasis on values and processes has
overshadowed the recognition of the existence of various groups
in the organisation, their antagonisms and the ensuing distributional features of such antagonisms (unequal distribution of
power, prestige and other rewards).[32]

The way in which Parsons treats the problem of organisational power is a very good illustration of the way in which he
overemphasises values. As has already been said, for Parsons,
power is the capacity to mobilise resources for the attainment
of organisational goals. Such a definition identifies power with
goal attainment. It leaves out of consideration the possibility
of the above capacity being used in a way which is in flagrant
contradiction to organisational goals (e.g. organisational power

used for the attainment of the narrow interests of a dominant group).

This curious limitation of the concept of power can be explained by the fact that Parsons is more interested in the production than in the distribution of power. He does not subscribe to the so-called zero-sum theory of power – a theory which conceives power as being of a limited quantity, so that what one party gains the other loses and vice versa. This way of conceiving power implies of course, the possibility of conflict, dominance and submission. Parsons prefers to look at the problem of power in another way. Instead of dominance over others power can be seen as the capacity, with others, to implement collective goals.[33]

Now it is evident that both the zero-sum and the capacity for resource mobilisation theories have something valid in them. They are both currently used in political sociology.[34] However, the latter theory is more relevant in a context when all the subunits of the social system have the same interests and profit equally from the achievement of collective goals. On the other hand in social systems, as in most organisations where interests are conflicting, where groups are hierarchically situated, to ignore the distributional aspects of power tends to give an illusory harmonious image to a conflictual situation.

Of course, Parsons does not ignore the existence of antagonistic groups in organisations and in society. Moreover his fifth pattern variable (self *v.* collectivity orientation) points to the possibility of subsystems being exclusively guided by their narrow interests to the detriment of the system's more general goals. But what makes him underemphasise the above possibility is again the exaggerated importance that he gives to the role of values as controlling mechanism imposing collectivity orientation on subsystems.[35]

In order to show how exaggerated the Parsonian emphasis on the integrative character of values is, one has only to point to such extreme organisational cases where one can hardly talk about system values at all. For instance, in prisons or concentration camps, what are the common values which keep the prisoners and their guardians together? Obviously what accounts for order and stability in this case is not any value system shared by the various subsystems but the distribution of power between them and the coercive situation which ensues.

Moreover, even when common values exist among organisational subsystems, the Parsonian scheme neglects the fact that certain 'groups or aggregates of people either tend to enjoy privileges or suffer deprivations by virtue of the prevalent norms';[36] that the organisational values may support a *status quo* where the self-orientation of the dominant subsystem may be institutionalised. This possibility can be more clearly seen when one shifts the level of analysis and takes the whole society as the system referent and the organisation as a unit. But in this case as well, Parsons puts his faith in the societal value system as an effective check to the self-orientation tendencies of organisational units. But why not come back to Marx and consider the possibility of societal values, not as a kind of divine providence caring for the welfare of all subsystems, but as the dominant ideology which might in fact legitimise and impose as general interest the narrow interests of certain groups.

In conclusion, the point of the argument is not to prove that organisations are less collectivity oriented than Parsons thinks they are (after all this is an empirical question which can only be settled by research); neither does it intend to reopen the sterile argument of whether interests and power relations are at the basis of values or vice versa. Rather, the intention is to show the partiality of Parsons' analysis which, by emphasising values, has neglected the equal importance (from a logical and empirical point of view) of the organisational power-structure.

3. THE ORGANISATION IN TERMS OF POWER AND CONFLICT

For Parsons structural differentiation centres around the processes which cope with the four functional problems of the organisation. Another way by which we can look at the organisation's social structure is in terms of groups (or quasi-groups) and their interrelationships. Of course, there are many ways in which organisation members group together or in which a social scientist can group them into categories. The range goes from relational configurations (real groups) to quasi-groups[37] and mere statistical categories (e.g. all people of the same sex or the same hair colour).

Of course, the problem in this kind of approach to social structure is to choose a differentiating criterion for grouping or categorising people which should be the most relevant for understanding the significant ways in which members are related to each other and which therefore should help us to see what really goes on in the organisation. It is in this context that the concept of power plays such a crucial role. Indeed individuals and groups have differential control over decision and policy-making as well as differential access to organisational resources. The distribution of control over resources and over the behaviour of others, and the ensuing formation of interest groups – competing with each other in their attempt to preserve or change in their favour the above distribution, are crucial clues for understanding organisational reality.[38] The belated but growing realisation of the above point undoubtedly constitutes one of the most significant theoretical developments in recent organisation theory.[39]

Of course, as far as a general theory of organisational conflict and power is concerned, we are very far from having a conceptual framework which can be compared with the Parsonian one in thoroughness and sophistication. Nevertheless some of the most important recent work in the organisational field centres around the problems of power and conflict. Such studies suggest lines of orientation and they provide very useful insights which may constitute a basis for the elaboration of a more general theory.

Thus Dalton, in a book based on his long experience as a participant-observer in six firms,[40] gives us the most revealing picture of the organisational structure in terms of conflicting cliques and their interminable struggles for gaining more power and ensuring a greater share of organisational rewards. It is literally revealing, because it brings to the surface all the day to day political activity of the organisation which is completely hidden from the outsider or even from the naïve sociologist who would base his study on interviews and questionnaires only.

Even if sometimes exaggerated, this analysis shows in a striking way to what extent organisational members and groups may be primarily interested in the rational pursuit of their narrow interests and the consolidation and improvement of their own power position, even at the expense of wider organisational interests. Moreover, it shows the all-pervasiveness and continuity of the ensuing struggles and their impact on every aspect of organisational life. Finally it shows how this intense political activity is scrupulously and skilfully camouflaged so that the resulting policies appear to be in harmony with the official ideology and the organisational codebook.

Dalton's powerful insight into the 'dirty linen' aspect of the organisation, its incessant intricacies and petty struggles causes him to give less importance to such larger antagonisms as staff *v.* line or management *v.* workers. According to him, although such broad divisions can be identified in the organisational structure, neat lines of demarcation are blurred as numerous cliques within and across the major blocks emerge and fight each other – without regard to all-embracing and abstract ideologies.[41] Thus the organisational image which finally emerges from Dalton's analysis, is a bewildering mosaic of swiftly changing and conflicting cliques,[42] which cut across departmental and other traditional loyalties and which, in the last analysis, account for organisational order and disorder.

Crozier's more recent study of two French government agencies is a second very important step in the analysis of organisational power and conflict.[43] He shows how indispensable for the comprehension of bureaucratic structure and change is the study of power relations between groups and the wider cultural and historical context within which such relations are articulated.

The type of organisation that Crozier examines presents a power-structure and a situation of conflict quite different from that studied by Dalton. Here the social structure is delineated in terms of occupational highly cohesive groups, each one presenting a unified and rather hostile front to the others. In such a stabilised and stratified conflictual situation, the further differentiation of the social structure into cliques within and across the occupational strata is excluded, every individual following faithfully his group strategy.

The strategy consists in the manipulation of rules as means of enhancing group prerogatives and independence from every direct and arbitrary interference from those higher up. But as rules can never regulate everything and eliminate all arbitrariness, areas of uncertainty always emerge which constitute the focal structural points around which collective conflicts become acute and instances of direct dominance and subordination re-emerge. In such cases the group which, by its position in the occupational structure can control the un-regulated area, has a great strategic advantage which is naturally used in order to improve its power position and ensure a greater share of organisational rewards.[44]

The above considerations do not give an exhaustive review of all recent writings dealing with organisational power and conflict. However, by referring selectively to some of the most important studies in this field, it is hoped that a very significant change of outlook, which has occurred and which seems to be gaining momentum, has been underlined. This change, which refers to the growing realisation of the central importance of the organisation's political structure, opens a new perspective in organisation analysis. To the image of the organisation man as an agent of sentiments seeking friendship and emotional security (human relations), and to Simon's problem-solver and decision-maker (organisation theory), is added the new image of a political man primarily interested in the individual and collective pursuit of power for the promotion of his interests. This new dimension of organisa-tional behaviour, as long as it is not followed singlemindedly, will certainly contribute to a more inclusive and realistic approach to the study of organisations.

Already, the new way of looking at organisational reality has redirected research to problems which have been long neglected. Moreover, it has shed fresh light in or has reinter-preted many well-established propositions. For instance, Merton's theory about the impact of the bureaucratic structure on the individual personality (ritualism and inflexibility of bureaucratic behaviour)[45] was seriously challenged by Crozier. The latter thinks that the caste spirit of the bureaucrat, his tendency to take means for ends and to stick to the letter of the rules and so on, do not come as a result of a profound and permanent transformation of his personality. They are often rational strategies by which bureaucrats try to affirm their independence and to impose or consolidate their power position.[46]

In the same line of thought, another interesting reinterpretation concerns Whyte's *Patterns of Industrial Peace*.[47] This book describes in interaction terms how the industrial relations of a firm passed from a phase of disorganised conflict to one of organised conflict and finally to a state of co-operation and good interpersonal relations (the passage from the one phase to the other being explained in terms of betterment in human relations). In criticising the above study, Sheppard[48] remarked that Whyte does not really explain why there was a change in union-management relations but that he simply gives a superficial description of it. The real cause of the change, according to Sheppard, is to be found in the dynamics of the power relations between the two antagonistic parties: as the union gradually gained more power, management was forced to take it more into consideration and thus the relations between the two became more harmonious.[49]

Of course, one could prolong the list of such reinterpretations. Such an exercise could be very fruitful, especially in the field of communication studies where many students seem to be blissfully unaware of the power aspects of an organisation's communication problems. In this context, as an illustration of how different may seem communication problems from a political angle, it is sufficient to refer to Kerr's suggestion for another way of looking at deficient communications and their relevance to conflict. He pointed out that bad communications and the ensuing misunderstandings are not always conducive to organisational conflict, as human relations manuals triumphantly declare; they can equally well operate as dampers of conflict – in so far as they prevent organisational members from finding out about their interest position and forming groups for its promotion. Such a hypothesis reminds one of the Marxist distinction between an individual's objective social position and interests and his subjective awareness of being in such a position (his class consciousness). This leads the student to look for organisational mechanisms, set up intentionally or unintentionally (e.g. human relations propaganda) to prevent people who have the same interests becoming fully aware of their actual or potential power positions.

There is no need to stress further that serious research along the above lines could be extremely useful from a theoretical and from a practical point of view – and this whatever the ideological orientation of the researcher. If not for any other reason, it is badly needed in order to reinvigorate organisation theory and re-establish the balance which, unfortunately at present, tips heavily on the side of conservatism and triviality. From this point of view, it is much to be hoped that the recent emphasis on organisation power and conflict may constitute a fruitful framework guiding research to an empirical but profound re-examination of the organisational problems of our civilisation – along the lines traced long ago by Marx, Weber and Michels.

For the moment, there are some faint indications of such orientations, but it is still difficult to assert their future development and potentialities. For instance a recent book by Blauner uses the concept of alienation, which is so central in Marxist thought, in an attempt to assess empirically the alienative effects of various technological and organisational structures on workers.[50] In spite of its clarity and interesting insights, there is no serious attempt to link the problem of the individual's alienation with problems of power and control of the larger institutional structure of capitalism within which the industrial organisations studied were embedded. This omission, because of the nature of the problem treated, seriously handicaps a study which seemed, at first sight, so promising.[51]

As a matter of fact, what is most needed in the present context, is to combine in a more systematic way this new awareness of the internal power-structure of an organisation with the wider problems of power in modern societies (whether capitalist or non-capitalist). In other terms, it is time for organisational theory to stop its excessive preoccupation with

Towards a Broadening of Scope

the problems in which managers are interested (efficiency) and to pose anew problems which are more relevant from a theoretical point of view[52] and more crucial for understanding the organisational features of the society in which we live. For such a theoretical reorientation, the recent trends examined in this chapter constitute quite favourable conditions. But there are some unfavourable conditions too – especially for the development of empirical studies in the field of organisational politics.

Apart from the theoretical difficulties of treating in an empirical way organisational problems which systematically refer to wider societal and historic contexts, there are many obstacles of a more practical nature. Field-work in organisations is expensive and usually research workers rely on the co-operation and financial support of those who control the organisations (at least this is true for the bulk of studies which are concerned with industrial organisations). Under such circumstances, it is evident that the necessary support is given only to research projects which seem useful or at least not harmful from the point of view of those who have power in the organisation. From this perspective it is quite certain that many groups would systematically oppose and hinder the sociologist's indiscreet attempts to bring into the open the power-structure and the political struggles taking place in the organisation.

Moreover, the researcher faces additional difficulties of an ethical nature. He has to decide whether or not he should disclose his intentions to his subjects. The widespread and rather fashionable practice of making quite clear to all organisation members what the research is about, might ethically be an excellent attitude, but severely restricts the range of topics that one can pursue (i.e. only those which seem quite harmless to all concerned). For instance, if Dalton had made public the intentions of his study in advance, I do not think that he would ever have gained management's consent for such a research project. Similarly, I see no reason why, in Crozier's book, the group of maintenance workers (which was depicted as taking advantage of an area of uncertitude under their control in order to impose their will on the production workers)[53]

163

would have agreed to co-operate with the author, if they had known what the research was about.

As to the human relations view that the social scientist should behave towards his subjects as a doctor towards his patients – that is, that he should reveal to them, in an objective way unpleasant truths which, in the long term, will help them to improve their situation – enough has been said about the organisational power-structure to show the ambiguity and dangers of such parallelisms. For it is quite evident that when an organisation is composed of groups with conflicting interests, the feedback effects of communicating the research results to all concerned may threaten the interests of some groups and enhance those of others. Under such circumstances, it makes very little sense to speak about the therapeutic role of the researcher (therapy for whom and for what?).

Unfortunately, as with so many other problems in organisation, there is no magic formula which will permit us to eat the cake and have it too. There is no way by which the organisation theorist can please everybody and at the same time perform his task seriously. As it has been said, in many cases (especially in the applied field), there are ethical and political problems about which the sociologist must make his position clear. He cannot avoid this by retreating to a misconceived notion of scientific neutrality (cf. concluding chapter).

4. CONCLUDING REMARKS

In examining the broadening of scope within organisational theory and its recent orientation to a more sociological approach, the distinction has been made between the value-integration and the power-conflict outlook in the literature. Of course, these two ways of looking at organisations are neither contradictory nor clearly distinct in actual writings. If for expository reasons we have contrasted Parsons' highly abstract and harmonious image of the organisation with Dalton's more concrete and conflict-stricken one, it is obvious that these two views refer to complementary aspects of an organisation. And although writers tend to emphasise more the one or the other of the above aspects, one can hardly find any important book which is absolutely one-sided in this matter.

Moreover, it is quite evident that in certain types of organisations the conflict outlook might be more relevant (e.g. firms, prisons), while in others the integrative approach seems more useful (e.g. youth organisations). From this point of view, the importance of a comparative approach to the study of organisations becomes evident.[54] It is also evident that a general theory which could account equally well for both the integrative and the conflict aspects of social systems is one of the major requirements in the study of organisations and of sociology in general. Of course, for the construction of such a general theory, it is not enough to affirm that there is no inherent contradiction between the social system and the conflict approach and that somehow the two approaches can be combined. Whether or not the present state of research is adequate for an effective integration, such an enterprise presents great theoretical difficulties and constitutes one of the most challenging tasks to both organisation and general sociological theory.

CONCLUSION

It is time to pull the various threads of the exposition together and to draw some general conclusions about the state and perspectives of organisation theory. In this study an attempt has been made to delineate and analyse critically the development of two long traditions of thought in organisation literature.

We have traced the starting point of the bureaucracy tradition to Marx, Weber and Michels. In a very general way, these writers have tried to analyse and provide solutions for the crucial problems created by an industrial and organisational civilisation. For Marx the problem of bureaucracy does not occupy the central place in his criticism of industrial society. The problems of bureaucracy and the ensuing alienation is one instance, one aspect of the more general problem of class domination – the source of all alienations, of all social ills. The abolition of classes is the general remedy which will put an end to every kind of alienation. Thus in the communist society bureaucratic domination disappears and social conditions provide a framework within which individual freedom is possible for the first time in man's history.

Marx's optimism, his faith in a classless society, prevented him from identifying organisational problems which are common both to capitalist and non-capitalist industrial societies. It is in this sense that the analyses of Weber and Michels are complementary to the Marxist critique of the strictly capitalist aspects of modern society. In their studies it is the organisational aspect of our society which comes to the fore. There is the same concern with the problems of alienation and freedom but these problems take a different form. The problem is not so much class domination but bureaucratic domination – the totalitarian tendencies of large-

Conclusion

scale organisations which threaten the democratic institutions of the western world and, on the individual level, man's potentialities for reason and free choice.

But the common element in the work of both Marx and Weber is their broad scope and their historical perspective. It is only when a whole society is the main unit of analysis and when its social structure is seen in an historical and developmental context that the sort of problems with which the classical writers were concerned arise and can be confronted. Such problems imply a strong humanist orientation, a deep concern with the human condition in a world dominated by forces which prevent the application of reason in human affairs. In a word, the classical writers are mainly concerned with the problems of power, with the crucial problem of alienation and freedom in society. Together, the analyses of Marx and Weber constitute the most profound diagnosis and criticism of modern society.

As we have seen, the post-Weberian writers shifted their focus of analysis from the societal to the organisational level. Taking as their starting point Weber's ideal type of bureaucracy (which was used by Weber for broad cross-cultural and historic comparisons) they tried to modify it and build a more empirical model of bureaucracy, more suitable for an analysis of the internal structure of bureaucratic organisations. Within this narrow context, they re-examined in a more rigorous and empirical manner some of the problems posed by the classical writers (especially the problems of democracy and individual freedom in a bureaucratised society).

The other line of organisational writings, both in terms of values, intellectual preoccupations and conceptual framework has a totally different starting point. Taylorism and the movement of scientific management reflects the confident ideology of American capitalism before the crisis of the thirties.[1] The main concern here is not any longer the problem of individual freedom and democracy but the problem of productivity in the firm. The main focus of analysis is not society as a whole but the individual worker, the organisational member seen as a tool which can be manipulated for the purpose of increased productivity. The formal theories of administration complement Taylorism as they carry its spirit of rationalisation and its concern with efficiency[2] from the workshop to the organisation as a whole. In this approach as well, the implicit model of the organisational member is an instrumental one. The principles of sound management take no account of the individual frame of reference and of the recalcitrance of people about their use as tools.

It is the human relations school which has provided a more inclusive framework in the above sense. Reacting against the formalism of the universalist, it tries to study in a concrete way how people behave in organisations. From this perspective the individual is seen as an agent with feelings and private goals, often in conflict with organisational goals. But in spite of the humanistic flavour of the approach and Mayo's concern with the problems of an anomic industrial society, the practical problems and preoccupations of the manager (productivity) remain the main concern of this school. Thus the main insights about informal organisation, leadership and morale are often seen as additional factors to be taken into consideration in shaping managerial policy. The same can be said about *organisation theory* (decision-making) which re-emphasises the rational aspects of the organisation, and has provided a framework for integrating the human relations and the formal management approach.

The narrow scope of both these developments, their emphasis on the social psychology of organisational behaviour and their consequent neglect of the whole organisation and its environment have distracted attention from the problems of social power and conflict which become more apparent when a broader scope is adopted. In that sense and because productivity and efficiency are the central preoccupations, the human relations and the decision-making approach have been seen as a part of a changing managerial ideology in a neo-capitalist context – in a context where the self-confident and authoritarian capitalist-entrepreneur is replaced by the professional and manipulative manager.[3]

Finally we have seen how recent developments in the human relations approach on the one hand (broader scope, consideration of conflict, of the formal structure of the organisation, etc.) and in bureaucracy writings on the other (beyond the formal-informal model) had as a result a certain convergence of these two theoretical traditions. Thus the interchange of methods and ideas has blurred boundaries between schools and has contributed to the adoption of a broader scope (seeing the whole organisation as a social system) and to the realisation of the crucial importance of power and conflict for understanding organisational behaviour. These new developments have definitely given to the study of organisations a more sociological character (as compared with the psychological and sociopsychological approach of human relations and organisation theory). At the same time, as theoretical interest has been focused on various types of non-industrial organisations (hospitals, schools, prisons, etc.) the problem of productivity seems to loose its previous importance and there is a shift of emphasis from an applied to a more theoretical approach (more emphasis on how an organisation functions and less on how to increase its efficiency).

In conclusion, looking at the global development of the bureaucracy and the managerial traditions, we can schematically represent it by two lines having diametrically opposed starting points (the one starting with society as its basic unit of analysis, the other with the single individual) and gradually tending to converge somewhere in the middle – i.e. major emphasis is put on the organisational level of analysis.

As we have seen, at each level values and intellectual preoccupations on the one hand, conceptual tools and methodology on the other are interrelated thus giving to each approach its distinctive character. At the one extreme, the values of human freedom and reason cause the classical writers to be concerned with the impact of bureaucratisation on the power-structure of society – and for such problems a broad conceptual framework and the comparative historical method is used. At the other, accepting implicitly the values of the *status quo* and being concerned with the limited problems of productivity, the managerial writers adopt a narrow scope and, in the case of the human relations and *organisation theory*, a rigorous methodology. This being the case, something must be said in this concluding chapter about the problem of values and their influence on research findings.

2. THEORY OF ORGANISATIONS AND THE PROBLEM OF VALUES

I think that so much, perhaps too much,[4] has been written about whether or not sociology is a value-free science that it is not necessary to repeat all the arguments here. But as most criticisms of organisation writings, especially of the managerial variety, evolve around this prolonged controversy, a few remarks are relevant at this point.

On the one hand, a point which seems to gain the consensus of most social scientists is that the attempt to disguise one's values under a pseudo-scientific cloak is misleading and useless. Although value judgements are evidently related to facts,[5] and although they can be studied from the outside as facts, they cannot be reduced to factual propositions (in the sense that they are not as the latter amenable to objective validation or rejection by experiment). From this point of view the attempt of some managerial theorists (Taylor and to a certain extent some human relationists) to disguise their value judgements under the cover of scientific objectivity, their claim to provide scientific solutions to power conflicts arising from antagonistic interests is not only naïve, it is also one of the main causes for the total rejection of their writings by those who do not have the patience to discriminate what is valid from what is invalid in their approach.[6]

On the other hand, it becomes increasingly clear that one is not obliged to disguise one's values and preferences or to make them somehow disappear from one's research in order to be objective. In spite of the fact that values inevitably play a role in the determination of the problems to be examined and even of the conceptual tools which are used, they do not necessarily distort social research (in the sense of automatically falsifying its results). For instance, even if we admit that human relations students have pro-managerial values and that such values have determined the problems studied (how to increase productivity) and the conceptual framework used (narrow scope, functional model), this is not a reason to dismiss *a priori* their statements as false.

Of course, I do not want to deny the fact that often a certain conceptual framework may be completely inadequate for coping with certain problems. For instance, a conceptual scheme which does not take seriously into consideration organisational conflict would be of little use in dealing with the problem of industrial democracy. But on the other hand, the same framework may be useful enough in cases where structural conflict plays a lesser role.

Moreover, the fact that research results very often have political implications (e.g. favouring conservative or radical groups), does not by itself tell us anything about their validity or falseness as scientific propositions. The statement for instance that in certain cases organisational changes, which make factory work less brutalising, are obstructed because they are against the interests of some minority groups, might be very valid, in spite of its political implications. In a similar manner, the fact that human relations findings might help the employer to manipulate his employees in a more effective way, does not destroy their scientific validity (on the contrary, if he really succeeds in his purposes – and this has not been clearly established – there are more chances that these findings are valid).

Of course, as was shown in the chapter on the human relations writers, their results were often disappointing. But that was not so much due to their values. It was due to the fact that they have adopted the wrong level of analysis even for the sort of problems they have chosen to tackle. This consideration raises a second crucial question – that of the multiplicity of levels of analysis in the study of organisations.

3. THEORY OF ORGANISATIONS AND LEVELS OF ANALYSIS

In the previous chapter we have dealt with the conception of an organisation as a social system containing within itself various subsystems (groups, individuals) and being embedded in wider systems (community, society). In examining the various approaches and the levels on which they focused their analysis, we have pointed out the reductionist tendencies of certain theorists and we have emphasised the ensuing fallacies.

The first principle in sociological analysis to be found in any basic textbook is that society is more than an agglomeration of individuals. Failure to take this principle seriously and to follow its implications in a thorough manner seems to me one of the main sources of confusion in the managerial tradition of writings.[7] This basic sociological postulate is not as simple as it appears at first sight. In an organisational context the problem is not simply to see the relationship between the individual and the larger collectivity. There are many collectivities within an organisation. And as you cannot reduce the analysis of an organisational group to a psychological study of its members, in the same manner you cannot reduce the study of the whole organisation or of a larger department to the mere study of the groups within it. As one moves from less to more inclusive systems, at each higher level of analysis new phenomena emerge which cannot be examined properly if we limit our analysis to an inferior level. As Parsons has rightly pointed out, although there is relative interdependence between larger systems and their subsystems there is also relative autonomy – the degree of autonomy or interdependence being an empirical question. The greater the autonomy between the system and its subsystem, the greater the probability of going astray by jumping from one level to the next without paying attention to the emergence of new system problems which cannot be understood on the subsystem level.

It is worth insisting on this point because if on the one hand reductionism makes things look simpler (by ignoring the complexity arising out of the multiplicity of levels of analysis), on the other hand and in another sense, it makes them look hopelessly complicated.

Indeed, organisation writers with a reductionist, psychologistic bias have often a very peculiar conception about the accumulation of knowledge in the social sciences. Usually, being strict empiricists, they try to operationalise their concepts and to quantify their data by studying as closely as possible concrete individual behaviour. On the basis of such solid data they hope gradually to develop propositions of a very limited

Conclusion

and modest scope which will constitute the building blocks for generalisations of a broader character. The implication of all this is that one should not start building the first floor before the ground floor is finished. In other terms, one should not venture to study such larger social systems as whole societies or organisations before enough building blocks, enough solid knowledge has been accumulated about less inclusive and complex systems. Of course, when one takes into consideration the multiplicity of levels of analysis and the irreducibility of the higher to the lower, one sees the absurdity of such a strategy and the unnecessary restrictions that it imposes on social research.

There is no doubt that in the present state of organisational research, much more emphasis than before must be given to the organisation as a whole, to its environment and the organisational features of society as a whole. There are two main reasons for giving priority to such a broader scope.

First, if by focusing on the individual or group level the organisational structure and its environment are not seriously considered, one risks the eventuality of a complete failure and loss of time and energy, (in the case when group phenomena are very dependent on extra group forces – cf. chapter 5).

Second, with a broader scope one has more chances for studying important problems, problems which are crucial for understanding our civilisation and its present crisis. Of course, what one considers as important and crucial, another may find trivial or irrelevant to his preoccupations. Without denying the underlying value judgement of my position, it seems to me that the most vital problems today are similar to those that the classical writers of bureaucracy have dealt with, and for such problems a broad theoretical scope is needed.

Indeed at the present moment the problems of organisational power and freedom seem to me more important than the problems of productivity. The crucial problem today is not so much how to increase what Mannheim calls the functional rationality of modern bureaucracies but rather how to safeguard within the increasing functional rationalisation of the world a minimum of substantive rationality[8] and individual initiative; not how to make people more contented and co-operative with management but rather how to prevent them from becoming happy automatons in a 'brave new world'. These were precisely the problems which preoccupied the classical sociologists and the same problems need reformulation and exhaustive analysis today.

Unfortunately such problems are left in the main to the journalists, novelists and philosophers. Most organisation theorists are too busy with problems set out for them by managers or government officials. This is a great pity, as there is no one better situated for the study of such crucial problems than the sociologist of organisations. Indeed modern large-scale organisations constitute the most strategic site for the empirical study of how broad structural features and changes in society enhance alienation and threaten to reduce man to a simple cog in a machine.

4. THEORY OF ORGANISATIONS AND THE COMPARATIVE APPROACH

We have argued the necessity of adopting a broader scope in studying the organisational problems of modern society. But the only way in which this can be done effectively is when one does not limit one's investigations within the context of a single national unit. The only way to understand the organisational features which are specific in one society is to compare them with the organisational features in other societies. The best way to understand English or American bureaucracy is to compare it with bureaucracy in other cultures and in societies which are at a different level of economic development.

Such a comparative approach would induce the organisation student to abandon his narrow scope. Indeed one of the reasons for the neglect of the organisation's larger environment is the ethnocentric character of present theory (empirical research being mainly restricted to the study of American and English organisations).[9] Once a cross-cultural approach is adopted, it is not possible any more to explain systematically differences in organisational features and functioning without reference to differences in the total culture and social structure in which organisations are embedded.

Of course, the need for a more comparative approach is

Conclusion

not only great in the cross-cultural field. As we have emphasised earlier (chapter 3), within one society, systematic comparisons between different types of organisations are extremely fruitful and relatively scarce.[10]

5. THEORY OF ORGANISATIONS AND HISTORY

Finally, the plea for a comparative approach in terms of locale is at the same time a plea for a comparative approach in terms of time. Indeed present organisation theory is not only predominantly ethnocentric but ahistorical as well. The organisations studied seem to exist in a timeless dimension. Generalisations about organisational behaviour do not take seriously into account that such behaviour is inextricably linked with a historically specific social structure and culture. They are presented as having universal applicability in terms of time and space.

Actually, as in the cross-cultural case, the present lack of a broad historical perspective is closely linked with the narrow emphasis of organisation theory on the social psychology of individual behaviour and on small groups. It must be hoped that a real shift away from the present myopic approach will give to the theory of organisations a more historical character.

In this area the potentialities are immense. There is a tremendous amount of material on the historical development of various types of organisations.[11] Of course, since they are written by historians, such works do not usually have a socio-logical perspective. That is to say, they do not attempt to link in a systematic way organisational developments within a certain institutional context with developments in other parts of the social structure. As their approach to human affairs has a rather descriptive and particularistic character, one often feels submerged in an ocean of details, acts of parliament, dates and names. By reading such histories, one feels strongly the need for a sociological framework within which all this material which is so rich in detail would be handled in a more analytic and theoretical manner.[12]

What sort of conceptual framework would be adequate

175

for such a task? In what way can sociological theory take history systematically into account? In other terms, what tools are necessary for directing empirical research towards long-range historical developments? In this context, the renewed theoretical interest in social evolution is of particular importance.[13] The recent theoretical attempts to revalue the nineteenth-century evolutionary theories may prove to be one of the major breakthroughs in sociological theory.

Briefly, the neo-evolutionists claim that the total rejection of classical evolutionary theories was an extreme reaction which operated as a blinker to what was valid in such theories and which had as a result the neglect of problems of social development and historical change. Indeed, according to the neo-evolutionists, if such notions as the inevitability of human progress or the idea of unilinear evolution cannot be seriously sustained any longer, this does not exclude the possibility of fruitful thinking along evolutionary lines.

As far as I can understand, the basic differences between classical and modern evolutionists is that the latter have abandoned the attempt to discover any set of universal stages or laws with which one could *a priori* account for man's evolution. Rather, present efforts seem to concentrate on the elaboration of concepts providing a framework within which limited questions about social development can be asked; a framework which does not give ready-made explanations but induces the researcher always to keep in mind that some social changes imply a certain continuity in their direction, that often, in order to understand a present form of social organisation, it is necessary to see how it is connected with and how it has developed from antecedent forms.[14] The basic postulates which seem to underlie the above considerations are first, that 'genuine parallels of form and function develop in historically independent sequences or cultural traditions', and second, that these parallels can be explained 'by the independent operation of identical causality in each case'.[15]

The relevance of such theoretical developments to the study of organisations is direct and quite obvious. For instance, as we have said at the beginning of this study, Weber's concept of bureaucracy was mainly constructed as a tool for cross-

Conclusion

cultural and historical comparisons between various types of administrative apparatus. Moreover, his idea of a universal trend towards increasing bureaucratisation implies the notion of direction in social change. As far as modern western society is concerned, the bureaucratic type of administration which has predominated can be best understood by contrasting it to the feudal administration from which it has evolved. Who would deny the usefulness of a conceptual scheme which would induce the researcher to look for sequences of types of administration and for the mechanisms of change by which we pass from the one to the other.

In conclusion, a developmental or evolutionary framework, when sufficiently developed, seems to be one of the most adequate ways in which the sociologist can acquire a sense of history. Such an insight might not only give his theories a more dynamic and developmental character, it might also help him to become interested in less abstract, more significant and real problems – real in the sense that they arise within a certain historical and cultural context and are relevant to the pre-occupations of men and women living in such a culture. For instance, I do not see any reason why more attention should be given to such abstract problems as the relationship between organisational productivity and morale in general, and not to more topical and concrete problems such as the organisational dynamics of the CND movement.

6. THE RELEVANCE OF THEORY

In emphasing the importance of a historical perspective and of a shift in attention from a quest for abstract and universal regularities between organisational phenomena to more concrete and specific problems, the intention is not to attack the sort of abstract theory with which Parsons, for instance, is concerned. I do not agree with those who consider this type of theory (pejoratively called 'grand theory') a sterile exercise in the manipulation of abstract and empty concepts.

Those who criticise the pretentiousness of Grand Theory, its alleged ambition to give a universal solution to the problems of society[16] simply misunderstand its nature and aims. Its aim is not to provide ready-made solutions to the problems of social order and disorder, or the discovery of Newtonian-like laws. The claims of Grand Theory are much more limited and modest. Basically it tries to elaborate conceptual tools which might help the sociologist in his empirical investigations by suggesting useful ways of looking at social reality. Such tools do not provide prefabricated answers to social problems, they simply prepare the ground for their adequate handling.

Of course, one may criticise Parsons' attempts to provide a general theory of social action as being obscure, partial or even completely inadequate to serve as a guide to research. But one cannot reject as easily the kind of work in which Parsons is interested. Sociological theory *per se* need not be obscure or conservatively oriented. If Parsons' name has been identified with it, one must not forget that he is not the only one who is engaged in this sort of theoretical work. Who would, for instance, deny the utility of Nadel's *On the Theory of Social Structure*. Yet his work is as abstract as Parsons'. When Nadel writes about the social structure, he does not refer to a specific social structure, he speaks about social structure in general. But this does not mean that he tries to give universal solutions to the problems arising within specific social structures.

From the above discussion it becomes clear that it is one thing to speak of an abstract theory when the term theory is used in its *conceptual framework* meaning, and another thing when the *content* meaning of theory is implied (i.e. 'an interconnected set of generalisations concerned with a particular problem area and meant to account for the empirical facts in it').[17] It is in the latter case that criticisms against high abstraction are relevant and often valid. Failure to make the above distinction has created this sort of indiscriminate hostility against all types of theoretical abstractions.

Moreover, I think it is the same confusion between these two types of theory which is at the basis of the frequent objection that attempts at constructing a 'grand theory' in sociology are premature at the present state of our knowledge. It is argued that only with the prior accumulation of more findings of a limited type will it become possible to elaborate theories on such a high level of abstraction. This is another case of misapplication of the building block conception about how to accumulate sociological knowledge.

Although, of course, there is no clear-cut distinction between framework theory and content theory, and although advances in the one bring changes in the other, the building block argument is not very relevant to the former type of theory. For instance if, as was said in the previous chapter, the conflict model and the integration model have not yet been systematically brought together into a single framework, I do not think that such a task is mainly obstructed by a lack of research findings and that it should be postponed till enough findings have been accumulated. On the contrary, I think that a synthesis is possible and will be extremely useful for the advancement of sociology in general and for organisation theory in particular.[18] Of course, it is not necessary to emphasise that such conceptualisations are never definite and settled once and for all. They are, and must be, subject to continual alterations, elaborations and refinements – all this being necessary in order to keep theory always at the service of empirical research.

In conclusion, it is hoped that this study, in analysing critically some approaches to the study of organisation, has shown sufficiently the crucial importance of general sociological theory to this kind of study. If at the present moment our knowledge about organisations seems scattered and unsystematic, this is due to a great extent to the neglect of this kind of theory. Knowledge about organisations cannot be systematised and grow by the mere accumulation of rigorously tested myopic statements; nor, even by studying in an *ad hoc* manner important problems without any theoretical awareness of the conceptual framework which is used – its shortcomings and its links with general theory. Moreover, the sort of homespun casual theorising which does not take into consideration existing theory, and which one finds in the introductory chapters of many organisation books will not do. Such conceptualisations do not imply originality but intellectual laziness. At their best, they simply repeat in a crude and more confusing manner already existing ideas. If present Grand Theory is unsatisfactory, the way to go on is not to ignore it but rather to show systematically where its shortcomings lie and how to overcome them. Without disregarding the importance of empirical research, I believe that at the present moment, what is greatly needed is closer contact of organisation students with developments in general sociological theory.

NOTES

(All books published in London unless
otherwise stated)

INTRODUCTION

1 A. Etzioni, *Modern Organizations*, New Jersey, 1964, p. 1.

2 R. Presthus, *The Organizational Society*, N.Y., 1962.

3 cf. P. Blau and W. R. Scott, *Formal Organizations*, 1961, p. 258.

4 S. F. Nadel, *The Theory of Social Structure*, 1962, p. 1.

5 In contrast to such social units as the neighbourhood for instance, which seems to emerge in spontaneous, non-purposive manner.

6 As both the degree of purposiveness and of goal-specificity may vary from one organisation to another, in certain limit cases it is difficult to decide whether or not a social unit can be usefully identified as an organisation. Thus all formal organisations do not present the same amount of conscious co-ordination of their activities. Some seem more to appear and grow in a spontaneous, unplanned way, as far as their goals and their internal organisation is concerned. Others, on the contrary, are highly planned even in the smaller details. This contrast is clearly seen in the ways political parties originate and evolve. For example, compare the gradual emergence of the British Conservative Party with the systematic and rapid construction of a modern communist or fascist party (cf. M. Duverger, *Les Partis politiques*, Paris, 1951, pp. 1–34). But such difficulties do not present any serious problems once it is made clear that the criteria of purposiveness and goal specificity must be used in a flexible way and that the difference between organisations and other groups is one of emphasis or degree.

(For definitions on these lines cf. Blau and Scott, pp. 2–8; Etzioni, pp. 3–4; T. Parsons, *Structure and Process in Modern Societies*, Ill., 1960, p. 17; for a very sophisticated analysis of the ways in which organisations differ from communities and institutions cf F. Bates, 'Institutions, Organisations and Communities', *Pacific Sociological Review*, vol. 3 (1960), No. 2, pp. 59–70.)

CHAPTER ONE

1 K. Marx, 'Critique de la philosophie de l'état de Hegel', in *Oeuvres philosophiques*, translation by Molitor, Paris, 1937, vol. 4, pp. 96–104.

2 *ibid*. p. 100.

3 For a more extensive exposition of Marx's views on bureaucracy and the state cf. P. Naville, *Le Nouveau Leviathan: de l'aliénation à la jouissance*, Paris, 1957, pp. 70–124.

4 This notion is very close to the concept of goal displacement which was systematically analysed by more recent students of bureaucracy (Michels, Merton, Selznick, etc.). For an extensive treatment of Marx's

Notes to pages 10–15

notion of alienation cf. J. Calvez, *La Pensée de Karl Marx*, Paris, 1956, pp. 41–334.

5   Marx, p. 102.

6   Quoted from S. M. Lipset, 'Political Sociology', in R. K. Merton *et al.* (eds.), *Sociology Today*, N.Y., 1959, p. 85.

7   Marx has avoided the detailed description of the political and administrative features of the future stateless society. His definitions of a communist society have mainly a negative character (in the sense that they refer more to what institutions will disappear in such a society rather than to what new institutional forms will take their place).

For a relatively detailed and clear exposition of how Marx conceived the 'withering away' of the state and its bureaucracy cf. V. Lenin, 'The State and Revolution' in *Essentials of Lenin*, 1947, pp. 164–78 and 197–210.

8   Lenin, pp. 167–78.

9   *ibid.* p. 194.

10   cf. V. Lenin, 'The Tax in Kind', in *Essentials of Lenin*, p. 178.

11   *ibid.* pp. 719 ff. Another Marxist revolutionary who follows a line of thought similar to Lenin's is N. Bukharin. He takes up the problems of bureaucracy and tries to give an answer to Michels 'Iron Law of Oligarchy' (cf. section 3) and to all those who were criticising the oligarchic tendencies of the Soviet régime. Faithful to the basic Marxist scheme, he attributes, like Lenin, the increasing bureaucratisation to the extreme difficulties that the régime has to face in the transition period from capitalism to socialism. It is such difficulties which bring about the increasing domination of the bureaucracy, a tendency leading to political degeneration. But Bukharin, having more faith than Lenin in the spontaneity of the masses, believes that the major counter attack against bureaucracy will come with the increasing education of the people as well as with the improvement of their economic position.

12   We shall treat the Trotskyist position in some detail as, even today, many Marxists adopt his views in explaining Soviet bureaucracy (e.g. cf. P. Naville, 'La Bureaucratie et la Révolution' in *Arguments*, No. 1, 1960).

13   cf. L. Trotsky, *The Permanent Revolution*, 1931.

14   As a matter of fact, the Stalinist dictatorship had nothing in common with the Marxist dictatorship of the proletariat. The latter means the domination of the workers as a class over all other classes. At the same time it implies an internal democracy among the proletarians. So for Trotsky, it is clear that the Soviet régime has ceased to be a dictatorship of the workers and has become the dictatorship of bureaucracy and of Stalin.

15   cf. L. Trotsky, *The Revolution Betrayed*, 1937, pp. 222–42; 268–74.

16   In order to be more precise, it should be mentioned that both Marx and Lenin were aware of the possibility of certain societies developing into directions other than the capitalist or the socialist one. Thus they both dealt in their writings with the famous problems of the 'Asiatic mode of production' which could not fit very well in their 'five stages' developmental scheme. But, as Wittfogel shows very clearly, eventually both Marx and Lenin have chosen to ignore the problem altogether as it was not in

harmony with their general theoretical framework (cf. K. Wittfogel, *Oriental Despotism*, N.Y., 1955, pp. 369–411).

17 M. Weber, *The Theory of Social and Economic Organisation*, translated by A. Henderson and T. Parsons, 1947, p. 139.

18 For a general definition of the organisation as the link between leaders and led cf. Max Weber, 'On law in Economy and Society', M. Rheinstein (ed.), Cambridge, Mass., 1954, p. 221.

19 cf. Weber. *op. cit.*, pp. 329–33.

20 *ibid.* pp. 313 ff.

21 cf. H. H. Gerth and C. Wright Mills (eds.), *From Max Weber: Essays in Sociology*, 1961, pp. 221–4.

22 Weber identifies three main factors which favoured the development of modern bureaucracy:

Firstly the development of a money economy. Money does not only facilitate and rationalise economic transactions. In the case of bureaucracy, it replaces the remuneration of officials in kind, a mode of remuneration which favours decentralisation of authority and thus the undermining of bureaucratic administration.

Secondly the quantitative and qualitative increase of the modern state's administrative tasks. Indeed, according to Weber, only a bureaucratic type of organisation can cope with the enormous complexity and scale of such tasks.

Thirdly the technical superiority (in terms of efficiency) of the bureaucratic type of administration has been an internal autonomous force contributing to its prevalence.

'The decisive reason for the advance of bureaucratic organisation has always been its purely technical superiority over any other form of organisation' (Gerth and Mills, p. 214). Of course, when western bureaucracy is seen as one of the many facets of the increasing rationalism in our civilisation, its less immediate causes are identified with general preconditions which gave rise to western rationalism. In this case, the whole work of Weber can be considered as an attempt to account for this process of rationalisation.

23 *ibid.* p. 261.

24 *ibid.* pp. 70–4, cf. also A. Salomon, 'M. Weber's political ideas', *Social Research*, vol. 2 (1935), p. 378.

25 Gerth and Mills, p. 293.

26 *ibid.*

27 *ibid.* pp. 70–4.

28 However, his pessimistic view of the historic process must be qualified:

– Firstly, Weber was against sweeping generalisations and theoretical attempts aiming at the discovery of the direction or the laws of the historic movement. Thus he was always very cautious in avoiding any dogmatic or even systematic exposition of his views about the general course of history.

– Secondly, although he clearly identified a trend towards increasing bureaucratisation in western civilisation, this by no means implies a unilineal interpretation of history. The charismatic, traditional and legal-bureaucratic types of domination do not constitute successive stages through which all societies will pass sooner or later. The construction of the above typology was due to purely analytical purposes. It was not based on any preconception about the direction and meaning of the historic movement. – Finally, the trend towards increasing bureaucratisation does not have the inevitable character which the advent of communism and the disappearance of bureaucracy has in Marx's deterministic conception of history.

29 The ambivalence of Weber's position on this subject can be seen in a nutshell in one of his political speeches published by J. P. Mayer in his *Max Weber and German Politics*, 1955, Appendix I, pp. 95–9.

30 cf. R. Bendix, *Max Weber: an Intellectual Portrait*, N.Y., 1962, pp. 493 ff.

31 According to Weber, these problems are not only limited in the public administration context. One finds similar dilemmas between the specialised salaried manager and the shareholders or even the board of directors who lack the expert knowledge necessary for the control of management (cf. Gerth and Mills, p. 91).

32 *ibid.* p. 235.

33 For example, one major conditional factor determining whether bureaucracy in a modern democratic régime will remain a tool or not, is the relative strength and vitality of parliament. When the parliament has not only formal power, effective control of the state administration can be achieved through such devices as special commissions inquiring into the functioning of various governmental branches. In these parliamentary bodies the politicians are gradually trained and become acquainted with the complexities of the administrative problems. By such a political education they become more professional and more capable of controlling the bureaucratic experts.

34 *ibid.* p. 224.

35 *ibid.* p. 221.

36 Alexis de Tocqueville, *Democracy in America*, 1961, vol. I, pp. 265–70; pp. 86–97.

37 This gradual shift away from a too democratic type of administration and the increasing theoretical preoccupation with the political domination of bureaucracy, is very well reflected in the study of public administration.

(a) In its initial stages this discipline was stressing the importance of making the administration as representative as possible (by the election of officials for short terms of office and by increasing the direct power of the legislature and the people over the bureaucrats). This system, when concretely applied, brought confusion and corruption. Electioneering and the interference of local politicians in the administration (spoils system, etc.) have so weakened the position of the public official that the need for a more autonomous bureaucracy was widely acknowledged.

(b) Thus the theme of representativeness was replaced by the theme of political neutrality. In this case the major principle was the clear separation of politics and administration (as in Weber's ideal distinction between bureaucrat and politician). The politician decides about policy and the administrator executes it. Moreover, according to the same theory, in order to function efficiently, bureaucracy needed further centralisation, the appointment of officials and the stabilisation and autonomy of its position. But if by this manner the state bureaucracy became more efficient and protected itself from external powers which tried to invade it, the opposite danger became evident, that is the possibility that the state apparatus would become an autonomous centre of power, too independent from the people or their elected politicians.

(c) Thus, on the theoretical level, it was gradually realised that, in concrete reality, it is not possible to distinguish between policy and administration and that one cannot study public administration and its principles in isolation from the problems of power in the wider sociopolitical system. (cf. D. Waldo, *The administrative State*, N.Y., 1948 and H. Kaufman, 'Conflict, in Doctrines of Public Administration', *American Political Science Review*, vol. 50 (1956), pp. 1057–73).

38   cf. Gerth and Mills, pp. 228–30.

39   *ibid.* p. 229.

40   *ibid.* pp. 70–4.

41   R. Michels, *Political Parties. A Sociological Study of the Oligarchic tendencies of Modern Democracy*, N.Y., 1962.

42   In this new context, before discussing these theories, we must say a few words about Machiavellianism, a system of ideas which is relevant to our problem. The Machiavellian tradition refers to a group of political theorists who have more or less a view of political life, first formulated by N. Machiavelli. (According to J. Burnham, the most prominent Machiavellians are: G. Mosca, R. Michels, W. Pareto – cf. *The Machiavellians: Defenders of Freedom*, 1943).

These writers conceive the political structure of society as a dichotomy between élites and non-élites. From their point of view, the most important task in political science is the intensive study of this élite (its structure, its relations with the non-élites), as it constitutes the ruling minority which imposes its will on the politically passive masses. The rule of the élite is ultimately based on force, even when this force is hidden. Moreover, even when not conscious, there is always an element of fraud at the basis of its domination. By elaborating appropriate ideologies, the rulers will try to hide their true motives about the aims of their rule (i.e. self-interest). They will invariably present themselves as striving for the general interest. Under such circumstances, the degree of exploitation of the ruled by the rulers depends on the extent to which the self-interest of the élite coincides with the interest of the whole political community.

Also, the existence or non-existence of other autonomous centres of power, is another determinant of the degree of exploitation. Indeed the existence of such power centres contributes to the division of the ruling class into factions striving for power. When this happens, the competing élites, in their struggle against each other, seek the support of the masses. Thus a pluralistic system of power, although it does not bring true democracy (i.e. the direct participation of the masses in the political decision-making), is the best guarantee against the arbitrariness of the rulers.

Finally, when the élite–non-élite relation is seen in the context of social change, no ruling class is absolutely stable in its domination. There are always two opposing tendencies operating within an élite, an aristocratic tendency, hindering the access of outsiders, and a democratic tendency facilitating it. Whether the one or the other tendency prevails, in the long run there is always a process of circulation of élites by which decadent élites are gradually (or abruptly, by revolution) replaced by new forces (cf. Burnham, pp. 20–55 and 164–73).

43 *ibid.* pp. 63–77. For a very vivid account of the insurmountable difficulties that early trade unions were facing in trying to reconcile direct democracy (i.e. such devices as the referendum and the initiative) with the increasing complexity of modern administration, cf. S and B. Webb, *Industrial Democracy*, 1897, pp. 3–37.

44 Michels, pp. 107–52.

45 *ibid.* p. 19.

46 *ibid.* p. 371.

47 R. Michels, *First Lectures in Political Sociology*, Minneapolis, 1949.

48 cf. R. Bendix, 'Bureaucracy: The Problem and its setting', *American Sociological Review*, vol. 12 (1947), pp. 493–507.

49 L. Von Mises, *Bureaucracy*, New Haven, 1944.

50 F. H. Hayek, *The Road to Serfdom*, 1944.

51 F. Neumann, *Behemoth: The Structure and Practice of National Socialism*, 1942.

52 R. Brady, *Business as a system of Power*, N.Y., 1943.

53 It is interesting at this point to mention J. Schumpeter's thesis about the gradual decline of capitalism due to its very success in promoting rational ways of life and thought. According to this theory, big business, rather than the entrepreneurial class behind it, instead of becoming a dominant force in society loses its power position by its very success. Indeed the 'perfectly bureaucratised giant unit' destroys its creator, the entrepreneur, by bureaucratising his main function: innovation. In other terms, as the process of technical progress and change becomes increasingly routinised and impersonal, the main *raison d'être* of the entrepreneur disappears. 'The very success of the business class in developing the productive powers of this country and the very fact that this success has created a new standard of life for all classes has paradoxically undermined the social and political position of the same business class whose economic function, though not obsolete, tends to become obsolescent and amenable to bureaucratisation' (*Capitalism, Socialism and Democracy*, 1965, p. 417).

54 M. Djilas' *New Class*, a violent critique of Yugoslavia's socialist régime, is not very different from Rizzi's analysis of the Soviet bureaucracy. They both assume that it is the party bureaucracy which has concentrated all power in its hands and which constitutes the new class.

In this context the problem arises as to whether one can say that the ultimate rulers in the socialist countries are the party bureaucrats i.e. to what extent the actual top leaders are bureaucrats in the strict sense of the word. For two opposing positions on this problem cf. T. B. Bottomore, *Elites and Society*, 1964, pp. 77–9 and J. A. Armstrong, *The Soviet Bureaucratic Elite: A Case Study of the Ukranian Apparatus*, 1959.

55 J. Burnham, *The Managerial Revolution*, N.Y., 1960.

56 Burnham's definition of the manager is more restricted and specific than that of Rizzi's bureaucrat. Indeed, the former distinguishes the function of the manager (administration, co-ordination) from those functions which necessitate 'elaborate training in the physical sciences and engineering' (*Managerial Revolution*, p. 75).

57 *ibid.* p. 70.

CHAPTER TWO

1 cf. M. Weber, *On the Methodology of the Social Sciences*, Glencoe, Ill., 1949, pp. 90–3.

2 Weber, *The Theory of Social and Economic Organization*, p. 311.

3 'Traditional Authority is bound to the precedents handed down from the past and to this extent is also oriented to rules,' *ibid.* p. 322.

4 'Bureaucracy and rationality in Weber's organisation theory: an empirical study', *American Sociological Review*, vol. 24 (1959), pp. 791–5.

5 For example M. Berger in constituting a bureaucratic scale, has used hierarchy as one of the criteria of bureaucratisation. He defines it in such general terms as emphasis upon the prerogatives of position, upon authority and obedience. But one could object that a feudal administration or any other type of administration has also a hierarchy emphasising prerogatives and obedience (cf. M. Berger, *Bureaucracy and Society in Modern Egypt*, Princeton, 1957, p. 49).

6 Weber, *Theory of Social and Economic Organization*, p. 344.

7 Berger, p. 49.

8 Weber, *Theory of Social and Economic Organization*, p. 303.

9 Gerth and Mills, p. 228.

10 cf. Gerth and Mills, pp. 209 ff.

11 For an interesting discussion of this problem cf. A. Etzioni (ed.) *A Comparative Analysis of Complex Organizations*, N.Y., 1964, pp. 15–19.

12 cf. for example A. W. Gouldner, *Patterns of Industrial Bureaucracy*, Glencoe, Ill., 1954.

13 cf. Parsons, p. 65.

From this point of view organisations do not differ only according to their goals but also according to the way in which they articulate their various subsystems with each other and with the larger societal environment (for instance the break in authority and generally the interrelationships between the technical and the managerial subsystem in an army and in a school are quite different).

For a more detailed exposition and discussion of Parsons' contribution to the theory of organisations cf. chapter 7.

14 cf. for example P. Selznick, 'An Approach to the Theory of Bureaucracy', *American Sociological Review*, vol. 8 (1943), p. 47; and his 'Foundations of the Theory of Organization', *American Sociological Review*, vol. 13 (1948), pp. 25–35; also cf. R. Merton, *Social Theory and Social Structure*, 2nd ed. 1957, Glencoe, Ill., pp. 50–4.

15 Udy, pp. 791 ff.

16 Weber, *Methodology of the Social Sciences*, p. 93.

17 cf. C. Hempel, 'Problems of Concept and Theory Formation in the Social Sciences', in *Science, Language and Human Rights*, American Philosophical Association, Philadelphia, 1952, p. 66.

18 The various racial typologies in physical anthropology are good examples of this kind of classification.

19 cf. J. McKinney, 'The Typological Tradition', in J. S. Rouček (ed.), *Readings in Contemporary American Sociology*, Paterson N.J., 1962, p. 557.

20 So, for example, Riesman's types of other-directed and inner-directed people, although in their extreme formulations do not correspond to any real concrete instances, they are useful for ordering concrete individuals as more or less near the one or the other pole (cf. David Riesman *et al.*, *The Lonely Crowd*, Yale, 1952).

21 cf. Weber, *Methodology of the Social Sciences*, p. 90. Also cf. T. Parsons *The Structure of Social Action*, 1937, pp. 601 ff. and C. Friedrich, 'Some Observations on Weber's analysis of Bureaucracy', in R. K. Merton *et al.* (eds.), *Reader in Bureaucracy*, Glencoe, 1963, p. 28.

22 cf. Weber, *Methodology of the Social Sciences*, p. 90.

23 The term 'ideal' refers precisely to this sort of exaggeration of empirical features. Of course this use of the term differs from its everyday usage (the latter referring to an actual thing which serves as a standard of imitation).

24 cf. Weber, *Methodology of the Social Sciences*, p. 91.

25 D. Martindale, 'Sociological Theory and the Ideal Type', in L. Gross (ed.), *Symposium on Sociological Theory*, N.Y., 1959, p. 72.

26 cf. T. Abel, 'The Operation called Verstehen', in H. Feigl and M. Brodbeck (eds.), *Readings in the Philosophy of Science*, N.Y., 1953.

27 cf. chapter 3, introduction.

28 cf. his introduction in Weber's *The Theory of Social and Economic Organization*, pp. 58–60, footnote 4.

29 Gouldner, p. 22.

30 i.e. The conflict between the professional specialist and the administrator (the staff and 'line' controversy in management theory – cf. chapter 4).

31 As H. Becker, another proponent of ideal types points out, the constructed or ideal type has a negative utility. It draws our attention to the investigation of all those factors which distort the ideal form of social configurations and make social reality so different from them, cf. *Through Values to Social Interpretation*, Durham, N.C., 1950, pp. 259–64.

32 The above remarks do not apply to all kinds of ideal types. For example, what J. Watkins calls individualistic ideal types are logically acceptable and methodologically useful for the explanation of specific cases (cf. 'Ideal Types and Historical Explanation' in Feigl and Brodbeck, p. 275). These types consist in the construction of the rational behaviour of an actor by deducing it from a set of given premises postulating the actor's preferences and information – e.g. the economic man construct in economics.

But the ideal type of bureaucracy cannot be considered as a similar construct.

33 cf. Gerth and Mills, p. 57.

34 Martindale, p. 88.

35 S. Andreski, 'Method and substantive Theory in M. Weber', *British Journal of Sociology*, vol. 15 (1964), p. 4.

36 After all, Weber devotes only a few pages in his vast work to the discussion of the characteristics and internal structure of bureaucracy.

37 R. Hall has made up a detailed catalogue of bureaucratic characteristics as listed by major authors (Friedrich, Merton, Udy, Heady, Parsons, Berger, Michels, Dimock). cf. 'A concept of bureaucracy: An Empirical Assessment', *American Journal of Sociology*, vol. 69 (1963), pp. 32–40.

38 cf. Hall.

39 Gerth and Mills, pp. 214–16.

40 In contradiction to substantive rationality which refers to an 'act of thought which reveals intelligent insight into the interrelations of events in a given situation . . .' (K. Mannheim, *Man and Society in an Age of Reconstruction*, 1948, pp. 51 ff).

41 P. Blau, *The Dynamics of Bureaucracy*, 1955, p. 60.

42 *ibid.* p. 61.

43 cf. J. Woodward, *Management and Technology*, H.M.S.O., 1958.

44 For various 'political' definitions of the term cf: W. A. Robson, *Civil Service in Great Britain and France*, 1956; H. Laski, 'Bureaucracy', in *Encyclopedia Britannica*.

45 cf. W. Delany, 'Patrimonial and Bureaucratic Administration', *Administrative Science Quarterly*, vol. 8 (1963), p. 459.

CHAPTER THREE

1 R. K. Merton, 'Bureaucratic Structure and Personality', in *Reader in Bureaucracy*, pp. 261–372.

2 cf. chapter 1, section 4.

3 He did not base his writings on bureaucracy on any specific research findings.

4 As a matter of fact, Blau and Gouldner, two of the most influential modern writers on bureaucracy, have been Merton's disciples. Of course another great influence, accounting for the empirical character of their

work, has come from the extensive empirical studies of behaviour in industrial settings which have their starting point in Hawthorne (cf. chapter 5, 'The Human Relations approach to the Organisation').

5 Thus although in a way every empirical study ultimately and unavoidably will have to deal with concrete individual behaviour, it is the manner and the angle from which one looks at it, which determines whether one's main interest is the individual, the group, or the organisation as a unit. Contrary to human relations writers (cf. chapter 6), modern writers on bureaucracy, although speaking of groups and individuals, concentrate their analysis on the organisational level. Lipset provides an example: 'The fact that the present study includes a sample of individuals from the union, and that part of the analysis is one of individual behaviour, must not be allowed to confuse the issue. The focus of analysis is not the individual but the organisation as a whole' (S. M. Lipset, M. A. Trow and J. S. Coleman, *Union Democracy*, Glencoe, Ill., 1956, p. 425).

6 cf. for example Gouldner.

7 cf. for example R. G. Francis and R. C. Stone, *Service and Procedure in Bureaucracy*, Minneapolis, 1956.

8 cf. H. M. Johnson, *Sociology: A Systematic Introduction*, 1964, p. 51.

9 Of course, the term 'need' in this context must be understood in a metaphorical sense. It does not imply that the organisation is an organism in any biological sense.

10 Thus, for example, in Merton's analysis previously cited, if strict control by rules is seen as a part of the bureaucratic system, it had both functional results (satisfaction of the predictability need of the system) and dysfunctional (frustration of the flexibility need). Merton's famous paradigm of functional analysis (cf. *Social Theory and Social Structure*, pp. 50–5) has become the main source of inspiration for subsequent analysts of bureaucracy. But each writer uses the functional method in a somewhat different manner. Some of these differences (in the terms used, in the emphasis on various aspects of the method) will be shown below.

11 cf. Merton, *Social Theory and Social Structure*, p. 51.

12 To take an example from the organisational literature: the introduction of statistical performance records in an office, by intensifying inter-employee competition, had the latent function of discouraging racial discrimination towards clients. Indeed discriminating practices were detrimental to individual productivity. Thus the employees, desirous to maximise their results, were tending to treat negroes and whites on an equal footing. These consequences of the statistical records were latent in the sense that they were neither intended nor recognised by the employees (cf. Blau, pp. 90–4).

13 For a more detailed analysis of the concept of formal structure cf. chapter 4.

14 Thus, for example, we may say that the organisational goal of a shoe factory is to produce and sell shoes. But for the worker or the owner-manager, the production of shoes is simply a means through which the former achieves his wage goal and the latter his profit goal.

15 cf. Selznick, 'Foundations', pp. 26–9.

16 Of course, writers on bureaucracy do not limit themselves to the examination of the formal-informal conflict. Although the above conflict (under its various forms) occupies the central place in their theories, other types of strains and tensions are also analysed. For a systematic enumeration of them cf. A. Gouldner, 'Organisational Analysis', in *Sociology Today*, pp. 400–28; cf. also his 'Cosmopolitans and Locals: Toward an Analysis of Latent Social Roles – I, II', *Administrative Science Quarterly*, vol. 2 (1957–8), pp. 287–306 and pp. 444–80.

17 Blau, in a slightly different manner, examines the same phenomenon (pp. 36–43).

18 For a schematic representation of this model cf. J. G. March and H. A. Simon, *Organizations*, N.Y., 1958, p. 45.

19 A. Gouldner, *Wildcat Strike*, Yellow Springs, Ohio, 1954.

20 Thus increasing market competition (threat to management) combined with a personnel change in top management, bring close supervision as a means of increasing productivity (management's defence mechanism). But tight control upsets the indulgency pattern (i.e. mutual toleration of small infractions to the formal rules) in the plant. This supervisory policy of the new management is perceived as threatening by the workers. The wildcat strike is a response to the above threat. The reduction of tension (temporary re-equilibrium) is brought about by a workers-management agreement which substitutes the old informal relations between the two parties (the indulgency pattern) with bureaucratic rules regulating future relationships in detail.

21 cf. Selznick, 'An Approach', pp. 47 ff; and 'Foundations'.

22 A similar, but more abstract analysis, between centripetal and centrifugal tactics and strategies of organisational subunits is to be found in A. Gouldner's 'Reciprocity and Autonomy in Functional Theory', in Gross, pp. 256 ff.

23 Moreover, according to Selznick, powerful interest groups in the periphery of bureaucracy may as well become sources of deviation from organisational objectives. In his study of a New Deal federal agency, he shows how this organisation, in its efforts to compromise and accommodate itself with local interests, undertook a series of commitments which gradually led it to change its initial progressive policies and goals (cf. *TVA and the Grass Roots*, Berkeley, 1949). A similar change in organisational policy is successfully analysed by S. M. Lipset in his *Agrarian Socialism*, Berkeley, 1950. Following Weber's and Michels' tradition, he shows in a more precise way the structural constraints which forced an agrarian socialist party, when in power, to abandon its radical ideals and adopt conservative policies.

24 cf. Selznick, 'Foundations', p. 30.

25 cf. A. Gouldner, 'Metaphysical Pathos and the Theory of Bureaucracy', *American Political Science Review*, vol. 49 (1955), pp. 496–507.

26 Gouldner, *Patterns of Industrial Bureaucracy*, p. 29.

27 cf. especially Blau, pp. 162–82.

28 On the concept of rationality, as a conscious effort to shape the organisational structure according to our aims and values cf. chapter 2, section 3.

29 Gouldner distinguishes a third type of rules: the mock rules which are imposed by an agency outside the organisation and which are discarded by managers and workers alike (cf. *Patterns of Industrial Bureaucracy* pp. 182–7).

30 A similar argument is to be found in modern management textbooks which have drawn their conclusions from the great bulk of industrial sociopsychological studies of the 'human relations' school. (For a detailed exposition and criticism cf. chapter 5.)

31 cf. R. Likert, *New Patterns of Management*, N.Y., 1961; P. R. Lawrence, *The Changing of Organizational Behaviour Patterns*, Boston, 1958; R. H. Guest, *Organizational Change: The Effect of Successful Leadership*, Homewood, Ill., 1962; T. Burns and G. M. Stalker, *The Management of Innovation*, 1955.

32 cf. M. Janowitz, 'Changing Patterns of Organizational Authority: The Military Establishment', *Administrative Science Quarterly*, vol. 3 (1959), 473–93; also cf. his *Professional Soldier*, Glencoe, Ill., 1960, and *Sociology and the Military Establishment*, N.Y., 1959.

33 cf. R. Blauner, *Alienation, Freedom and Technology*, Chicago, 1964.

34 Lipset *et al.*

35 They pointed out that a decentralised system of authority increases the power of the locals and thus constitutes the basis for a pluralistic system of power (which is a necessary prerequisite for the existence of a legitimised opposition). Furthermore, the autonomy of the locals is usually determined by whether the national union emerged through alliances of pre-existing local organisations (the case of the ITU) or whether the locals were created from the top, i.e. after the establishment of a powerful central unit (cf. Lipset *et al.* pp. 33–66, 364–89 and p. 414). For a similar argument cf. also Duverger pp. 1–34.

36 When the gap between the status of the leader and the status of the led is small, there are more chances that the former will accept more easily the possibility of losing his position. Moreover, when there is a wide distribution of leadership skills among union members, the chances of democratic rotation of personnel at the top increase (cf. pp. 201–333).

37 Usually a high degree of participation and interest in the union's activities enhances the democratic process. In turn such participation depends on the existence of a strong occupational community which can provide many occasions for its members to meet and discuss union problems. By such informal discussions and meetings, interest in union politics is sustained (cf. pp. 69–122; for a more general treatment of political apathy in a mass society, cf. W. Kornhauser, *The Politics of Mass Society*, 1960).

38 Political behaviour in the trade union depends greatly on the system of beliefs and values of the organisation. If the culture of the union legitimises the functions of the opposition, the suppression of the latter and the establishment of oligarchic rule becomes very difficult. Usually

the institutionalisation of such values takes place when the faction in power cannot suppress the opposition without jeopardising the existence of the organisation itself (cf. pp. 238–73). For a more theoretical and concise treatment of all the above factors cf S. Lipset, 'The Political Process in Trade Unions: A Theoretical Statement', in M. Berger, *et al.* (eds.), *Freedom and Control in Modern Society*, N.Y., 1954, pp. 82–124.

39 Lipset *et al.* p. 405.

40 cf. Duverger; S. Neumann (ed.) '*Modern Political Parties: Approaches to Comparative Politics*, Chicago, 1956.

41 Thus Michels' theory cannot account for significant variations between parties. For example it has been shown that the internal political structure of American parties allows more conflict and change of leadership than European (continental) parties. This is explained partly by the fact that the two-party system as well as various constitutional rules make a definite scission of warring factions into two or more separate parties almost impossible. On the contrary, in a multiparty system various interest groups have their own party with less internal conflict and a more stable leadership (cf. S. Lipset, 'Party Systems and the Representation of Social Groups', *European Journal of Sociology*, vol. 1, (1960), pp. 50–8).

42 cf. W. Leiserson, *American Trade Union Democracy*, N.Y., 1959.

43 O. Garcean, *The Political Life of the American Medical Association*, Hawden, Conn., 1961; B. Barber, 'Participation and Mass Apathy in Associations', in A. Gouldner (ed.), *Studies in Leadership*, N.Y., 1950, pp. 477–504; P.M. Harrison, *Authority and Power in the Free Church Tradition*, Princeton, 1959.

44 Particularly where unionism is concerned, they point out that the crucial problem in a union's political system is not the existence of an institutionalised opposition but the question of the 'representativeness' of its policies. To what extent does the leadership represent the interests of the led? This is the most important consideration. To quote V. L. Allen, 'the end of trade union activity is to protect and improve the general standards of its members and not to provide workers with exercise in self-government'. (*Power in Trade Unions*, 1957, p. 15.)

If these ends are systematically and successfully pursued, that is, if the union leaders really represent the interests of the rank and file, there is no need for internal democracy. If they do not, there are other mechanisms which could check the abuse of power: as in many other voluntary associations, whenever the leader adopts wrong policies, membership decreases. As a consequence, the leader is obliged to change his policies if he wants his organisation to survive.

Of course, although the argument has a degree of validity, it has no application in all those cases where participation in the organisation is not voluntary but obligatory (e.g. closed shop system). Moreover, the vagueness of organisational objectives, the immeasurability of results achieved and the impossibility for the rank and file to assess the real achievements of the leadership (especially when the means of propaganda are monopolised by the latter), makes fluctuations of membership participation a very weak mechanism of control. As proof of this, there are numerous examples of cases where union leaders were pursuing policies which were opposite to what their rank and file members considered as the appropriate policy for the defence of their interests.

Thus, for example, a survey of the member attitudes in the British Medical Association at a time when its leaders were against nationalisation, showed that the great majority of the rank and file was in favour of the government's proposals and against their leaders' policies (cf. H. Eckstein, 'The Politics of the British Medical Association', *The Political Quarterly*, vol. 26, (1955), pp. 345–59).

The above arguments bring us finally to a brief consideration of the effects of organisational oligarchy on society as a whole.

Michels thought that organisational oligarchy necessarily brings societal oligarchy. Although much research is still needed on the precise mechanisms which link the organisational to the general political system of a society, some modern writers see no radical incompatibility between non-democratic voluntary organisations and democratic government. According to these theorists such oligarchic large-scale organisations as unions and even political parties can very well constitute autonomous and antagonistic centres of power. Such forces, in the pursuit of their particular interests, sustain the pluralistic system of democratic régimes.

Indeed, it is because of this pluralistic system of power that the structural differentiation (accentuated by the growth of large bureaucracies) between masses and élites does not necessarily lead to the unlimited manipulation of the former by the latter. The so-called élitist theory of democracy maintains that in spite of the non-active participation of the masses in the political process, as competing élites need electoral support, they are forced to take into consideration other interests than their own (cf. S. Lipset, *Political Man*, N.Y., 1960, pp. 45–6).

Of course, the debate does not end here. 'Democratic pluralism' is attacked by those who do not think that the multiplicity of centres of power is a sufficient condition for democracy. As Bottomore puts it, 'it is one of the political myths of our age that democracy is protected and sustained principally or solely by the competition between élites, which balance and limit each other's power,' and he goes on to argue that the 'Preservation, and especially the development and improvement, of a democratic system of government does not depend primarily upon fostering the competition between small élite groups whose activities are carried on in realms far removed from the observation and control of ordinary citizens, but upon creating and establishing the conditions in which a large majority of citizens, if not all citizens, can take part in deciding those social issues which vitally affect their lives – at work, in the local community and in the nation . . .' (pp. 118–19.) For another systematic analysis and criticism of the Pluralist theories of democracy cf. Shin'ya Oho, 'The Limits of Bourgeois Pluralism', *Studies of the Left*, vol. 5, (1965), pp. 46–72. Moreover, the various theorists who advocate the democratic control of industry – industrial democracy – as a prerequisite for a really democratic régime can be situated in this context (cf. W. Scott, *Industrial Democracy: A Revaluation*, Liverpool, 1955).

As to the tool or master problem of the public bureaucracy, it has also been re-examined in a more cautious and empirical manner. As with the problem of internal democracy, there is a definite dampening of the deterministic rigour of Rizzi's and Burnham's theories. The sweeping generalisations about a new bureaucratic or managerial class and its inevitable oligarchic domination are met with great scepticism. (For a criticism of Burnham's thesis cf. G. H. Gerth and C. W. Mills, 'A Marx for the Managers' in *Reader in Bureaucracy*, pp. 165–79).

In this context as well, the main focus of attention in recent writings is on the identification of the social conditions under which bureaucratic organisations tend to a usurpation of power, and those conditions which favour their control (cf. S. N. Eisenstadt, 'Bureaucracy and Bureaucratisation', *Current Sociology*, vol. 7 (1958) pp. 99–164; as well as his 'Bureaucracy, Bureaucratisation and Debureaucratisation', *Administrative Science Quarterly*, vol. 4 (1959), pp. 302–20; cf. also S. Lipset, *op. cit.* pp. 273 ff. and Bendix, 'Bureaucracy and the Problem of Power', *Public Administration Review*, vol. 5 (1945) pp. 194–209).

45 The work by Lipset *et al.* is a very good example of this use of historical information. But generally and unfortunately the 'historic' perspective is not much used in writings on bureaucracy (cf. concluding chapter).

46 'The more highly stratified an occupation is, the more intense and rigid will be its political cleavages if its union has democratic policies.' (Lipset *et al.* p. 426.)

47 As a matter of fact, too often in the literature of bureaucracy generalisations are formulated without any reference to the conditions under which they hold true. They thus give the false impression of being universally valid. Although modern writers are more cautious in this respect than their predecessors, the tendency to over-generalisation still persists. (For example, the fact that many generalisations are built up exclusively from the observation of American or North European organisations is rarely made explicit, neither is the pressing need to study bureaucracy in different cultures – cf. Part III.)

48 For example, the relationship between organisational size (in terms of units produced, or number of employees) and the growth of the administrative apparatus of a firm, or the ratio of women employees to the whole personnel population of the firm, etc.

In Great Britain P. S. Florence and his collaborators have made considerable contributions to this kind of organisational knowledge (cf. *Economics and Sociology of Industry*, 1964; cf. also T. R. Anderson and S. Warkov, 'Organizational Size and Functional Complexity', *American Sociological Review*, vol. 26 (1961), pp. 23–8).

49 cf. Johnson, *Sociology*, pp. 56–66. Of course, in this context one should not underestimate the potentiality of such methods as multivariate factor analysis in accounting quantitatively for more than two structural variables

Notes to pages 69–73

(cf. P. Lazarsfeld, 'Problems in Methodology' in *Sociology Today*, pp. 39–78).

Moreoever, sociometric techniques make possible the construction of the social structure of an organisation (rather some aspects of its social structure) on the basis of questionnaires (cf. R. S. Weiss and E. Jacobson, 'A Method for the Analysis of the Structure of Complex Organisations' in Etzioni, *Complex Organizations*, pp. 464–77, and R. Weiss, *Processes of Organization*, Ann Arbor, Michigan, 1956).

50 For an account of unsuccessful survey studies in industrial settings, cf. chapter 5, section 3.

51 The classification proposed by Blau and Scott is a good example of such a typology. The authors distinguish four types of organisations according the *cui bono* criterion, i.e. according the kind of persons who are the primary beneficiaries of the organisational activities: (a) The mutual-benefit association where the prime beneficiary is the member, the rank and file of the organisation (e.g. a trade union); (b) business organisations where the owners are the primary beneficiaries; (c) service organisations where the public, the clients are the primary beneficiaries (e.g. a governmental welfare agency); (d) communal organisations which are supposed to serve primarily the public at large (e.g. the police organisation).

This typology seems very useful as each organisational type faces specific problems which require specific structural arrangements for their solution.

For an exposition of various typologies according other organisational criteria cf. Blau and Scott, pp. 70 ff.

52 cf. D. Martindale, *The Nature and Types of Sociological Theory*, Boston, 1960, pp. 441–501.

53 Indeed it is not only the modern 'bureaucracy' theorists who use systematically functional-structural analysis but many other organisation theorists as well (cf. chapter 6).

54 For further criticism of the formal-informal dichotomy cf. chapter 5, section 2 and chapter 7, section 2.

55 cf. Merton, *Social Theory and Social Structure*, pp. 60–4.

56 cf. Gouldner, *Patterns of Industrial Bureaucracy*, p. 25.

57 For example, the statistical performance records, in the federal agency studied by Blau, were purposively introduced in order to increase employee productivity (or, we could say, in order to satisfy the organisational need for increased productivity), cf. Blau, pp. 36–43.

58 Thus the statement 'The introduction of statistical records of performance had the *latent function* of decreasing racial discrimination', can be replaced by the statement: 'The introduction of statistical records of performance had as an effect the decrease of racial discrimination.'

59 J. Rex, *Key Problems of Sociological Theory*, 1963, pp. 60–77.

60 cf. E. Nagel, 'Teleological Explanation and Teleological Systems', in Feigl and Brodbeck, pp. 537–58.

61 Merton has made it very clear that the concept of function must not be confused with such subjective categories as intentions or purposes. But, by not making explicit the fact that we can only use the functional

methods when we analyse self-maintaining systems, he did not meet the most serious objections to functionalism.

62   In much the same way, when biologists speak of the functions of a human organ, they do not ascribe to it, in an anthropomorphic way, purposes and intentions. They simply imply that this organ is part of a system (the human body) which is directly organised with respect to some of its properties (e.g. its temperature).

63   cf. K. Brown, *Explanation in Social Science*, 1963, p. 130.

Of course, it must be made clear that when we speak of the existence of system needs and of feedback mechanisms regulating them, we do not mean that somehow needs directly create the social patterns which will cope with them. The simple presence of a need does not, by itself, guarantee or fully explain the appearance of a variable with functional consequences with respect to this need. In other words, contrary to a law statement, a functional statement is not of the form: 'When need A then functional variable B'. The need is neither a sufficient nor a necessary condition for the appearance of a functional variable.

It is not a necessary condition in the sense that we cannot say that such a need will bring forth a corresponding specific functional variable (or any variable). And it is not a sufficient condition because the existence of a need, even when a functional variable appears, cannot fully explain the appearance of this variable. A functional statement gives only a limited explanation to the appearance of a variable. It may partially explain why a variable persists in a social system; it may also, in a negative way, tell us why certain social patterns do not appear to take root in certain social systems (when they are in disaccord with the dominant needs of a system).

64   cf. E. Nagel, *Logic without Metaphysics*, 1957, chapter 10.

65   And if it were possible, one should even try to find a way to measure these variables. By such a measurement, one could establish their range of variation within which the system retains its self-maintaining aspects. For example, we can imagine a management's authoritarian personnel policy going beyond a certain limit of tolerance, in which case the system, as far as productivity is concerned, breaks down (strike). The problem in such a case should be to identify the range of values that the variable management policy can take which will keep productivity within certain limits.

For a more detailed and formalised exposition of the above stringent conditions of a successful functional analysis, cf. Nagel, pp. 247–86. Of course, in the social sciences, this sort of quantification seems rather a remote possibility.

CHAPTER FOUR

1   G. Friedmann, *Industrial Society*, N.Y., 1955, p. 27.

2   M. Nadworny, *Scientific Management and the Unions, 1900–1932*, Cambridge, Mass., 1955, p. 1.

3 cf. H. Aitken, *Taylorism, at Watertown Arsenal*, Cambridge, Mass. 1960, pp. 17–18.

4 Taylor had originally named his system task management. The label 'scientific management' was first used by L. Brandeis in 1910.

5 F. Taylor, *The Principles of Scientific Management*, N.Y., 1945, pp. 36 ff.

6 After Taylor, the methods of registration and timing of work were extensively elaborated and refined, especially by Frank and Lilian Gilbreth.

7 The exposition of this system was in the first formal paper presented by Taylor to the American Society of Mechanical Engineers in 1895.

8 cf. Nadworny, p. 49.

9 Quotation taken from Nadworny, p. 5.

10 Van Alstyne, Brandeis and Valentine were among the first Taylorites to show their sympathy for the unions, cf. Nadworny, pp. 75, 97–121.

11 The quotation is taken from Waldo, p. 53.

12 Quoted from Friedmann, p. 56.

13 cf. C. Myers, *Business Rationalisation*, 1932.

14 Friedmann, pp. 60–5.

15 March and Simon (pp. 15–22) have conveniently summarised some of the valid contributions of Taylorism in various research areas:

(a) *Speed:* Findings about the speed characteristics of the human organism (e.g. how fast individuals with varying degrees of effort or skill can perform a certain task).

As to time study, its main goal – not yet fully achieved – is to find a set of basic activities and unit times for each of them. If this could be achieved it would become possible to find the standard time of a more complex activity by simply reducing it to its basic components. So, they were efforts to establish a set of basic movements (Gilbreth's 'therblings'), as well as complicated tables with movement and time measurements. The main difficulty with all these attempts is the fact that a therbling (i.e. a basic movement) is not a homogenous unit; its performance time varies widely and depends on a multiplicity of factors (skill, effort, etc). In consequence, the establishment of time standards in industry is at present usually estimated directly by a stop-watch, instead of being synthetised with the aid of tables.

(b) *Capacity:* The main focus in this area is on the identification of the limits of the production rate, as well as in the discovery of ways of reducing the unused capacity of the working organism.

(c) *Effort and fatigue:* In this domain lies the most sophisticated part of the literature of the physiological organisation theory: statements of general relationships between manual activities and muscular groups, between fatigue and activity, between work-time and rest-time.

16 For a definition of technicism, cf. Friedmann, p. 32.

17 cf. N. Person, 'Fayolism as the necessary complement of Taylorism', *American Political Science Review*, vol. 39 (1945), p. 68; also E. Hunt (ed.) *Scientific Management since Taylor*, N.Y., 1924, pp. 63–147.

18 Taylor elaborated the so-called principle of functional foremanship: instead of attaching one foreman to a limited number of workers, Taylor

proposed that the job of the foreman should be broken down to its simpler components so that each foreman could be specialised in performing one very simple supervisory task over a great number of workers. By this specialisation the productivity of the foreman was expected to increase.

19 His main work, *Administration Industrielle et Générale* was presented as a paper to the Congress of the Société de l'Industrie Minérale in 1908.

20 Main contributors to this type of approach: W. Robinson, L. Urwick, J. Mooney and A. Reiley, Alvin Brown, etc.

21 cf. E. Dale, *The Great Organizers*, 1960, pp. 5–11.

22 cf. A. Lepawsky, *Administration*, N.Y., 1949, p. 653; D. Waldo, *The Study of Public Administration*, N.Y., 1955, p. 56; for the impact of scientific management on public administration, cf. Waldo, *The Administrative State*, pp. 47–64.

23 This chapter focuses mainly on the business administration field.

24 cf. E. Brech, *Organization: The Framework of Management*, 1957, pp. 27–9.

25 cf. March and Simon, pp. 22–9.

26 In this context we must emphasise that very often in writings on management there is no clear-cut distinction between description and prescription – between how things are and how they ought to be. For instance very often, when one reads in textbooks on business or public administration about the functions of a department or of the executive, one is not sure if reference is made to what the executive does or to what he should do. Many universalists seem to move from the descriptive to the prescriptive level without giving adequate warning to the reader (cf. K. Brown, pp. 124–5).

27 It can be referred to as the scalar principle, cf. J. Mooney, *The Principles of Organization*, N.Y., 1947, pp. 14–27.

28 Fayol distinguished six basic functions of an enterprise (technical, commercial, financial, accounting, administrative and of security).

29 The range of variability goes from one basic principle (Mooney's co-ordination, subdivided ultimately to secondary principles) to ninety-six (cf. A. Brown, *Organization of Industry*, 1947).

30 H. Koontz, 'Making Sense of Management Theory', *Harvard Business Review*, vol. 40 (1962), p. 25.

31 cf. Fayol, pp. 16–77.

32 The number of these activities varies according to the author. This variation is mainly due to differences in definition. Other activities typically included in the process of management: forecasting, organising, commanding, staffing.

33 cf. B. Goetz, *Management, Planning and Control*, 1949, pp. 229–67.

34 cf. H. Betham, 'Control', in E. Brech (ed.), *The Principles and Practice of Management*, 1963, pp. 633–841.

35 cf. E. Wilkinson and R. Foster, *Management Principles and Practice*, 1963.

36 Koontz, *op. cit.*

37 cf. On this point the criticism in March and Simon p. 30.

38 For example Mooney and Rei!ley define as principle 'any underlying cause of more or less correlated acts in any particular field of investigation' (*Onward Industry*, 1931, p. 17). One can hardly see how their co-ordination or functional principle can fit this definition.

39 In this case it is called a principle, as it embodies a fundamental truth or generalisation.

40 cf. E. Stene, 'An approach to a Science of Administration', *American Political Science Review*, vol. 34 (1940), pp. 1127–37. Although this kind of formulation seems to approach the style of the laws in the exact sciences, the similarity is rather superficial as the statements are platitudinous: e.g. 'The degree to which a given organization approaches the full realization of its objectives tends to vary directly with the co-ordination of individual efforts within that organization'.

41 cf. L. White, *Introduction to the Study of Public Administration*, 1948,

42 cf. V. Graicunas, 'Relationship in Organization', in L. Gulick and L. Urwick (eds.), *Papers on the Science of Administration*, pp. 181–7.

43 cf. Fayol, pp. 19–20; L. Urwick, 'Public Administration and Business Administration', *Public Administration Review*, vol. 17 (1957), pp. 78–9; and Brech, *Organization*, p. 86.

44 cf. M. Haire, 'The Concept of Power and the Concept of Man', in G. Strother (ed.), *Social Science Approaches to Business Behaviour*, 1962, p. 172.

45 'It is clearly wrong to assign a task and then fail to provide the powers and sanctions needed to implement it,' D. Clough, *Concepts in Management Science*, N.J., 1963, p. 23.

46 cf. E. Dale, 'The Functional Approach to Management', in H. Koontz (ed.), *Toward a Unified Theory of Management*, N.Y., 1964, p. 30.

47 Koontz, *art. cit.* p. 38.

48 cf. H. Simon, *Administrative Behaviour*, N.Y., 1948, pp. 20–36.

49 cf. W. Taylor, pp. 98–9.

50 For a more sensible approach to the problem of principles cf. J. Woodward *Industrial Organization*, 1965. Woodward argues that principles of successful management change from one technological context to another. Thus she shows convincingly that the sort of principles elaborated by clsssical management theorists are *only* relevant in mass production factories.

51 cf. Brech, *Organization*, p. 363.

CHAPTER FIVE

1 cf. Friedmann, pp. 43–51.

2 *ibid.* pp. 261 ff.

3 J. A. C. Brown, *The Social Psychology of Industry*, 1962, p. 17.

4 Friedmann, p. 294.

5   cf. R. Girod, *Attitudes collectives et relations humaines*, Paris, 1953, p. 17.

6   These studies, a co-operative five year enterprise between the company and a Harvard Business School team (1927–32), were extensively reported by F. J. Roethlisberger and W. J. Dickson in *Management and the Worker*, Cambridge, Mass., 1939.

7   Roethlisberger and Dickson, pp. 19–30.

8   *ibid*. pp. 189–255.

9   *ibid*. pp. 379–409.

10   cf. Blau and Scott, pp. 87–93.

11   The term is taken from C. Arensberg and G. Tootell, 'Plant Sociology: Real Discoveries and New Problems', in M. Kommarovsky (ed.), *Common Frontiers of the Social Sciences*, Glencoe, Ill., 1957, pp. 310–37.

12   F. J. Roethlisberger in Koontz, p. 45.

13   Thus, any activity or expressed attitude which deviates from the group's norms (threatening to disturb the existing state of relations), meets the disapproving reactions (sanctions, etc.) of the other members of the group, these reactions tending to redress the deviation (thus restoring the system to its previous state of equilibrium).

14   Roethlisberger in Koontz, pp. 46–8.

15   cf. Roethlisberger and Dickson, pp. 565–8. As we shall see later on, the confusion which this has brought was minimal, because most of the time the concept of social system was only applied on the group level.

16   Roethlisberger and Dickson, p. 564.

17   cf. E. Mayo and G. F. Lombard, 'Teamwork and Labor Turnover in the Aircraft Industry of Southern California', *Business Research Studies*, No. 32, Boston, 1944.

18   cf. E. Mayo, *The Human Problems of an Industrial Civilisation*, N.Y., 1933; also *The Social Problems of an Industrial Civilisation*, Boston, 1945.
Other works on the same style by members of the orthodox school:
N. T. Whitehead's *Leadership in a Free Society*, Cambridge, Mass., 1936.
F. J. Roethlisberger's *Management and Morale*, Cambridge, Mass., 1941.

19   This committee was organised in 1954 by W. Warner, who became chairman, with B. Gardner as executive secretary.
Other well known members: A. Davis, F. Harbison, E. Hughes, W. F. Whyte.

20   Warner's anthropological orientation and his functionalism has considerably influenced Mayo and contributed to the shaping of the social system approach (cf. E. Chapple, 'Applied Anthropology in Industry', in A. L. Kroeber (ed.), *Anthropology Today*, Chicago, 1953).

21   W. L. Warner and J. O. Low, *The Social System of the Modern Factory*, New Haven, 1947.

22   But it must also be said that Warner accepted Mayo's assumptions in a rather uncritical way and did not pay systematic attention to the internal structure of the organisation. His main emphasis is always upon the organisational environment, rather than upon the organisation itself.

23 cf. E. Hughes, *French Canada in Transition*, Chicago, 1943; W. F. Whyte, *Human Relations in the Restaurant Industry*, N.Y., 1948; W. F. Whyte (ed.), *Industry and Society*, N.Y., 1946.

24 Labour organisations did not fit very well into Mayo's general system of thought. The development of trade-unionism, according to Mayo and Whitehead, simply reflects the high degree of social disorganisation in the modern industrialised world; 'It is a revolt not against bad conditions but social isolation' (Whitehead, p. 144). Thus the role of the union will become superfluous if, by the application of human relations techniques, management establishes harmony and good morale in the plant. (*ibid.* p. 155.)

25 cf. B. Gardner, *Human Relations in Industry*, Chicago, 1945 (chapter V, 'The Union: Its Functions and Place in the Structure').

26 cf. W. F. Whyte, *Patterns of Industrial Peace*, N.Y., 1951; and by the same author, 'The impact of the Union on the Management Organization', in C. Arensberg *et al.* (eds.) *Research in Industrial Human Relations*, N.Y., 1957.

27 The main point of difference lies in the varying importance that each author gives to the concept of interaction and to the rigorous application of the operational method. From this point of view one can place these writers on a continuum, Chapple being at one end (he gives a great causal importance to the patterns of interaction which constitute more or less the permanent independent variable, sentiments being always a by-product of interaction); and Homans at the other (he attributes *a priori* equal importance to interactions, activities and sentiments, all of them being capable of becoming independent or dependent variables in the social system). Moreover, Homans is opposed to many other basic assumptions of the initial theory, as formulated by Chapple (cf. C. Argyris, *An Introduction to Field Theory and Interaction Theory*, New Haven, Connecticut, 1952).

28 The above is based on Whyte's conceptualisation of the social system. On the other hand, Homans sees an external social system (those sentiments, activities and interactions which enable the group to survive in its environment) and an internal one ('group behaviour that is an expression of the sentiments towards one another') (cf. *The Human Group*, 1951, p. 110). Whyte rejects the distinction as impractical and confusing (cf. *Man and Organization*, Illinois, 1959, p. 65). In a later publication Whyte includes a fourth element; the *symbols*, as links between the individual's sentiments and his social and physical world (cf. W. F. Whyte, 'An Interaction Approach to the Theory of Organization', in M. Haire (ed.), *Modern Organization Theory*, N.Y., 1959).

29 cf. Arensberg, p. 345.

30 cf. F. L. W. Richardson and C. Walker, *Human Relations in an Expanding Company*, New Haven, Connecticut, 1948.

31 Arensberg, p. 351.

32 The formal-informal dichotomy has had several uses in human relations literature: (a) In Roethlisberger and Dickson the formal organisation covers not only rules and official values but also concrete behaviour

which follows official rules (p. 566); (b) But this term has been most often used in a more restricted sense: it implies only official rules and policies in contrast to all concrete behaviour which goes under the label of informal organisation. It is in this second sense that the term is used when the behaviourists criticise the classical school of management of having concentrated its attention on the formal organisation; (c) With Arensberg, although both formal and informal concepts imply concrete interactions, the informal category becomes less important than in *Management and the Worker*; indeed these informal relationships become a dependent variable of interactions prescribed by rules and technology (cf. p. 351).

But whatever the distinction, as in concrete cases it becomes impossible to distinguish clearly official from unofficial behaviour and rules, this dichotomy, if it is not misleading, is most certainly confusing (cf. chapter 7).

33   cf. Chapple, pp. 819 ff.

34   *Micro-interaction analysis* is the 'detailed measurement of the interaction of two or more persons within any simple contact or event'. As to the *interaction chronograph*, it is a computing machine 'measuring the quantitative aspect of the adjustment of two or more persons' (cf. E. Chapple, *Measuring Human Relations: An Introduction to the Study of the Interaction of Individuals*, Genetic Psychology Monographs, 22, 1940, pp. 3–147).

35   Indeed as sociometric methods were very often applied to industrial settings, and as there are many similarities between the Mayo and the Moreno school, it is interesting to state briefly some relevant aspects of sociometric theory.

(a) By its various techniques, sociometry tries to bring to the surface and measure quantitatively that part of social reality which consists of the intricate interpersonal relations between group members. As it is from such basic relations and interactions that group life emerges, the sociometric approach complements the study of informal groups by a depth analysis of its 'infrastructure', i.e. the invisible repulsion-attraction network of organisational members (cf. M. Rogers, 'Problems of Human Relations in Industry', *Sociometry*, vol. 9 (1946), pp. 350 ff).

(b) The sociometric school was also interested in group leadership: authoritarian and *laissez faire* atmospheres, etc. (cf. L. Moreno, 'Advances of Sociometric Techniques', *Sociometric Review*, February, 1936). It seems that such studies have influenced Lewin's experiments in group leadership, experiments which had an important impact on organisational research about supervisory practice and participation.

(c) Moreover, Moreno has had preoccupations about society as a whole similar to those of Mayo. Like Mayo, he is alarmed by the problems of our technical civilisation and by the increasing alienation of man (his loss of spontaneity and freedom). The solution of the problem is sociometry: i.e. the sociometric knowledge and transformation of social reality on the microscopic level, so that maximum spontaneity and freedom is assured for every individual in his immediate social environment. Such a transformation is a prerequisite for bigger changes on the societal level (cf. *Who Shall Survive*, Washington, 1934, pp. 551–611).

– For an important application of sociometric techniques in an organisational context, cf. Weiss.

36 cf. Arensberg, pp. 324–54. In a later publication Arensberg has elaborated in more detail the various phases of this process of successful change (cf. Arensberg and Tootell, pp. 315–19).

37 Very often it is even difficult to decide to which school an author belongs. For example, W. F. Whyte, a disciple of Chapple, has later joined the committee of Human Relations, at Chicago, thus contributing considerably to both subschools and combining their methods.

38 cf. H. Landsberger, *Hawthorne Revisited*, 1958, p. 93.

39 For example in the 'Bank Wiring Room Experiment' (Roethlisberger and Dickson, Ch. XVII), there was systematic analysis of: the physical and technological context in which the group operated (pp. 394–403), the common beliefs and unofficial rules (412–26), common patterns of behaviour (500–2), structural relationships between group positions (449–53), clique relations (508–10), etc.

40 Mainly problems of supervision and morale and their impact on productivity (cf. D. Miller and W. Form, *Industrial Sociology*, N.Y., 1964).

41 Actually, in Roethlisberger and Dickson, although there is much attention given to the first level supervisor and his problems, the authors are not very optimistic about the potentialities of skilful supervision in solving the problems of the plant (cf. p. 536). It is only later studies of the Mayo orthodox school which emphasise supervision as the solution to the problems of productivity and morale (cf. for example J. C. Scott and G. C. Homans, 'Reflections on the Wildcat Strike', *American Sociological Review*, vol. 12 (1947), pp. 278–87; Mayo and Lombard).

42 cf. K. Lewin, R. Lippit, and S. K. Escalona, *Studies in Topological and Vector Psychology*, Iowa, 1940 and R. Lippitt and R. K. White, 'The Social Climate of Children's Group' in R. G. Barker *et al.* (eds.), *Child Behaviour and Development*, N.Y., 1943, pp. 485–508.

43 For an extensive presentation of such findings and relevant bibliography cf. Likert; Blau and Scott; M. Viteles, *Motivation and Morale in Industry*, N.Y., 1953.

44 Landsberger pp. 85 ff. Actually, the quick and uncritical acceptance of these tentative conclusions on supervisory skills and training manifest if nothing else, the widespread craving among business circles for a new management ethic and for an easy, unpainful solution of industrial conflict.

45 cf. E. Fleishman, E. Harris and E. Burtt, *Leadership and Supervision in Industry, an evaluation of a supervisory training program*, Columbia, Ohio, 1955. F. Mann, 'Studying and Creating Change, a means to understanding social organization', in *Human Relations in an Industrial Setting*, N.Y., 1957, p. 146–67; J. Goldthorpe, 'La Conception des conflits du travail dans l'enseignement des relations humaines', *Sociologie du Travail*, vol. 4 (1962), pp. 1–17.

46 cf. Survey Research Centre, *Productivity, Supervision and Morale among Railroad Workers*, Human Relations Series 2, Report 3, Ann Arbor, 1950, p. 51. N. C. Morse, *Satisfaction in the White Collar Job*, Ann Arbor, 1953, p. 137.

47 cf. C. W. Mills, *The Contributions of Sociology to Studies of Industrial Relations*, Proceedings of the First Annual Meeting, Industrial Relations Research Association, vol. 2, 1948, pp. 199–222.

48. cf. J. R. P. French, J. Israel, and D. Aas, 'An Experiment on Participation in a Norwegian Factory', *Human Relations*, vol. 13 (1960), pp. 3–19.

49 cf. R. Golembiewski, *Behaviour and Organization*, Chicago, 1962, p. 119.

50 cf. Likert, pp. 15–16.

51 L. R. Sayles, *Behaviour of Industrial Groups*, N.Y., 1958. The new emphasis on technology is oriented towards the importance of technological impact on group structure rather than on interaction (Chapple), or on individual personality [industrial psychology] and productivity (Taylor).

52 It is only the supervisor with influence on his superiors who can instigate favourable attitudes to his subordinates by permissive leadership, cf. D. C. Pelz, 'Leadership within a Hierarchical Organization', in A. H. Rubenstein and C. J. Haberstroh (eds.), *Some Theories of Organization*, Homewood, Ill., pp. 203–9.

53 D. Katz, N. Maccoby and N. Morse, *Productivity, Supervision and Morale in an Office Situation*, Ann Arbor, 1950.

54 cf. Landsberger, pp. 102 ff.

55 Indeed problems which are systematically examined by bureaucracy theorists and which have recently attracted the attention of human relations students, can be found in nascent form in Roethlisberger and Dickson (e.g. the conflict between locals and cosmopolitans, p. 353, between Shop and Office Workers, pp. 360–3, between specialist and line personnel, pp. 563–78, etc.).

56 cf. W. F. Whyte, 'Human Relations Theory', *Harvard Business Review* (1956), pp. 125 ff.

57 Chris Argyris has treated extensively the conflict between the individual's social and psychological needs and the exigencies of the organisation. Moreover his work reflects faithfully the patterns of change described in this paragraph.

In his early writings he stresses the importance of supervisory training (cf. *Role Playing in Action*, Ithaca, N.Y. State School of Industrial and Labor Relations at Cornell University, Bulletin No. 16, 1951). Then he becomes interested in changing attitudes and behaviour on the higher levels of management (*Executive Leadership*, N.Y., 1953). Finally, he turns his attention to the frustrations of the individual personality resulting from the authority and technological structure of modern organisations (cf. *Personality and Organization*, N.Y., 1957 and *Integrating the Individual and the Organization*, N.Y., 1964).

58 According to Landsberger (p. 48), most of the criticisms are addressed to Mayo's and Whitehead's philosophical ideas which are in no way shared by all human relations students.

59 cf. A. Siegel, 'The Economic Environment in Human Relations Research', in Arensberg *et al.* p. 86 ff.

60 Of course, as in all generalisations, one may find exceptions. But I

think that when one looks at the human relations literature as a whole, the exceptions are very few. Even in Roethlisberger and Dickson, where there is a whole chapter dealing with the analysis of the whole organisation as a social system, the real research and observation had the group and the individual's definition of the situation as their main focus of attention. Their remarks on the organisation as a whole were rather casual generalisations based on group findings.

61 Roethlisberger, p. 59.

62 *ibid*. p. 62.

63 cf. C. Kerr and L. Fisher, 'Plant Sociology: The Elite and the Aborigines', in Kommarovsky pp. 287–309, and S. Krupp, *Patterns in Organization Analysis*, N.Y., 1961.

64 cf. P. Drucker, *The Practice of Management*, 1961, p. 246.

65 cf. A. Tannenbaum and B. Georgopoulos, 'The Distribution of Control in Formal Organizations', *Social Forces*, vol. 36 (1957), pp. 44–50.

66 Indeed it is often analytically useful to distinguish more than three levels in organisation analysis (individual, interpersonal, group, intergroup, organisational, interorganisational, etc.); at each level new phenomena and problems emerge which cannot be reduced to similar problems at lower levels. For example, although at the group level, the more the group is cohesive the more effective it is in pursuing its proper goals; on the intergroup level many cohesive groups have difficulties in co-operating and are rather ineffective in combining and defending their common interests (cf. Sayles pp. 76–9). Of course, the passage from one level to another is possible, but it is not automatic. It requires adequate tools and special attention.

67 'The Inter-industry Propensity to Strike – An International Comparison', in A. Kornhauser *et al.* (eds.), *Industrial Conflict*, N.Y., 1954, pp. 199–212.

CHAPTER SIX

1 The 'organisation theory' label has two meanings in organisational literature. In its broader sense, it refers to all kinds of studies on formal organisations. In its restrictive sense it refers to a specific approach to the study of organisation that we shall examine in this chapter. *Thus, whenever reference is made to its second meaning it will be in italics.*

2 cf. H. A. Simon, *Models of Man*, N.Y., 1957, p. 1; also *Administrative Behaviour*, N.Y., 1961, Introduction to the second edition, pp. xxii–xxxiii; J. Litterer (ed.), *Organizations: Structure and Behaviour*, 1963, p. 19.

3 C. Barnard, *The Functions of the Executive*, Oxford, 1938, p. 73.

4 cf. Simon, *Administrative Behaviour*, p. xxiii.

5 cf. Mayo, *Social Problems*, pp. 41–4.

6 At this point it would be interesting to compare Simon's and Mayo's criticisms of the economic man model. Mayo and his disciples in the human

relations school mainly challenged the motivational assumptions of economic theory. They emphasised the fact that economic gain (profit or wage maximisation) is not the only one or even the most important motive in determining behaviour in industrial organisations. (They have shown the importance of status, approval, power seeking, etc.) Simon, on the other hand criticises more the cognitive assumptions of the economic model, those which refer to the perfect knowledge and the unlimited computational capacities of the entrepreneur or the consumer.

7 The same can be said about statistical decision-making, game theory and other similar approaches to the study of rational choice; in spite of their spectacular development and their successful managerial applications, they have a similar normative, non-empirical character (cf. H. A. Simon, *The New Science of Management Decision*, N.Y. 1960, p. 8).

8 cf. H. Leibenstein, *Economic Theory and Organizational Analysis*, N.Y., 1960, Introduction.

9 cf. Simon, *Administrative Behaviour*, p. xxiii.

10 *ibid.* p. xxv.

11 H. Simon, 'Recent Advances in Organization Theory', in *Research frontiers in Politics and Government*, Brookings Lectures, Brookings Institution, 1955, p. 30.

12 A factual proposition is a statement about the 'observable world and the way in which it operates' (*Administrative Behaviour*, p. 45). A value statement has an imperative, ethical character. As such, it does not refer to what is but rather to what ought to be. Although Simon admits that in concrete decision-making situations it is difficult to distinguish the factual from the ethical element, he considers the distinction as analytically possible and useful.

13 Simon is careful enough to point out that there is no strict correspondence between factual-value premises and means-ends relationships. Indeed, when a goal is given (value premise), in the choice of means for its achievement, value considerations cannot be avoided. Moreover, in a means-end chain an intermediate goal is a means to a more distant one. Thus, the choice of the lower level goal might be guided by factual considerations (cf. *Administrative Behaviour*, pp. 62–6).

14 Thus, two unrelated decision-makers who are confronted with exactly the same sets of value and factual premises (i.e. who have the same decisional environment), if they are rational, will necessarily decide in the same way (cf. *Administrative Behaviour*, p. 223).

15 For Simon decision-making is not limited to conscious, deliberate thinking and choosing. For him all behaviour involves selection of a course of action among all those alternative courses which are physically possible to the actor (whether or not the actor is conscious of all the alternatives). Thus, the term 'selection' does not imply any deliberate process, it simply refers to the fact that 'if the individual follows one particular course of action, there are other courses of action that he thereby foregoes'. (*Administrative Behaviour*, p. 3).

16 Indeed the difficulty is not only to predict the possible consequences

but also to evaluate them – i.e. to imagine how much you would like or dislike a future state of affairs.

17 The concept of the satisfying behaviour becomes clearer when one realises that in a problem solving situation the decision-maker is not simply concerned with the attainment of a unitary, isolated goal. Rather he is confronted with the problem of finding an alternative which will satisfy a series of goals. For instance, it may be that the problem is an alternative plan for the production of a machine (main goal) which must be subject to the following constraints: it must not cost more than a certain amount of money, it must be constructed within a short time period, and so on. The above constraints can be viewed equally as goals which the decision-maker must take into consideration in searching for an alternative plan. Thus, if he seeks a satisfactory solution, he will stop the search as soon as he finds a plan which meets the above specifications. On the other hand, if he wants to find the optimal plan, he must go on searching until he finds all the plans possible which satisfy the specifications and, among them, he will choose the most economic.

18 Barnard pp. 56–9, 139–60.

19 For a more clearly elaborated exposition of the contribution-inducement theory cf. March and Simon pp. 84–110.

20 Thus in a firm the employees contribute their work and receive a salary (or other inducements), which come from the contribution of clients (they pay a price), who receive as inducement the product of the firm. We can think in the same way about other categories of participants (stockholders, suppliers, etc.) cf. Simon, *Administrative Behaviour*, pp. 119–20.

21 The great importance of authority for decision-making lies in the fact that, contrary to other types of influence (persuasion, expertise), it permits a decision to be taken and executed even if the inferior does not agree with it. In other terms, the inferior decision-maker, by accepting authority, partially suspends his judgement and leaves the superior to set some of the premises of his decisional environment. Of course, this arbitrary character of authority has its limits. According to Simon, such limits delineate an individual's area of indifference. Beyond this area the individual will refuse to comply with the orders of his superior.

22 Of course, when we speak of an organisation as a unit taking decisions, the danger of reification arises. The impression is easily created of an anthropomorphic entity over and above individual members which has goals and solves problems. This danger is avoided when one bears in mind that such concepts are constructed for analytic and expository convenience and do not refer to concrete entities but to social processes and configurations which have always at their basis interacting individuals. (For example, when we talk of the organisation's searching for an alternative solution, this should be understood as a convenient way of referring in an aggregate manner to the various search activities undertaken by different departments or individuals scattered all over the organisation.)

23 cf. for example, Leibenstein; R. M. Cyert and J. G. March, *A Behavioural Theory of the Firm*, Englewood Cliffs, N.J., 1963; R. M. Cyert,

E. A. Feigenbaum and J. G. March, 'Models of a Behavioural Theory of the Firm', *Behavioural Science*, vol. 40 (1959), pp. 81–95; R. M. Cyert, H. A. Simon and D. B. Trow, 'Observations of a Business Decision', *Journal of Business*, vol. 29 (1956), pp. 237–48.

24 cf. Cyert and March, pp. 128–48.

25 *ibid.* pp. 114–27.

26 And as there is no single goal, there is not either a simple decision-maker (as in micro-economics) but a series of decision-makers who are only loosely connected and whose value premises are not totally co-ordinated (so there is not a clear preference ordering of the organisation as a whole).

27 Thus, for instance, an agreement between firms to reduce competition makes the environment more stable (it achieves a negotiated environment) as it permits the accurate prediction of the competitor's moves.

In a sense, internal planning, the establishment of programmes, standard procedures and decision rules are also attempts to stabilise or negotiate the internal environment of the organization. In this way, subunits, in making decisions, avoid uncertainty as to the reactions of other subunits – they know what to expect from them.

28 For instance, it tries to find the cause of a problem in the neighbourhood of its symptoms and it looks for a satisfactory alternative near the alternative adopted by the organisation in the past. In other words the organisational assumptions in this case are that a cause must be sought near its effect and a new solution near the old one. Thus, time-consuming and overcomplicated searches of all the alternatives and other totally radical solutions are avoided in concrete organisational situations.

Of course, whenever such search procedures do not yield satisfactory results, search becomes more complicated (consideration of more distant alternatives and consequences).

cf. R. M. Cyert and J. G. March, 'The Behavioural Theory of the Firm: A Behavioural Science – Economics Amalgam', in W. W. Cooper *et al.* (eds.), *New Perspectives in Organization Research*, N.Y., 1964, pp. 294–6.

29 Thus, search rules or attention rules (i.e. rules determining to which parts of the environment organisational attention and energies are directed) may be changed when repeatedly unsuccessful. And whenever such changes still do not meet the new difficulties, the adoption of less ambitious goals (reduction of aspiration levels) might become necessary.

30 It is mainly, although not exclusively, in management science writings that such a framework can be seen. Management scientists or systems analysts are quantitatively oriented scientists who emphasise the importance of seeing the whole organisation as a system of interconnected parts. (According to them, any managerial problem must be placed in such a broad context.) Their main task is to elaborate mathematical tools which would help the manager to take rational decisions in very complex situations. According to Simon their approach is not very different from the operations research method, as applied to industrial problems.

cf. Simon, *The New Science*, p. 15, cf. also G. E. Briggs, 'Engineering

Systems approaches to Organizations', in Cooper *et al.*, pp. 479–92). Another field of study which is closely linked with the present approach is General System Theory. Its purpose is the examination of systems in all spheres of reality – social, psychological, biological, physical. By such an examination it is hoped that organisational universals, regularities common to every kind of system or organisation (in the large sense), can be established (cf. L. Von Bertalanffy, 'An Outline of General System Theory', *The British Journal for the Philosophy of Science*, vol. 1, No. 2, 1950; M. D. Mesarovic, J. L. Sanders and C. F. Sprague, 'An Axiomatic Approach to Organizations from a General Systems Viewpoint', in Cooper *et al.* pp. 493–512).

31 cf. S. Beer, *Cybernetics and Management*, 1959, p. 7; G. T. Guilbrand, *What is Cybernetics?*, 1959.

32 The vocabulary in this field is not uniform. For instance, some writers speak as well of a 'goal setter' as distinct from the governor (cf. D. J. Clough, *Concepts in Management Science*, Englewood Cliffs, N.J., 1963, pp. 80–5). A transmitter, having the function of simply transmitting messages, is another concept usually found in the literature (cf. K. Boulding, *The Organizational Revolution*, N.Y., 1953, p. xxviii).

33 cf. A. Kuhn, *The Study of Society*, Homewood, Ill., 1963, pp. 52–3.

34 cf. previous section.

35 cf. K. W. Deutsch, *The Nerves of Government*, 1963, pp. 187–92.

36 cf. Clough, pp. 85–97.

37 cf. J. T. Dorsey Jr., 'A Communication Model for Administration', *Administrative Science Quarterly*, vol. 2 (1957), pp. 307–24.

38 As a matter of fact the choice of a design is one of the most crucial organisational decisions; as such, a design may directly determine what sort of problems shall be emphasised in an organisation, how and by whom they will be considered, and so on. Consider for instance the so-called 'Gresham's law of planning', which stipulates that routine chases away non-routine activities in organisations. If the systematic considerations of long term problems and plans is considered vital for an organisation's goals, the design of such an organisation should be such that it counteracts Gresham's law of planning. This can be achieved for example, by creating a special planning department – specialising in non-routine activities (cf. R. M. Cyert and J. G. March, 'Organizational Design', in Cooper *et al.* pp. 565 ff). In this context one should mention Burns and Stalker's ideal type distinction between the mechanistic and the organic system of organisation. The former, having relatively fixed and stable goals and operating in a predictable environment, is characterised by rigid division of labour and a monolithic authority structure. The latter refers to organisations whose structure is flexible enough to cope effectively with new problems emerging from a rapidly changing environment (cf. pp. 6 ff).

39 For an example cf. B. M. Bass, 'Production Organization Exercise: An application of Experimental Techniques to Business Games', in Cooper *et al.* pp. 97–114.

40 Indeed, the laboratory method usually consists of a series of short

trials during which the behaviour of the subjects is highly regularised. The subjects are not left free to play a prolonged and complicated game (cf. J. E. McGrath, 'Towards a "Theory of Method", for Research in Organizations', in Cooper *et al.* pp. 437 ff).

41 For a simple example cf. C. P. Bonini, 'Stimulating Organizational Behaviour', in Cooper *et al.* pp. 276–88.

42 Thus computer simulation is used a great deal by organisation theorists who try to identify the process of organisational decision-making (cf. section 3A). For example, Cyert, March and Moore tried to simulate by computer the decision-making process of a department store as it was related to price and output determination. By means of such a model they were able to predict with a close approximation the future output and pricing of the firm (cf. Cyert and March, *op. cit.* chapter 7).

43 Of course here, as well, the usual reservations must be made as to the interpretation of various approaches and the impossibility of drawing rigid boundaries (cf. chapter 5).

44 cf. T. Burns, 'The Sociology of Industry', in A. T. Welford *et al.* (eds.), *Society*, 1962, p. 204.

45 March and Simon, p. 2 (underlining mine).

46 And this, in spite of the fact that in March and Simon a whole chapter is dedicated to the problems of organisational conflict (pp. 113–36).

47 Another index of Simon's superficial consideration of differences between individual and group phenomena, is his criticism of the role concept (cf. *Administrative Behaviour*, Introduction to the 2nd edition, pp. xxx–xxxi). He suggests that a decision premise, as a smaller unit of analysis, is a better tool for explaining human behaviour than the concept of the role. The latter not only is vague, but whenever, at its best, it implies a specification of some of the premises influencing behaviour, it leases out other premises which may greatly determine the behaviour of the role player (e.g. his idiosyncrasy, the way he acts a role, etc.).

But no sociologist has ever claimed that knowledge of a person's role is enough for explaining *in detail* his concrete behaviour; neither is it the purpose of the role concept to perform such a task. If we take Simon's example, the fact of knowing the role of a policeman will perhaps not be enough for the exact prediction of how a specific policeman X will act in a specific situation Y. But a sociologist might be less interested in policeman X and his specific reactions and more interested in the policeman in general or in the police force as a professional group. Indeed, the role concept cannot be so easily dismissed. If, in spite of its vagueness, it is so widely used by so many social scientists, especially sociologists, it is because it has the great advantage (which the decision premise does not have) of showing how the individual as a personality system is linked and integrated into the social system. As a matter of fact, the role concept is the most convenient bridge from the individual to the group, organisation and societal level in social analysis.

48 March and Simon, p. 5.

49 For a summary and a bibliography of the controversy about the

nature and functions of the economic man assumptions cf. Cyert and March *op. cit.* chapter 2; cf. also Krupp pp. 3–11.
   50 cf. R. B. Braithwaite, *Scientific Explanation*, Cambridge, 1964, pp. 76–8; G. Ryle, *Dilemmas*, 1962, pp. 82–92.

CHAPTER SEVEN

   1 cf. H. Simon, 'Approaching the Theory of Management' in Koontz *op. cit.* pp. 79 ff.
   2 cf. R. Dahrendorf, 'Out of Utopia: Towards a Re-Orientation of Sociological Analysis', *American Journal of Sociology*, vol. 64 (1958); L. A. Coser, *The Functions of Social Conflict*, 1956, Introduction. For a discussion of these tendencies in general sociology cf. Dahrendorf.
   3 Two recent textbooks in industrial sociology reflect pretty well these tendencies in organisational research.
   (a) E. V. Schneider, *Industrial Sociology*, N.Y., 1957.
   Schneider, a pupil of Parsons, shifts the analysis from the workplace and its impact on workers' attitude to a broader examination of the organisation as a social system.
   (b) M. J. Vincent and J. Mayers, *New Foundations for Industrial Sociology*, N.Y., 1959.
   As the authors explicitly state in their preface, 'This book distinguishes itself from other books in this field by its persistent emphasis on power group relations – on the roles of unions, management and government' (p.v.). (For a review of the above books and for a critical discussion of their implication cf. J. H. Smith 'New Ways in Industrial Sociology', *British Journal of Sociology*, vol. 10 (1959), pp. 244–52).
   Moreover, the same theoretical trends are reflected in the significant research in industrial sociology carried out at the University of Liverpool. In all these writings one can clearly discern:
   (a) a broader conceptual framework: the organisation as a whole is the main unit of analysis
   (b) a more systematic consideration of the problems of organisational conflict. (For a critical review of the 'Liverpool' studies cf. R. K. Brown, 'Participation, Conflict and Change in Industry', *The Sociological Review*, vol. 13 (1965), pp. 272–95.)
   4 This does not, of course, mean that the relationship between individual and organisation is neglected, that the emphasis on the social structure brings about a shadow image of an organisation deserted by real people. It simply means that the organisation-individual relationship is seen from a different angle: the emphasis is not any more on the individual but on the organisation pole of the relationship. The organisation has ceased to be in the background and has become the main focus of analysis. In more concrete terms, instead of asking 'How does the individual perceive, and is affected by the organisation?' one tends more to pose questions like

'What is the significance of the individual's behaviour from the point of view of the organisation, how does the organisation motivate the individual to participate?', etc.

5 Partially as a result of the above development, organisation theory has stopped being exclusively interested in the study of industrial or profit organisations. Studies of schools, universities, hospitals and many other types of large-scale organisations indicate an increased awareness of the inadequacy and narrowness of concepts developed in industrial settings. (For a bibliography of research in various types of organisations cf. Miller and Form pp. xv–xix.)

6 cf. chapter 5, section 3.

7 cf. for instance Sayles, and R. L. Kahn and E. Boulding (eds.), *Power and Conflict in Organizations*, 1964; D. Cartwright, *Studies in Social Power*, Ann Arbor, 1959.

8 cf. chapter 5, section 3.

9 cf. E. W. Bakke, 'The Concept of the Social Organization', in Haire, p. 45.

10 It is in this sense that so many authors, starting with Mayo, speak about the inevitability and usefulness of the informal organisation.

11 For the various ways in which human relations students use the formal-informal dichotomy cf chapter 5, footnote 31.

12 cf. for instance W. Scott, J. A. Banks, A. H. Halsey and T. Lupton, *Technical Change and Industrial Relations*, Liverpool, 1956, pp. 263–82.

13 cf. for instance E. Jacques, *The Changing Culture of a Factory*, 1952, pp. 249–56; cf. also Bakke, pp. 45 ff.

14 cf. T. Parsons, 'Suggestions for a Sociological Approach to the Theory of Organizations', *Administrative Science Quarterly*, vol. I (1956), Nos. 1 and 2, pp. 63–85 and 224–39; 'Some Ingredients of a General Theory of Formal Organization', in A. W. Halpin (ed.), *Administrative Theory in Education*, Chicago, 1958, pp. 40–72. 'The Mental Hospital as a Type of Organization', in M. Greenblott, D. Levinson and R. H. Williams (eds.), *The Patient and the Mental Hospital*, Glencoe, Ill., 1957, pp. 109–29.

15 T. Parsons, R. F. Bales and E. A. Shils, *Working Papers in the theory of Action*, Glencoe, Ill., 1953, pp. 172 ff.

16 Very often, when Parsons talks about the mechanisms (or processes) relevant to each functional problem, it is very difficult to see whether he refers to the minimum processes required for organisational survival, to concrete mechanisms existing in real organisations, or to ideal mechanisms which should be necessary if the organisation were to function in a smooth way. Parsons shifts (without warning) from the one position to the other (cf. H. Landsberger, 'Parsons' Theory of Organization', in M. Black (ed.), *The Social Theories of Talcott Parsons*, Englewood Cliffs, N.J., 1961, pp. 225–6).

17 In a way this distinction corresponds to Homan's distinction between external and internal system (cf. chapter 5, footnote 28).

18 Parsons distinguishes three types of decisions:

policy decisions which trace the main ways by which organisational goals will be implemented

allocative decisions referring to the distribution of financial resources and responsibilities

co-ordinative decisions

19 Parsons, 'Suggestions', p. 228.

20 Actually in analysing the organisation's integration problem, Parsons has moved to a higher level. When he speaks of the integration problem, he does not refer to the organisation's internal integration but to the integrative requirements of the larger system: 'So far two problems have been dealt with, that of the adaptation of an organisation to the situation in which it must operate, and that of its operative goal attainment mechanisms. There is, however, another central problem area which is not covered by these considerations, namely that of the mechanisms by which the organisation is integrated with other organisations and other types of collectivity in the total social system.'

Because of this jumping of levels the problem of internal integration as well as the problem of latency are treated, as far as I can judge, in the goal attainment sector (cf. Parsons, 'Suggestions', pp. 70–85).

The above considerations illustrate well the ambiguity which characterises most of Parsons' work and which is particularly marked in his writings on organisations.

21 cf. Parsons, *Structure and Process*, pp. 44–7.

22 The five dichotomous variables which refer to the basic and universal dilemmas that any actor faces in a social situation are:

Affectivity	– Affective neutrality
Specificity	– Diffuseness
Universalism	– Particularism
Quality	– Performance
Self-orientation	– Collectivity-orientation.

23 cf. E. C. Devereux Jr., 'Parsons' Sociological Theory', in Black p. 39.

24 As a matter of fact, the organisation cannot concentrate its energies and attention on all four functional problems at once. Maximising efforts in one direction intensifies functional requirements in another. The main antagonism seems to be between instrumental requirements (adaptation and goal achievement) and expressive or socio-emotional requirements (integration and latency). This organisational dilemma is met by a temporal sequence of phases during which the organisation's attention shifts from one functional problem to another. Thus the four functional problems point to two types of differentiation in the social system:

(a) A *temporal* differentiation into four phases, each one corresponding to the functional problem with which, at a certain time, the organisation is mainly occupied.

(b) A *structural* differentiation, as according to Parsons, there is a tendency for the development of separate subsystems, each specialised in the solution of one functional problem (this tendency can be more clearly seen on the societal level). On the organisational level it is not very marked. Consequently the four organisational subsectors – each referring to processes which deal with the four functional problems – have rather an analytic character (i.e. they do not correspond to concrete sub-collectivities).

25 cf. Landsberger, *art. cit.*, pp. 219–20.

26 For example, if the chief of the sales department, in his policy making, is exclusively preoccupied with the interests of his department and not with those of the entire organisation, we can say that the department, as a unit is self-oriented (of course, in a similar way we can define departmental role expectations and values).

27 In another context, Parsons is less concerned with functional requirements and with processes necessary to cope with them and pays more attention to the hierarchical structure of the organisation. Here, his main insight is to point out a three level break in the hierarchy of an organisation and to different modes of articulation of authority relations that exist among these three levels. Thus he distinguishes between the *technical* level, the *managerial* level and *institutional* level of formal organisations. He examines the boundary interchanges between these three subsystems and the larger context within which they operate. On the basis of such distinctions, he proposes some new ways for constructing organisational typologies (cf. chapter 2, section 1c).

28 It is significant in this context that Parsons' influence has been greater in those organisational fields which were less established as areas of research (hospitals, schools, etc.) – cf. Landsberger, *art. cit.*, p. 218.

29 Actually most studies dealing with extraorganisational collectivities are mainly tracing their impact on the individual's behaviour (cf. chapter 5, section 2B). They are not referring to the relations between the organisation as a *social unit* to other types of social units. For a discussion of this problem cf. Etzioni, 'New Directions in the Study of Organizations and Society', in *Social Research*, vol. 27 (1960), pp. 223–8; cf. also his 'Industrial Sociology: The Study of Economic Organizations', *Social Research*, vol. 25 (1958), pp. 303–24.

30 Actually this Parsonian distinction has been used in leadership studies where, instead of speaking about formal or informal leadership, one uses the concept of task oriented and socio-emotional leader (cf. Etzioni, *Complex Organisations*, p. 93).

31 cf. For instance Kroeber and Parsons 'The Concepts of Culture and Social System', *American Sociological Review*, vol. 23 (1958), pp. 582–3; and Kluckhohn, Clyde and Kelly, 'The Concept of Culture', in R. Linton (ed.), *The Science of Man in the World Crisis*, N.Y., 1945, pp. 78–106.

32 cf. D. Lockwood, 'Some Remarks on "The Social System" ', *British Journal of Sociology*, vol. 7 (1956), no. 2.

33 cf. T. Parsons, 'The Distribution of Power in American Society', *World Politics*, vol. 10 (1957), pp. 108–29. For a similar approach to the concept of power cf. R. S. Lynd, 'Power in American Society as Resource

and Problem', in A. Kornhauser (ed.), *Problems of Power in American Society*, Detroit, 1957.

34 cf. Lipset, 'Political Sociology, pp. 105–7.

35 This is clearly seen when Parsons refers to the collectivity orientation of business organisations cf Landsberger *art. cit.* pp. 221–7.

36 R. Dahrendorf, *Class and Class Conflict in Industrial Society*, 1959, p. 96.

37 For a definition of the concept of quasi-group cf. M. Ginsberg, *Reason and Unreason in Society*, 1956, pp. 12–15.

38 It is not by chance that in one of the most incisive works on the theory of social structure, power (i.e. control over resources and the behaviour of others) is considered the central concept for understanding and comparing social structures (cf. Nadel). For another general work emphasising the theoretical importance of the concepts of power and conflict cf. Coser.

39 cf. M. Crozier, *Le Phénomène bureaucratique*, Paris, 1963, pp. 200 ff; 'De l'étude des relations de pouvoir', *Sociologie du Travail*, vol. 3 (1961), pp. 80–3; also Miller and Form pp. 694–6.

40 M. Dalton, *Men who Manage*, N.Y. 1959.

41 'The point to be stressed is that not just the lukewarm, but also the militant members of the union, those who criticised others for not "sticking together", practised this behaviour (drive for personal advantage). To labour the point, though unions were a legally established powerful force in these plants, and were made up of persons who clung together in crises, still the sincerest of these members as persons with private interests might on occasion behave in a manner contrary to group expectations,' *ibid.* p. 114.

42 Dalton defines a clique as 'the informal association of two or more persons to realise some ends'. This conception of the clique, in contradistinction to Mayo's informal group, has usually a more purposive character (i.e. the rational pursuit of definite goals).

43 Crozier, *op. cit.*

44 *ibid.* pp. 193–222.

45 cf. Merton, *Social Theory*, pp. 195–205.

46 cf. Crozier, *op. cit.* pp. 261 ff.

47 cf. W. F. Whyte, *Patterns of Industrial Peace*, N.Y., 1951.

48 H. L. Sheppard, 'Approaches to Conflict in American Industrial Sociology', *British Journal of Sociology*, vol. 5 (1954), pp. 324–40.

49 This much more plausible hypothesis is in accord with the insights of Michels who has shown how trade unions and political organisations with a revolutinary or radical ideology lose their radicalism as soon as they become established and legitimate centres of power (cf. chapter I).

50 Blauner.

51 For instance, Blauner does not examine the problem of workers' participation and ownership of the means of production – so central to the theories of Marx and Weber – simply because the American workers are not interested in such problems. Yet, in another context, he admits the possibility of workers being content in an alienated (self-estranging) manner (p. 29).

Notes to pages 163–70

Thus, it is not surprising that the author finally, after his long excursion into the realm of facts and statistics, seems to place his hopes in the advent of automation, which in a smooth and painless way, might provide a non-alienated working environment for man. Of course in all this discussion there is not much concern about the crucial question of under whose control the coming process of automation will be, or what will be the impact of this new technological revolution on the social structure of our society. Marx, in such a study of alienation, would have surely posed the simple but critical problem of whether automation would control man or man automation. One would expect that even if such questions were of no interest to the American workers, at least they should interest American sociologists – especially when they claim to operationalise and test empirically Marx's insights on alienation.

52   Although quite evident, it is very often forgotten that problems which are theoretically important and crucial for the development of organisation theory do not necessarily coincide with what the administrator considers important.

Of course, by this we do not try to deny how important it is both practically and theoretically for the sociologist to be concerned with the day to day practical problems with which men of action are faced. What is criticised is the overemphasis on this kind of problem at the expense of more basic research. At the present moment, as Thompson states, 'when industrial administrators are vexed by the changing role of foremen, we get a rash of research on this topic; and when these same administrators begin to puzzle over resistance to change, we flood the market with research and theories designed to overcome resistance to change '(cf. J. D. Thompson, 'Modern Approaches to Theory in Administration', in Halpin.

53   Crozier, *op. cit.* pp. 203–8.

54   cf. concluding chapter, sections 2, 3.

CONCLUSION

1   cf. Crozier, *op. cit.* p. 195.

2   Of course in this context efficiency does not have the technical meaning that Barnard gave to the term. It is used in its commonsense meaning.

3   cf. Crozier *op. cit.* pp. 195–6; R. Bendix, *Work and Authority in Industry,* 1956; C. W. Mills, *The Sociological Imagination,* N.Y., 1959, pp. 99 ff.

4   What seems to me surprising about this tortuous and prolonged battle is that it still goes on and gains in momentum, not so much because of the fundamental disagreement between the two camps but because of a curious lack of communication between them. Each one, in order to defend its position builds up a straw man that it savagely attacks without paying much attention to what is valid in the opponent's arguments. The one emphasises that values are inescapable, the other that objectivity in

Notes to pages 170–6

sociology is possible and the controversy goes on indefinitely because not much attention is given to the question of what sort of values are inescapable or what sort of objectivity is possible. It seems to me that the present extraordinary agitation about the value problem in sociology is due first to semantic confusion, and second to a misconception of how the researcher in the physical or exact sciences works (the myth that somehow values do not intrude at all in his work).

5 For instance, a better knowledge of the facts, of the real state of affairs in a certain context may make a writer change his value judgements.

6 At this juncture it might be useful to point out that scientism, the tendency to present value judgement as scientific propositions, has not been monopolised by conservative thinkers. This type of extreme positivism is one of the weakest points in Marx's work.

7 As we have repeatedly pointed out, in such studies there is a tendency to focus the analysis on the individual or the group level and then, on the basis of such a limited analysis, to formulate generalisations and solutions referring to the organisation as a whole (thus implying that an organisation is an aggregate of individuals or groups).

8 For the definition of functional and substantive rationality cf. Mannheim, pp. 51 ff.

9 For a bibliography on comparative public administration cf. F. J. Tickner, 'A Survey and Evaluation of Comparative Research', in *Public Administration Review*, vol. 19 (1959), pp. 19–25; R. V. Presthus, 'Behaviour and Bureaucracy in Many Cultures', *ibid.* pp. 25–35 and F. Heady, 'Recent Literature on Comparative Public Administration', *Administrative Science Quarterly*, vol. 5 (1960), pp. 137–57.

10 From the point of view of providing a conceptual framework as a guide to comparative research, the following writings seem very useful:
Etzioni, *Complex Organisations*.
Parsons, 'Suggestions'.
D. S. Pugh *et al.*, 'A Conceptual Scheme for Organizational Analysis', in *Administrative Science Quarterly*, vol. 8 (1963–4), pp. 289–315.

11 For an extended bibliography of historical writings dealing mainly with state bureaucracies in various civilisations cf. S. N. Eisenstadt, *The Political Systems of Empires*, Glencoe, Ill., 1962, especially chapter 10.

12 Of course this is not an attempt to discredit historical work as unsystematic or trivial. As was said earlier (cf. chapter 3), often the sociologist and the historian look at social reality from different angles and with different interests and problems in their minds. Thus, what seems significant to a historian might seem trivial for the sociologist and vice versa. But whether or not one accepts that there is, or should be, a distinction and a division of labour between the sociologist and the historian, the fact remains that the sociologist of organisations will have a great deal to gain by taking historical material more into consideration and by being more aware of history when he looks at modern organisational structures.

13 cf. M. D. Sahlins and E. R. Service (eds.), *Evolution and Culture*, Ann Arbor, 1960; S. N. Eisenstadt, 'Social Change, Differentiation and

220

Evolution', *American Sociological Review*, vol. 29 (1964), pp. 375–85; D. MacRae, *Ideology and Society*, 1961, pp. 137–50.

14 The term 'often' is used in order to indicate the relativity of the statement. That is to say in spite of the fact that the past is always relevant and necessary for the understanding of the present, in certain cases it can be more relevant and necessary than in others. This argument bears a similarity to the one stating that although knowledge of a more inclusive social system is always necessary for the understanding of its subsystems, this knowledge is more or less necessary according to the self-containment of the subunit (cf. chapter 6). The same can be said about the necessity of a historical perspective. One can imagine a case where the present social structure can be adequately explained without recourse to the past. But even in this extreme case a historical perspective is necessary in order to find out whether or not and how much the past is relevant.

As C. W. Mills has put it, sometimes we must know history in order to be able to get rid of it (pp. 155 ff).

15 J. H. Steward, 'Evolution and Process', in Kroeber *Anthropology Today*, p. 315.

16 cf. Mills pp. 46–7.

17 Nadel, p. 1.

18 An interesting attempt in this direction has been made by Gouldner, cf. Gross pp. 241–70.

INDEX

For Product Safety Concerns and Information please contact our EU
representative GPSR@taylorandfrancis.com
Taylor & Francis Verlag GmbH, Kaufingerstraße 24, 80331 München, Germany

www.ingramcontent.com/pod-product-compliance
Lightning Source LLC
Chambersburg PA
CBHW070404270326
41926CB00014B/2698

9 780415 863582